American Muslim Women,
Religious Authority, and Activism

BOOK TWENTY-EIGHT

Louann Atkins Temple Women & Culture Series
Books about women and families, and their changing role in society

American Muslim Women, Religious Authority, and Activism

More Than a Prayer

Juliane Hammer

University of Texas Press
Austin

*The Louann Atkins Temple Women & Culture Series
is supported by Allison, Doug, Taylor, and Andy Bacon;
Margaret, Lawrence, Will, John, and Annie Temple;
Larry Temple; the Temple-Inland Foundation;
and the National Endowment for the Humanities.*

Requests for permission to reproduce material from this work should be sent to:

    Permissions

    University of Texas Press

    P.O. Box 7819

    Austin, TX 78713–7819

    www.utexas.edu/utpress/about/bpermission.html

♾ The paper used in this book meets the minimum requirements
of ANSI/NISO Z39.48–1992 (R1997) (Permanence of Paper).

Library of Congress Cataloging-in-Publication Data

Hammer, Juliane.

American Muslim women, religious authority, and activism : more than a prayer /
Juliane Hammer. — 1st ed.

p.   cm. — (Louann Atkins Temple women & culture series ; bk. 28)

Includes bibliographical references and index.

ISBN 978-0-292-73555-2 (cloth : alk. paper) — ISBN 978-0-292-73557-6 (e-book)

1. Women in Islam—United States.   2. Muslim women—Political activity—United
States.   3. Feminism—Religious aspects—Islam.   I. Title.

BP173.4.H3654   2012

297.082′0973—dc23

      2011035820

In memory of Gerhart Fritzsche,
avid reader, gifted artist, and
loving grandfather (1921–2010).
Mein Opi.

Contents

Note on Transliteration

It is customary for Islamic studies scholars to explain their transliteration system, in part as proof that we are aware of the complex rules guiding our field and the languages associated with it. I have used a simplified transliteration system for Arabic words which indicates the difference between ' (ayn) and ' (hamza), but does not include indicators of long vowels and letters not found in the English alphabet. Those familiar with Arabic will easily identify the correct terms and those who are not will benefit more from the translation in parenthesis. In addition to ease of reading, I have refrained from using a more complicated system because American Muslims generally use simplified transliterations of key religious vocabulary that has been integrated into American Muslim English, including the use of English plurals for Arabic words.

Acknowledgments

There probably is no single phrase or sentence that has not been used before in the acknowledgments of an academic book. The gratitude and indebtedness I express here are nevertheless heartfelt and sincere. This book would not have been possible without the support and encouragement of many people.

I owe my deepest gratitude to my husband, Cemil, my beacon of support and understanding, no matter how complicated or confusing life gets. He doubles as my agent, most enthusiastic fan, editor, and thoughtful critic. My daughters, Leyla and Mehtap, cheered me on throughout the writing process and learned more than they will ever need to know about chapters and publishers unless they become scholars one day. I will always cherish the "Go Mama Go" picture hanging over my desk. This book is dedicated to them with much love.

My parents and sisters in Germany have followed my work from afar for many years; their love and their support for my quest for knowledge provided the foundation of my academic career.

The research project at the core of this book has been supported by a faculty research grant and a small grant from the College of Liberal Arts and Sciences at the University of North Carolina at Charlotte (UNCC) and a semester of faculty research leave from George Mason University. Much of the earlier work on the project was carried out when I was a visiting scholar in the Department of Near Eastern Studies at Princeton University. Special thanks to Sükrü Hanioğlu and Michael Cook for providing me with inspiring working conditions. I am also indebted to Brittany Huckabee, who graciously shared video footage of the woman-led prayer event in 2005.

I am grateful to my colleagues at Elon University for their early encouragement of this project, especially Lynn Huber for suggesting that this would be material for a book and Jeff Pugh and Toddie Peters for walking me through my early years as an American college professor.

The participants in several workshops, "Muslims in America" and "Muslims and Media" at Princeton University in 2008 and "Islam in/and America" at Columbia University in 2010, read drafts of chapters and provided valuable feedback. Their collegiality and willingness to think through my questions and long German sentences is very much appreciated. The participants in the conference and book project "Female Religious Leadership in Mosques and Madrasas" at Oxford University deserve special gratitude for redirecting some of my thoughts and helping me focus on questions of authority and leadership.

This book would not have been the same without the students in my Muslims in America courses at Elon, Princeton, UNCC, and George Mason. Each class has been helpful in thinking through my ideas and discussing aspects of this project. Special thanks go to Rachel Hinson for focusing her research project on Muslim women as scholar-activists. Our shared interest in the topic and subsequent work on American Muslim intellectuals paved the way for this book.

Many scholars, peers, and mentors deserve mention as steady providers of insight, ideas, and support in the process of writing this book: Muhammad Qasim Zaman, Carl Ernst, Omid Safi, Yvonne Haddad, Kecia Ali, Laury Silvers, Saʿdiyya Shaikh, Zain Abdullah, Edward Curtis, Zareena Grewal, Ahmet Karamustafa, Amaney Jamal, Nelly van Doorn Harder, Vincent and Rkia Cornell, Bruce Lawrence, Ayesha Chaudhry, Rumee Ahmed, Sarah Islam, Timur Yuskaev, Vincent Biondo, Kristin Sands, Kambiz GhaneaBassiri, and Riem Spielhaus. Their advice, thoughtful critiques, and encouragement are very much appreciated. Leigh Schmidt, Melani McAlister, and Marie Griffith were instrumental during my year at Princeton in shaping my thoughts on this project and deserve thanks for sharing their time and energy. I am grateful for the opportunity to meet David Watts and Laura Levitt, who have become more than valued colleagues since then.

Some of those who started out as colleagues have become friends over the years. They all deserve special gratitude for the many ways in which they have helped this project come to fruition. I am grateful to Omid Safi for his enthusiasm for my work. Saʿdiyya Shaikh has deeply influenced my thinking about Muslim feminisms and the beauty of Muslim sisterhood. Laury Silvers, Debra Majeed, Aysha Hidayatullah, Fatima Seedat, Kecia Ali, Zahra Ayubi, and Hina Azam embody this sisterhood in their lives, their work, and their presence in my life.

Rosemary Hicks has been a fountain of theoretical insight, a nurturing mind, a formidable critic, and a challenge to the things I take for granted. Working with her on workshops, panels, and writing projects has been like a writing group, an email list, and a close friend all in one. Homayra Ziad is always there when I need to talk and sends prayers and energy on demand. She is also one of my most honest critics, which I always appreciate a day or two after the fact. Special gratitude is due to the Zülfikar family, especially Cangüzel for many years of friendship and fellowship. Several of my friends deserve thanks for keeping me grounded and reminding me of what matters, especially Saghar Hanachi, Lama Najjar, Louise Puck, and Noha Bakr.

I am very grateful to Jim Burr, my editor at the University of Texas Press, for his trust in me and my project, his patience with delays and excuses, and his support beyond the call of duty.

I have worked with the writings of many American Muslim women authors, scholars, and activists. Some I have come to know in person; others I only know through their texts. It is my hope that they will find themselves in the pages of this book and that it opens the door to continued conversation on issues that are of concern to all of them. Of course, omissions here or in the pages that follow, as well as any mistakes, are my own.

American Muslim Women,
Religious Authority, and Activism

Introduction

Head to the ground
Even the floor she walks upon becomes sacred
She prays in prescribed form but knows
There is no language the Universe does not accept
There is no posture void of God

From "My Sister's Prayer" by Suheir Hammad

It was the prayer of a Muslim woman, standing, bowing, and prostrating "head to the ground," that would leave its mark on Muslim debates about gender, women, and tradition. Like the sister in Suheir Hammad's poem, she and those praying with her performed their prayer in the prescribed form, and yet some aspects were different. On March 18, 2005, Amina Wadud, professor of Islamic studies,[1] gave the Friday sermon to a mixed-gender congregation and subsequently led the same congregation in Friday prayer in New York City. While it was not the first time a Muslim woman led men and women in prayer, it was a highly publicized and highly debated act of religious, political, and symbolic significance. The 2005 prayer, itself part of a larger trajectory of events, debates, and developments, focused and changed existing intra-Muslim discussions and reflections on issues ranging from women's interpretation of the Qur'an, leadership, mosque space, and religious authority to gender activism and media representations. In this book I take the 2005 woman-led prayer event as the historical focus for these larger debates. This is why this book is about more than a prayer.

American Muslim Women's Writings and the Prayer Event

The research project this book is based on was initially not about the woman-led prayer at all. A broader interest in the intellectual production of American Muslims and their contributions to contemporary Muslim thought came together with a long-standing interest in gender debates and women's roles in Muslim societies. The result was a growing collection of texts written and published by American Muslim women. Two categories of texts emerged: (1) academic writings by Muslim women concerned with Muslim women and gender discourses; and (2) narrative and autobiographical materials. Some of the texts were products of the 1980s and 1990s. However, the bulk of the materials were published in the past decade, with a notable increase in quantity since 2001. It is easy and tempting to explain this surge with the events of September 11, 2001, but that may be too easy. It has become commonplace to describe 9/11 as a formative event not only for the world or the United States but also, and in particular, for American Muslims. And it is certainly the case that the aftermath of 9/11 saw increased scrutiny and indeed often collective persecution of American Muslims as internal security risks while also dramatically increasing interest in all things Islamic and Muslim, both in the American public sphere and in the world of academic inquiry. The growing academic interest (and its marketability) is amply demonstrated by the large volume of recent publications dedicated specifically to the study of American Muslims. Some of these academic works support the impression that 9/11 has forever changed the status of American Muslims in American society, as well as American Muslim attitudes, discourses, and practices. However, many of the debates and issues catapulted to the forefront of public interest and indeed many of the transformation processes that have taken place in American Muslim communities have trajectories that reach farther back and cannot solely be explained by the impact of 9/11. The existence of materials and texts by and about Muslim women dating to the early 1980s is a clear indication of this trend. The increase in the number of texts is more closely linked to increased public and publishing interest than to the absence or insignificance of gender discourses and transformations in the decades before 2001.

The second step of the project was to identify shared patterns and themes in the texts so as to analyze them as a body of materials with an inner cohesion beyond the shared identities of their authors as American Muslim women. Not unexpectedly, the scholarly materials in the first category were very different in style and content from the "speaking out" literature in the second category. And even the drawing of boundaries around the group "American Muslim women" was not quite as self-evident as expected. The authors are Muslim women because they identify as such in their writings, regardless of whether they perceive this identity as primary or more significant than other markers of identities. They are American in a very broad sense because they publish their writings in the North American academic and publishing context and thus address them to American audiences. Every other restriction of their Americanness would have become a matter of definition and thus by itself part of the naming process. This is not to say that no woman author was excluded. For a variety of reasons, some of which will be discussed below, I did not include every woman who identified as Muslim in her writings *and* has published in North America. Some of the reasons are a function of political preferences; others are a matter of methodology.[2]

The most significant pattern I recognized was the fact that all the texts demonstrate the investment of their authors in a triangle of self-understanding and textual production: they write for the sake of formulating, negotiating, and sometimes saving their faith and religious identities as Muslim women; they address intra-Muslim and communal audiences in an attempt to generate discussions about gender discourses, attitudes, and practices in those communities; and they are acutely aware of and directly involved in media representations of Muslims and Islam and/or the dynamics of authority and scholarship in the secular American academy. Each corner of this triangle influences the others in the ways in which the texts are produced, negotiated, and contested.

It soon became apparent that the number of authors and texts identified was too large to analyze in comprehensive and qualitative ways. Focusing on a particular historical event had the potential for a more focused and nuanced study of the larger topic. As I demonstrate, many of the authors discussed here were somehow connected to the 2005 woman-led prayer and the debates surrounding it, most notably Asra Nomani, the chief organizer, and Amina Wadud, the *imamah* (prayer leader) and *khatibah* (woman offering the Friday sermon) of the event. Although their writings have an important role in many chapters in this book, I have tried to avoid constructing the two women as archetypical in conveniently dichotomous (or complementary) pairs. The tendency and indeed temptation to "pitch" them as opposite poles—for example, born Muslim/convert, South Asian/African American, scholar/journalist—became quite evident in media coverage of the event. While some of those dichotomies reflect real issues and concerns within Muslim communities in North America, the focus on these two individuals and their struggles has overshadowed the intellectual, religious, and political communities that have sustained the discussions and debates on women and gender among American Muslims. Many other authors are discussed in this book in order to highlight their equally important perspectives and contributions.

Privileging Texts and Voices

In the process of writing this book I was criticized for giving too much credit and paying too much attention to the 2005 woman-led prayer and its organizers. Critics have argued that the event was blown out of proportion by the media (and the organizers themselves) and that it has had no lasting or significant impact. I disagree. The prayer event served as a catalyst for debates that were already under way among Muslims in North America. The event itself was an accident of history, initiated by particular individuals on a particular day in a particular place. However, if not with those individuals, that day, in that place, something like the March 18, 2005, woman-led prayer event would have happened as the logical culmination of a trajectory of events and debates in the decades before. All those—intellectuals, activists, and community members—arguing over gender equality, social justice, and the inclusion of women, whether they were male or female, had already paved the way for this step. Texts and events since March 2005 attest to the lasting impact of this symbolic event.

The focus on the prayer as a historical event calls into question the methodological focus on texts as opposed to a multilevel methodology that includes empirical research such as interviews and observations. It was not only the fact that I did not attend the 2005 prayer or that I did not develop a scholarly interest in the event and the debates until long after March 2005. It was also not only the methodological difficulty of "recording" or tracing something as fluid as gender discourses in Muslim communities and how they were and are translated into realities on the ground. Rather, it was my concern about how a more empirical approach as opposed to a textual one would limit and define the range of possible readings of the texts that swayed me in the direction of textual analysis. And it was my original interest in the intellectual production of American Muslims that is still significantly understudied that helped retain my focus on texts.

Based on a broad definition of the category "text," this study draws on books, journal articles, newspaper items, websites, and documentaries produced by and about American Muslim women since the early 1980s. It is in the nature of the texts, especially those of a scholarly nature, to easily move between the categories of primary and secondary sources. Throughout the book I have used academic writings by Muslim women scholars for analysis while also drawing on their analysis of the matters at hand. This approach creates productive tensions between the dynamics of scholarly authority and the "'reading'" of primary texts. It also reflects the dynamics of my own involvement in different communities. As an Islamic studies scholar I have encountered many of the intellectuals whose work I assess here as colleagues, mentors, and peers. Reading and analyzing the works of one's contemporaries comes with the hazard of attachment but also the very real possibility of being taken up on the invitation to engage in dialogue on their writings and my readings of them. I have found myself deeply involved in the very discourses and debates I am analyzing here, and thus this book is at once an analysis of and a contribution to the texts at the center of this study. My own work is as much invested in the triangle of faith, community, and representation as the texts and authors analyzed here.

The textual approach, the focus on the woman-led prayer, and the selection of works by women writers can produce the impression that this study privileges the ideas and contribution of a very specific segment of American Muslim communities: those commonly described as progressive or liberal. Both terms are immediately political, especially in discussions of "gender issues," in Islam as the status of women in Muslim societies has for more than a century been a litmus test of the ability of Muslims to be "modern." They are also of concern when state actors like the United States actively pursue the construction of different categories of Muslims, or what Mahmood Mamdani has termed the "good Muslim—bad Muslim" dichotomy.[3] Such labels, even when self-assigned, are even more complicated when they are used to dismiss or belittle contemporary Muslim projects of reform, transformation, or preservation. This privileging of certain 'voices' is in part a function of the texts themselves. Many of the texts by American Muslim women written in English and published by mainstream publishers are indeed more representative of a small spectrum of all American Muslim women. The dynamics of speaking for other Muslim women and standing in for them in media and textual representations is the subject of one chapter of this book. Rather than be overly critical of the progressive bent of many of the writings, it is important to recognize this "bias" as a research result in and of itself.

The focus on women's writings creates another limitation that is only partly addressed in this book. Foregrounding the texts authored by women has created a space for interactions and conversations between women authors while ostensibly ignoring that Muslim men have made significant contributions to gender debates and that women's ideas, projects, and critiques can only be understood in their interplay and interdependence with men's perspectives. This gender bias, even more than the progressive bias, has the potential to relegate women's contributions to the womens corner, away from the concerns of those outside it. The book, in sometimes ambivalent ways, includes men's perspectives and the contributions of male Muslim intellectuals to gender discourses while recognizing the power dynamics of using male perspectives to authenticate or legitimize women intellectuals and their ideas. Muslim women and men are increasingly conscious of the need to negotiate gender discourses among as well as between the sexes. The ultimate emphasis on women's texts and perspectives is a form of affirmative action: as long as women have to struggle for their concerns and ideas to be heard within Muslim communities, extra attention and analysis with a focus on precisely these concerns and ideas may help them take their place as half of their communities.

The focus on text should not be read as a dismissal of the various forms and projects of local, communal, and transnational activism that American Muslim women are involved in. There is a strong interdependence between formulating and negotiating discourses and translating them into actions. The prayer event itself as well as many other activist projects mentioned in this book are informed by gender discourses and debates while simultaneously informing and changing the discourses themselves.[4]

American and Transnational Dimensions

American Muslims are at once American and members of transnational Muslim networks. As such, their histories are interwoven with those of the United States and Canada (and the Americas), and they are equally intertwined with the modern and especially colonial and postcolonial histories of Muslim-majority countries halfway across the globe. The transnational dynamics of American Muslims' intellectual production and activism are hinted at in several places in this book, but more research is necessary to adequately assess the multiple ways in which American Muslim intellectuals are produced by and are producing contemporary Muslim thought.

Muslims are part of the fabric of American society, socially, economically, politically, and religiously, and they are struggling to be recognized

as equal members in it. As Americans and as Muslims they have to negotiate the environments, histories, and policies of a secular state with a liberal
ideology. While several chapters of this book are focused on intra-Muslim
debates and conversations, they are always framed by the particular American context in which they take place. For a better understanding of the
secular state–religious community dynamic, I draw in subtle ways on the
works of Talal Asad.[5] His assessment of the historical development of secular and liberal ideologies and practices and his critique of secular and liberal
frameworks as self-evident and uncontroversial sets of values have deeply
influenced my thinking about Muslims as a religious minority population in
North America.

Even more directly, the work of Saba Mahmood (who draws on Asad's
work herself) has provided avenues for situating this project. Initially, Mahmood's work on women in the piety movement in Egypt[6] appeared at one
end of the spectrum of how one can study Muslim women and gender discourses and thus worked as something of a mirror to my own concerns.
The women in Mahmood's study participated in religious education and
transformation through increased levels of piety and religious practice.
The women authors I studied situated themselves as part of American society, however critical they may have been of it, and employed decidedly
liberal frameworks to position themselves within their communities and
the larger society. Mahmood saw her work as a contribution to feminist
theory engaging with religious women, while some women authors in my
study themselves employed feminist theory and rhetoric to advance religious transformation. In *Politics of Piety* Mahmood describes the way one of
her informants, a woman preacher in a mosque in Cairo, insisted on leading women who were studying with her in prayer, despite the quite explicit
prohibition of such prayer leadership in Hanafi interpretations of Islamic
Law. Strikingly, the argument for her choice was the possibility of interpreting the law differently, thus assuming the authority to do so, but not any
liberally framed gender concern.[7] For American Muslim women writers the
prayer was all about gender and symbolic equality and not very much about
legal dynamics. Yet Mahmood's critique of the inability of liberal frameworks to acknowledge their own discursive power helped me understand
the ways in which the women (and men) in this study are influenced by such
frameworks and their inherent power dynamics.

Asad's work is foundational in yet another way for many of the topics discussed in this book. Asad has formulated the now commonly cited concept

of an "Islamic discursive tradition" (there can be a multitude of them in his view). In his seminal essay *The Idea of an Anthropology of Islam* he writes:

> A tradition consists essentially of discourses that seek to instruct practitioners regarding the correct form and purpose of a given practice that, precisely because it is established, has a history. These discourses relate conceptually to a past (when the practice was instituted, and from which the knowledge of its point and proper performance has been transmitted) and a future (how the point of that practice can best be secured in the short or long term, or why it should be modified and abandoned), through a present (how it is linked to other practices, institutions, and social conditions). An Islamic discursive tradition is simply a tradition of Muslim discourse that addresses itself to conceptions of the Islamic past and future, with reference to a particular Islamic practice in the present.[8]

Mahmood elaborates:

> Tradition, viewed in this way, is not a set of symbols and idioms that justify present practices, neither is it an unchanging set of cultural prescriptions that stand in contrast to what is changing, contemporary, or modern. Nor is it a historically fixed social structure. Rather, the past is the very ground through which the subjectivity and self-understanding of a tradition's adherents are constituted. An Islamic discursive tradition, in this view, is therefore a mode of discursive engagement with sacred texts, one effect of which is the creation of sensibilities and embodied capacities (of reason, affect, and volition) that in turn are the conditions for the tradition's reproduction.[9]

Such an understanding of the dynamics of text, interpretation, and history permeates the discourses and debates addressed in this book. Whether it is in attempts to reinterpret the Qur'an, rethink and restructure Islamic rituals such as congregational prayer, or make claims to religious and communal authority, the interplay of texts and interpretative presents and authoritative readings of the past are ever-present subtexts in those debates.

American Muslim women are part of the fabric of American society and history in yet another way. Not only does secular American feminism have its own trajectory and dynamics, but to a greater extent religious feminisms are a product of and in constant conversation with the concerns and investments in secular America and the secular feminist movement. Aysha Hidayatullah has traced the interactions of Muslim women feminist theologians with Jewish and Christian feminist thinkers in the United States and has argued that while other religious feminisms have had various interactions with Muslim feminist thinkers and their ideas, deep rifts and disconnects also need to be acknowledged.[10] Of particular importance is the tendency of American feminists, both secular and religious, to use Islam and Muslim women as a backdrop for their own conversation and as the other against which to define themselves. Even more difficult to escape is a sense of evolutionary hierarchy in which feminist projects and ideas are measured against a scale of developments in Christian and later Jewish feminism in which they can only be in a perpetual state of being behind. And while Muslim women scholars have been involved in feminist "interfaith" work for decades, they have also often insisted on their own circumstances, trajectories, and methods. Many Muslim women scholars are still debating the use of the term *feminist* for themselves and their works.

The Structure of the Book

This book is and is not about woman-led prayer. It uses the 2005 woman-led prayer in New York as the historical focus for an analysis of gender discourses in American Muslim communities as reflected in the scholarly and nonfiction writings of American Muslim women authors. The resulting structure of the book combines two focused chapters on the prayer event itself and the ensuing debate on woman-led prayer with six thematic chapters addressing a variety of themes that formed the subtext and framework of the debates.

Chapter 1 describes the prayer event on March 18, 2005. It also includes a partial transcript of Amina Wadud's Friday sermon and the first written reflections by some of those who organized and attended the event. Chapter 2 traces the debate surrounding the prayer event, starting with opinions expressed after the early announcement of the event and following the trail of opinion pieces, newspaper articles, and follow-up events into the summer of 2005. The chapter also identifies the themes guiding the remaining six chapters of the book and argues that the prayer acted as a lens that focused and advanced existing discussions on women and gender in American Muslim communities.

Chapter 3 presents a discussion of the exegetical projects developed by American Muslim women scholars in their hermeneutics and goals. It argues that the prayer event should be read as an embodiment of a *tafsir* (Qur'anic exegesis) of gender justice, which is at the center of women's interpretations of the Qur'an. The chapter also presents an analysis of two Friday *khutbahs* (sermons) offered by Amina Wadud, one in 1994 in South Africa and another at the prayer event in 2005. Both *khutbahs* are to be read as *tafasir* (pl. of *tafsir*) of gender justice and equality demonstrating the content and methods of Wadud's Qur'anic exegesis.

Chapter 4 engages with the legal dimensions of the prayer debate and develops a larger framework for women scholars' approaches to Islamic Law. Connecting the hadith of Umm Waraqa, often cited in discussions of the prayer, with the larger legal arguments for and against women's prayer leadership, the chapter then moves to the works of women scholars with particular interest in legal frameworks and legal reform, as well as women's scholarship within human rights frameworks. Finally, it addresses the identification and negotiation of historical role models for contemporary Muslim women, in particular a recent interest in the person of Hagar among several Muslim women writers.

Chapter 5 connects exegetical and legal projects to the overarching question of religious authority and the ways in which women scholars have stepped into the authority "voids" created by colonialism and modernity. Muslim religious authority is linked directly to the ongoing debate about the nature of the Islamic tradition and whether there is indeed a complete or even partial break between the "classical" and modern interpretations of textual sources and the application of hermeneutical methods. Discussions of Islam as tradition are inextricably linked to questions of authenticity. The idea of interpretive communities as the only way to make interpretations relevant is then connected to the multiple ways in which American Muslim women's ideas have contributed to the creation and sustenance of informal networks, communities, and structures.

Chapter 6 addresses another subtext of the prayer event: the quest of American Muslim women for full access to and equality in mosques and the debate about women's leadership roles within and outside mosques and formal community structures. If the prayer event "gave voice" to women's demands, it also claimed their right to both really and symbolically use their voices in worship and community politics. The chapter closes with a discussion of women's voices in both capacities.

Chapter 7 assesses the ways in which women have been framed by but have also challenged media representations of themselves as oppressed and silent. American Muslim women are uniquely situated to recognize and change media images and representations they perceive as false. However, their active self-representation does not necessarily change the ways in which they are determined by existing frames, and it can unintentionally create a new dichotomy between liberated, confident, and outspoken American Muslim women and their still oppressed counterparts in Muslim-majority societies.

Chapter 8 analyzes memoirs and narrative texts published by American Muslim women and discusses their entanglement in the politics of publishing and marketing in North America. The concluding chapter takes up dimensions and angles of the texts to be explored further: the issue of *hijab* (Muslim headscarf), the politics of American Muslim women's participation in the secular American academy, and matters of race and gender inclusion.

WHILE GENDER DISCOURSES and discussions among American Muslims are at the center of inquiry in this book, the themes addressed are also reflective of all the major issues in modern and/or contemporary Muslim thought, among them authority, tradition, Islamic Law, justice, and authenticity. The focus on gender acknowledges the centrality of this concept for modern intra-Muslim debates while simultaneously questioning its defining status. If the debates and discourses analyzed in this book prove one thing, it is that gender has become part of "mainstream" discourses among Muslims worldwide rather than the concern of a few privileged or activist women. Debates about authority, authenticity, and tradition cannot meaningfully take place any longer without taking gender issues into account. And while some still accuse those Muslims who advance gender conversations of having adopted a "Western" and thus inauthentic and alien concept, Muslims in an interdependent globalized world of intellectual exchange have taken ownership of gender debates and have taken it upon themselves to address issues of justice and human dignity from within their religion and communal structures.[11] This book demonstrates that gender debates are contextualized, framed, and negotiated through the particular histories, circumstances, and intellectual currents of Muslim societies and communities. American Muslims experience and advance gender discourses in particular American ways while simultaneously developing and sustaining transnational projects and networks that address gender dynamics worldwide.

1

A Woman-Led Friday Prayer

March 18, 2005

I was not there. I did not attend the mixed-gender congregational Friday prayer, led by Amina Wadud, on March 18, 2005. I am not sure whether I heard about the event when it was announced or whether I followed the debate at the time. It was early in 2006, in a conversation with one of my students, Rachel Hinson, that I first considered the event with academic interest. I was starting to experience tensions between my identity as a Muslim woman and the expectations of the secular study of religion. To address this tension I developed an interest in the work of American Muslim women and the diverse strategies for negotiating their religious identities within the academy. I was especially interested in women scholars who had found ways to make meaningful connections between their scholarship on gender issues and their activist engagement in Muslim communities. Conversations about these scholar-activists led to Rachel's decision to focus her independent research project on the 2005 prayer and the surrounding debate. When reading her paper, titled "Scholar Activism in Islam: Woman-Led Prayer Case Study," today I realize that many of the ideas we discussed have stayed relevant but that my perspectives have been transformed. What would have been different if I had known about the prayer? Would I have decided to make the trip to New York City and attend? Would I have participated? What impact might the prayer event have had on my convictions? How would I remember the event today? What impact would the debates in the media and among Muslims in the United States and abroad have had on my recollections?

Here I offer a description of the prayer event on March 18, 2005. In its format and perspective it resembles notes from a participant observation, containing the impressions and explanations of an observer present at the event combined with first thoughts on its significance and implications. When I decided that this book would use the prayer as a lens, I needed to locate information on what transpired in New York City that day. Sources were readily available in the form of reflective and narrative texts written and published by some of those who organized and/or attended the prayer event. However, video footage and photographs were surprisingly diffi-cult to obtain, despite the presence of dozens of journalists and cameras. It was Asra Nomani, an organizer of the prayer, who referred me to Brittany Huckabee, a documentary filmmaker who had accompanied Nomani to the event for a documentary film project—focused on Nomani—that she was working on at the time. The film, *The Mosque in Morgantown*, aired in June 2009 on PBS.[1] Huckabee shared with me several hours of unedited video footage, filmed with two cameras and following Nomani, before, during, and after the event. While very helpful and my only access to "what really happened," the footage is as skewed as the recollections of a particular ob-server. Instead of being able to decide where to be when, what to notice and what to leave out, and how to interpret the sequence of events, these deci-sions had been made for me.[2] I am including the lengthy description of the prayer event as a way for the reader to imagine what it may have been like to be there.[3] No such description has been published. The fierce debate over the symbolic significance and legal permissibility of woman-led prayer has since early 2005 overshadowed the details of the ritual acts, speeches, and bodily movements during the event itself.

The description of the prayer event is framed by thoughts on its historical context. I offer a brief account of Nomani's activities in 2004 and 2005 and point to earlier events in which Muslim women led prayers or participated in Islamic ritual in leadership positions. The description is followed by an analysis of several narratives published by organizers and participants.

A Historical Event?

Once every week, on Friday around noon, Muslims across the globe come together in mosques and prayer spaces to perform congregational prayers, known as *jum'a* (Friday) prayers. The ritual requirements, including ablu-tion, congregation size, and number of prayer units, are regulated by Islamic Law. Traditionally, only men are required to attend Friday prayers, but women at least in some geographic locations have also participated in them. Unlike the five daily prayers, Friday prayers cannot be performed individually. The congregational prayer is preceded by a khutbah (sermon), which may or may not be offered by the same person leading the congregation in Friday prayers (imam). The requirements and legal regulations associated with the prayer are, like many other aspects of Muslim worship, modeled after the practices of the Prophet Muhammad.

The Friday prayer on March 18, 2005, differed from established Muslim practices in several ways: the imam was a woman, Amina Wadud, who also delivered the khutbah; the congregation she addressed and led in prayer was not separated by gender;[4] and the *adhan* (call to prayer) was pronounced by a woman. It is in these three departures from established ritual practice that the March 18 prayer became an embodied performance of gender justice in the eyes of its organizers and participants. They symbolically challenged the exclusively male privilege of leading Muslims in ritual prayers and at the same time blurred the lines of gender segregation in ritual prayers.

There are many ways to see the woman-led prayer of 2005 as part of a larger historical contingency, as one event in a chain of developments concerned with the equality of Muslim women. One could think about the various attempts to reinterpret the Qur'an, carried out by both male and female Muslim scholars, with the intention of finding more egalitarian readings of the Islamic sacred text. The history of Muslim women's activism in North America would be another fruitful way to situate the prayer in a larger historical context. And not least, other, earlier events at which women led prayers or had leadership roles in Muslim communities across the globe would have to be seen as belonging to the same history. The trajectory of events leading to and beyond the March 2005 prayer event as narrated by Asra Nomani demonstrates how experiences and events built on each other to form a logical chain of activism and motivations. The chain of events is significant as the lens through which this book addresses gender discourses and debates. However, a similar event, elsewhere and at a different time, would have served the same catalyzing purpose building on existing dynamics. If not in March 2005 in New York City and initiated by Nomani, a public woman-led and mixed-gender congregational Friday prayer would have taken place eventually, triggering similar debates and emphasizing existing historical trajectories.

The organizers around Asra Nomani and Nomani herself perceived the prayer event on March 18, 2005, as part of a chain of events with Nomani at their center. Nomani's 2005 book, *Standing Alone in Mecca*, is the story of her pilgrimage to Mecca and her connected journey to a new Muslim woman's identity. She describes how her experiences in Mecca and in her hometown's Muslim community came together to form the seeds of her activist campaign in 2003. Having completed the pilgrimage with her parents and her son Shibli, Nomani asserted the significance of her Muslim identity for herself and for raising her son and decided to try to integrate herself into the Muslim community in Morgantown, West Virginia. Her resistance to gender discourses in the community was triggered when, in 2003, the community completed a new mosque building featuring a separate prayer space and a separate entrance for women. When Nomani was told to use the women's entrance she felt compelled to rethink the role of women in mosques and communities and subsequently decided to challenge the board and members of her mosque in Morgantown. After researching the topic and finding support for her position, Nomani initiated a series of events that eventually led to the prayer in New York City. In her own account the events developed organically and were based on her conviction that women are equal in worship and society.[5]

In June 2004 a group of Muslim women led by Nomani gathered in Morgantown for one of the five daily prayers. It was Nomani's way of taking her own critique of the mosque and community practices to a new level, by enlisting support and by making a first symbolic statement calling for women's equality in worship. Calling the small group "Daughters of Hajar: American Muslim Women Speak,"[6] Nomani organized her march on the mosque in Morgantown to demand prayer space for women in the main hall of the mosque. Before their march on the mosque, Nomani, her parents, and her son; Saleemah Abdul-Ghafur, editor of the book *Living Islam Out Loud*; Saleemah's mother, Nabeelah; Sarah Eltantawi, activist and writer; the poet Mohja Kahf; and the novelist Michael Muhammad Knight gathered at the West Virginia University School of Law to pray, led by Nabeelah Abdul-Ghafur. This prayer, with a woman leading a mixed-gender congregation, would be a prelude to the woman-led Friday prayer in March 2005. The group then walked to the mosque, entered through the main door, and prayed in the main prayer space.

In early March 2005 Nomani taped her "99 Precepts for Opening Hearts, Minds, and Doors in the Muslim World"[7] on the front door of the mosque in Morgantown. On March 18, 2005, the prayer event took place in New York City. It was organized by Nomani, Saleemah Abdul-Ghafur, Sarah Eltantawi, and Ahmed Nassef. Eltantawi and Nassef were among the four cofounders of the Progressive Muslim Union, and Nassef was also the cofounder of the progressive Muslim website MuslimWakeUp.[8] From March to June 2005 Nomani's "Muslim Women's Freedom Tour" took her to various mosques around the United States where she insisted on praying in the main prayer space, despite protest and resistance from imams and congregations. Also in 2005 Nomani led a mixed-gender prayer at Brandeis University in Boston.

Announcing the Prayer

The March 18 prayer was to take place in the Synod House of the Cathedral of St. John the Divine, mother church of the Episcopal Diocese of New York. Earlier the organizers had tried to find a mosque in New York City for the prayer but were unsuccessful. The second choice of venue was an art gallery, but threats moved the organizers to seek an alternative space, which they found at St. John's, despite prevailing security concerns. Police presence and security checks at the entrance attested to the fact that the organizers and the police took the threats seriously.[9]

The plans for the prayer were announced on the MuslimWakeUp website on March 7, 2005, calling for public endorsement on the same site from all those in support of the prayer event. The announcement read:

> As part of the Muslim Women's Freedom Tour, muslimwakeup.com will be sponsoring an event of historic proportions on Friday, March 18, 2005: a Jum'ah prayer in which a woman will deliver the khutbah and lead the prayer for a mixed-gender congregation. It will be the **first public Jum'ah prayer of its kind on record** since Prophet Muhammad, upon whom be peace and blessings, reportedly authorized Umm Waraqa to lead her household in prayer. The khutbah and prayer will be led by Dr. Amina Wadud, professor of Islamic Studies at Virginia Commonwealth University and internationally known Qur'an scholar.
>
> It took us 1,400 years to do it again. But this time, it's for keeps insha'allah.
>
> We are calling on everyone in our community to speak loud and clear in favor of reclaiming our faith of justice and compassion for all people, women and men, by endorsing the event, either individually or on behalf of your mosque or organization. Thousands of Muslim women and men in North America and around the world are looking for your leadership and vision.[10]

The 2005 debate about female prayer leadership was triggered by this announcement. The announcement was followed by a second statement from the organizers, posted on March 13, five days before the Friday prayer.[11]

This second statement responded to the ongoing and at times raging debate about women leading prayers and appealed to all involved in the conversation to accept differences of opinion and create spaces for open debate without threats. In it, security concerns were cited as the reason for changing the venue of the prayer event and for not announcing the new location publicly. Those interested in attending the prayer had to fill out a form on the MuslimWakeUp website and would subsequently be informed about the location. This sign-up list became important for security management, as the security personnel at the event allowed only those on a list of invited or confirmed participants to enter the premises of St. John the Divine. The statement also expressed gratitude for the worldwide support that the organizers had received for their endeavor. Both statements on the MuslimWakeUp website also functioned as announcements to media representatives and set the stage for the heavy media presence at the event. In an unusual move, on the morning of the event, the *New York Times* carried an article by Andrea Elliott, giving the organizers one more chance to publicize the prayer and its intentions. In her article, "Muslim Group Is Urging Women to Lead Prayers," Elliott chronicled the plans for the event, the motivations and arguments of the organizers, and some of the debate about women leading prayers while also announcing the location of the prayer. Quite possibly, it was this article that accounted for the presence of those vehemently opposed to the event demonstrating in front of the St. John compound on March 18. The protesters, too, were part of Elliott's vivid description of the prayer in a second article, published on March 19 in the *New York Times*:

> A woman, Dr. Amina Wadud, led the Muslim service after another woman sounded the call to prayer wearing no headscarf. More than a hundred men and women knelt in adjacent rows, with no curtain to divide them. They were surrounded by a bustling group of newspaper reporters, photographers and television cameras. And outside the service, which was held at the Synod House of the Cathedral of St. John the Divine, protesters held signs and cried out in disgust.[12]

The Press Conference

The prayer ceremony itself was preceded by a press conference at which several of the organizers, including Asra Nomani, Saleemah Abdul-Ghafur, Ahmed Nassef, Sarah Eltantawi, and Amina Wadud, spoke to the significance of the prayer. Even before the press conference Nomani gave several interviews to journalists and media representatives while trying to set up the main hall of the Synod House as a Muslim prayer space and while attending to a host of logistical issues involving security checks and safety measures in and around the compound. In one such interview, with Al-Jazeera Television, Nomani shared her excitement and explained her view of the significance of the prayer:

> Today is the dawn of a new day in the history of Islam. We are opening the door of the Muslim world to women and to people of all faith. This is not just about mosques, this is about our Muslim faiths, this is about our Muslim community. It is about opening up the doors of Islam to everyone. I am so excited about today. We are going to change history and the course of our Muslim world. . . . We have the right to stand without barriers. America and the West have to deal with glass ceilings; we have brick walls in front of us, and we are hammering them down. And it is so that we can bust open the Muslim world for a better day.[13]

Later in the same interview, Nomani referred to historical models for women's leadership, starting with Hajar, whom Nomani chose as the patron for her group Daughters of Hajar.

The press conference took place on the lower level of the Synod House and was attended by at least several dozen journalists and media representatives from the United States and around the world. Nomani, Wadud, Abdul-Ghafur, Eltantawi, Nassef, and Suhayla El-Attar, who would later sound the call for prayer, were assembled in front. Speaking for several minutes each, their comments highlighted the fact that each one of them may have had a different perspective on the meaning of and justification for the event but that they were brought together in an effort of temporary community building through their recognition of the symbolic significance and potential of the event. Their excitement was palpable in their short remarks and filled the room with a sense of importance and anticipation.

Eltantawi, who acted as host of the press conference, began by introducing herself and the Progressive Muslim Union, an American Muslim organization that was a cosponsor of the prayer event. She then proceeded to describe the prayer as a historic event—that is, the first time on historical record that a woman would lead a Friday prayer and give a khutbah. She then introduced each speaker.

Nomani explained again the significance of the event as one that would take American Muslim women to the front of the mosque and, symbolically at least, into leadership positions in Muslim communities, not just in America, but globally. She described the event as a victory for women, for Islam, and for world peace and included a sharp critique of the status of women in the Muslim world, which the prayer, if successful, would begin to rectify. She said:

> The voices of women have been silenced through centuries of man-made traditions, and we are saying, no more, enough is enough, we are going to take our rightful place in the Muslim world. We are reclaiming the place that the Prophet Muhammad and Islam gave us in the seventh century, and we are going to be part of the solution. . . . We are going to be cities of light to the Muslim world so that all can follow this lead.

Eltantawi then introduced Ahmed Nassef as a "tireless advocate for women's rights" and pointed out that his presence was a reflection of the fact that the prayer initiative had been supported by many Muslim men. Nassef emphasized that it had taken Muslims fourteen hundred years to come to this point when such a prayer was possible and claimed that equal space in the mosque and the Muslim community for men and women was a precondition for realizing what it means to be Muslim. Like Nomani, Nassef, too, referred to Muslim history and origins as justification for the prayer: "We are not trying to change Islam; we are going back to our roots of justice and compassion." Later he cited evidence from prophetic practice and the opinions of Al-Tabari (838–923 C.E.), a classical Islamic scholar, as support for the prayer by stating that the Prophet Muhammad had allowed a woman to lead a mixed congregation in prayer. He pointed to the inspiring and community-building rather than divisive nature of the prayer for those Muslims in America who had not attended communal prayers and had avoided their communities because they did not identify with their gender practices. Despite the fact that the prayer did not take place in a mosque, Nassef predicted that it would bring the majority of Muslims who are not attached to mosques and communities back into the fold of organized religion.

Nassef's comments were followed by those of Saleemah Abdul-Ghafur, a participant in Nomani's Muslim Women's Freedom Tour. Abdul-Ghafur read a prepared statement emphasizing the negative treatment of Muslim women throughout the world based on unequal readings of the religion of

Islam and called Muslims to reclaim the egalitarian and humanistic roots of Islam in order to improve Muslim women's lives and claim leadership in Muslim communities. Referring to Umm Waraqa again, Abdul-Ghafur insisted that women have the God-given right to lead. She promised that the organizers would "create a powerful and spiritual environment for our congregants" and that it would take place in a "safe and nurturing and inspiring space." In acknowledgment of earlier prayers led by women, she urged women and communities to take their private prayers public and encouraged those who had contemplated such acts to carry them out. She recounted nationwide and worldwide support for the event but also criticized opponents of the event for their "vitriolic attacks" against the organizers and supporters, expressed in hateful and threatening emails and messages.

In introducing Suhayla El-Attar, the young woman who would later offer the adhan, Eltantawi spoke of the importance of the call for prayer in the Islamic tradition and the spiritual impact it can have on Muslims: "The beautiful voices of women have been excluded from this beautiful ritual, and that, too, will end today with the brave participation of Suhayla El-Attar, who will be giving the call for us today." El-Attar attributed her call to her family legacy, especially her grandfather who was a well-known muezzin in Cairo, and described Islam as a religion that is not based on fear but on the quest for knowledge.

Eltantawi then introduced Amina Wadud as a historical figure for her intention to lead the prayer and for her reinterpretation of the Qur'an. She expressed her admiration and appreciation for Wadud's work but also for her courage in the face of threats. After thanking the organizers for the invitation, Wadud mentioned her earlier efforts to help Muslim women in "reclaiming their full human dignity" and emphasized its grounding in the Qur'an. "The basis of what I will present during the sermon," she said, "will be from the Qur'an, through the voice, experiences, reality, strength, and weakness of a woman." She also emphatically described herself as a lonely academic, much more comfortable in the peace and serenity of writing books than with standing "before so much technology." She pointed out that "advertising this event raises the stake several notches higher" than holding it in a private setting. She asked everyone to respect her decision not to be contacted, photographed, or interviewed after the event. For her, the prayer performance would be an act of "devotion to Allah," performed in the form of Friday prayers practiced by Muslims for many centuries— with "the notable distinction," she continued, "that I will act as leader of the prayer and as the person giving the sermon and I am a woman. And I hope therefore that the benefit will be felt by every woman, every Muslim woman, and by every Muslim man, as an act of devotion before Allah." She added, "I have never given a press conference before I went to pray!"

In a seamless transition to a question-and-answer period Wadud was approached by a man who challenged her position on woman-led prayer based on the example of Umm Waraqa by claiming that she had been ordered by the Prophet Muhammad to lead other women in prayer but not a mixed congregation. In response, Wadud said (after spelling "Umm Waraqa" for the journalists):

> This Umm Waraqa has been the subject of a tremendous amount of discourse over the last few weeks, and one thing is certain from the great diversity of responses to her role, her legacy, her significance, etc.: it is an aspect of the reality of humanity, including Muslims, and that is diversity and plurality. However, the basis of my articulation of the mandate to acknowledge Muslim women as spiritual equals and therefore competent not only in the realm of political and economic leadership but also, and more important to me, competent in the realm of spiritual and public ritual leadership will be on the basis of the Qur'an, and that I will speak about during the sermon.

Wadud was then asked what she wanted to change in Muslim mosques. She responded:

> I don't want to change Muslim mosques; I want to encourage the hearts of Muslims in both their public, private, and religious or ritual affairs to believe that they are one as equal to any other especially in the context of Islam and by accepting that to remove artificial and sometimes inconvenient restrictions on the entry and participation of women in that same devotion.

Other questions, addressed primarily to Wadud, included the choice of venue, perceptions of Wadud in the Muslim world, and a request to reiterate her justification for the importance and validity of the prayer, to which she responded:

> I would say I believe in Allah, I believe in the messenger of Allah, I believe in the unity of Muslims, and I believe that we are part of the agency or khilafah that Allah has assigned, and as a consequence we

will all be required to respond to the situations, the circumstances of our cultural and historical, very culturally diverse, presence as agents, and consequently we will be faced with many new and unprecedented circumstances for which we draw from our hearts and from our tradition in order to argue with the best of our intentions.

The press conference was then adjourned so that preparations for the prayer could be made.

Before the Prayer

Upstairs in the Synod House sky blue carpeting had been spread on the ground in order to visually designate the ritual space for the prayer. Nomani discussed with several people present—including Leila Ahmed, professor of women's studies at Harvard University—how to arrange the carpeting in order to have participants face the *qiblah* (direction of Mecca), as required for all Muslim prayers. Journalists were repeatedly instructed not to stand in front of the congregation in order to not obstruct the qiblah.

Worshipers—women and men—started to fill the prayer space, dressed in a variety of clothing, some women wearing headscarves while others were not. Standing in small groups and talking, or sitting on the carpet in anticipation of the prayer, here, too, a sense of excitement is palpable from the video. Nomani can be seen greeting incoming participants and getting embroiled in several conversations about the qiblah and the placement of the carpet. When asked if she wanted to have women on one side and men on the other, she replied that there should be a space in the middle for families to mix. The carpets were straightened, with the discussion echoing Wadud's concern about following established ritual practice in almost all aspects of the prayer, except those intentionally challenging such practice.

After some discussion about security concerns and the possibility of the prayer being infiltrated and disrupted by protesters, Nomani walked to the front of the congregation and greeted the waiting Muslim worshipers:

> Assalamu Alaykum, I cannot tell you how happy I am seeing all of you here today. I stood here yesterday, in an empty space, and I imagined the beauty of all those that would come here guided by light. I have out here all my friends, old and new, and I have with you a new vision for Islam in this world. My name is Asra Nomani. I am just an ordinary Muslim woman who has had the same crisis in faith that so many

women have had when they have felt that there was no place in the religion for them. Three years ago I went on the pilgrimage to Mecca, and I stood with my brothers and sisters in Islam, and I sat with them like we sit here today, without any barriers, without any partitions, without anything dividing us, connected by love and the oneness that is Islam. I am so proud to be here together with all of you. Last June five women and one man prayed on the banks of the Monongahela River in Morgantown, West Virginia, my hometown, and we broke the dawn with a prayer led by a woman and we had a dream. We had a dream that we would be able to take this vision of a world where women are leaders into our universe. We have made our dream come true, and you are part of that dream. And I know that this is the dream that women have not even believed that they could imagine.

Nomani then repeated parts of her "Islamic Bill of Rights for Women in the Mosque" from memory to the congregation and the reporters.[14] She went on to say:

I cheer all of you and I thank all of you because you are the new vision of Islam in this world. We are taking our faith and we are bringing it into the twenty-first century. We are erasing traditions that have denied the beauty of Islam in this world. Allahu Akbar to all of you! The Divine radiates from you, and we are a shining light to the world. My blessings to all of you! I am going to now introduce you to a phenomenon that we are not getting to hear in the Muslim world, and that is the sound of a woman calling us to prayer. Close your eyes if you wish, feel the echo of her sound, know the strengths and the echo of centuries of women before us from Hajar who stood alone in Mecca. And feel the strength of the pulse of the women of Islam in all of you, women, men, and children. We are all one.

El-Attar then sounded the first call to prayer from a microphone in front of the congregation. As Elliott pointed out in her article for the *New York Times*, El-Attar did not wear a hijab while performing her duty.

After walking to the front of the congregation, Saleemah Abdul-Ghafur instructed reporters again to move away from the front of the congregation, so as to allow for the creation of a sacred space for the ceremony. She also asked that they respect the congregation and not use flash for cameras. Now kneeling in front of the congregation, with microphone in hand,

Abdul-Ghafur faced the worshipers and introduced the plan to begin the worship with ten minutes of *dhikr* (invocation). She instructed the congregation to focus on their worship, forget the cameras, and not worry about doing everything right. Visibly nervous herself, she encouraged worshipers to focus on the meaning of their recitation and not their surroundings. Briefly explaining the meaning and sources of the worship exercises to follow, Abdul-Ghafur, with notes in her lap, then recited the opening chapter of the Qur'an, *al-Fatiha*, seven times, joined by members of the congregation, followed by thirty-three repetitions of the Qur'anic verse "Salamun Qawlan min Rabbi Raheem," translated by Abdul-Ghafur as "Peace—a word from the Lord, most Merciful."[15] This recitation was then followed by one hundred repetitions of one of the ninety-nine beautiful names or attributes of God, *an-Nur*, the Light, in the form of "Ya Nur" (Oh Light).[16] Given the fact that Nomani had repeatedly referred to the significance of being and/or following the light embedded in the prayer event and its symbolic meaning, the choice of this attribute was presumably deliberate and meaningful for the organizers. Nomani participated in the dhikr, first standing on the side and later sitting down in the front row of the congregation.

Abdul-Ghafur then handed the microphone to El-Attar, who sounded the second call for prayer while Amina Wadud came into the room and sat down, waiting for the adhan to end. Wadud stood up and walked to the front of the congregation, her prayer beads in one hand and a notepad in the other. Facing the congregation and with her back to the qiblah, Wadud began her sermon.

The Khutbah

The khutbah began with a standard greeting for the Prophet Muhammad, recited in Arabic, and followed by an English translation.[17] Wadud proceeded to recite several passages from the Qur'an, first in Arabic and then in her own English translation, including Q 62:9, 2:255, 33:35, and 2:286. The passages were selected because they address proper religious and ritual practice and the nature of God and, in the case of 33:35, because the verse addresses women and men separately. It is noteworthy that Wadud offered translations of the passages in which she used the pronouns "He" and "She" and on one occasion also "It" to refer to God. She explained later in the sermon that this choice reflected her understanding of the nongendered, transcendent nature of God and the grammatical but not divine limitations of using the Arabic pronoun *Huwa* for God. Her thoughts focused on the fact that the Qur'an assures Muslims repeatedly that He will not burden them beyond their ability to bear such burdens. She continued by reflecting on the presence of God's signs for humanity all around and inside of humanity. The central piece and argument of the sermon focused on Wadud's reflection on the nature of creation, especially humanity, and her "*tawhidic* paradigm," which emphasizes the "horizontal reciprocity between any two humans, especially between male and female humans."[18] This part of the khutbah reads:[19]

Qur'an 4:1
"And among his ayat or his signs is that She created you from a single nafs, a single soul and created with her its mate. And spread from those two countless men and women."

All humanity descended from a single soul. This unity of origin, I would say, affects to important implications about extensions of the foundational principle of *tawhid*. Those implications are, number one, of course, that Allah is One, *tawhid* means Allah is one. Allah is unique, Allah is united and Allah unifies. Number two, no human being is ever the same as Allah, is ever able to precisely know or understand all of Allah's intention for the creation of humans or of the entire cosmos. And yet, all human beings have been granted the potential to experience "at-onement" with Allah, for fleeting moments, in this creation and eternity, the Hereafter. Since humans, created from a single soul, by a single Lord of love, mercy and power, one dimension of experiencing that oneness, is by living before and in surrender to Allah Ta'ala, to practice the unity of human beings. Tawhid is the foundation of Muslim unity. Let's look a minute at this tawhid paradigm, especially as it relates to all human action and to our particular gathering here today.

Muslims constantly repeat *Allahu Akbar, Allahu Akbar, Allahu Akbar*, that Allah is the Greatest, there is nothing higher than Allah. The Qur'an says *"that there is no 'shay' or thing or manifestation in creation that Allah is like or that is like Allah."* Allah is unique. Allah also said, *"and from all 'shay,' created things we created the pair."* [She puts folder/pad down on the floor.] So you have in thinking about Allah's presence, which is everywhere, a guidepost that first distinguishes Allah from similitude with the cosmos or creation, and we have that every "shay" or every thing created is in pairs. The combination of *"that He is not like shay or created phenomenological reality"* and *"that from every shay created or phenomenological realities there are pairs."* The pair, for example, male and female, are features, characteristics, phenomena, realities, expressions of our being created. We are creatures of Allah. Pairedness or dualism is a feature of created things. Allah is not created and not like anything in creation and therefore cannot be limited to being either a he or a she because that would make similitude, *shirk*, it would make Allah like us. Many Muslims believe that Allah is male. There are certain grammatical reasons why this is so. But when the Qur'an categorically dismisses the similitude between Allah and creation and describes creation on the basis of pairs, then it is a violation of the integrity and the uniqueness and oneness or the tawhid of Allah to try and reduce Allah to half of what is the human creation.

And we said Allah is the Greatest. The Qur'an says, *"no three of you gather but Allah is the fourth, no four of you gather but Allah is the fifth."* In other words Allah is always present between any human interactions. So if Allah is the greatest and male and female as part of creation acknowledge, accept, respect, believe and surrender to Allah's greatness, then male and female can only ever exist on a line of horizontal reciprocity. So it matters not if the male is here and the female is here [indicating with her hands their horizontal alignment], or the female is here and the male is here, they are always on a horizontal line of reciprocity. Why? Because transcendentally the presence of Allah as Akbar, as Greatest, does not allow for a man to be on a vertical line vis-à-vis the woman, which is often what is meant when people say complementary. They have complementary roles. So if you put on your Armani suit and you have a matching necktie and handkerchief in your pocket, that handkerchief and that necktie complement your suit. That is not reciprocity. My understanding then of tawhid in action is that the necessity of being a pair, that is that Allah created *"min kulli shay'in zawjain,"* the necessity of being a pair means that we are both equally essential in creation and therefore reciprocally responsible for our relations with others. And you can extend this to issues of race, to class, to religion, to practicing, to nonpracticing, etc. In other words every human being against another human being can only exist on a line of horizontal reciprocity because Allah is Akbar. Now I don't mean to reduce Allah to a thing, but since Allah is present everywhere it means that whenever a man is in contact, in relationship, in thoughts, in philosophy, in deeds on a line with every woman, every man in relationship to every woman can only exist on a line of horizontal reciprocity because Allah is the greatest and Allah is always present whether we acknowledge it or not, whether we agree with it or not, and whether it is convenient for us or not, women and men both are necessary and essential to Allah's plan for creation, and women and men both have the capacity to reach moral excellence and to demonstrate that excellence by reciprocally participating in every action that they can. Sorry, you guys can't have kids, but you can't have everything. The level of reciprocal possibility and responsibility with regard to 1,426 years of the historical phenomenon of Islam because of course Allah existed before 1,426 years at the level of historical experience the removal of the active principle . . . [missing passage].

We all participate in the making of the basic paradigm that is the understanding of Islam. We, in the twenty-first century recognize this invisibility, this silence, this distortion where men get to tell us how to be women although they have never been women themselves, and then get to mark upon themselves a stamp of divine legitimacy and authority. People ask, well, what about *fiqh* [Islamic jurisprudence] and *fulan* [person x] and fulan and fulan, and I tell them fiqh is after the Prophet. I personally belong to the same *madhhab* [Islamic legal school] as the Prophet, and he didn't belong to a madhhab. So the whole idea of *madhahib* [pl. *madhhab*] with all its good intentions is in fact an innovation but a necessary and good innovation, with the exception of the fact that women were not allowed input into the articulations of the basic paradigms that determine what it means to be Muslim. We therefore claim at this time in history that we have primordial, preexistent mandates to correct this error and to acknowledge the reciprocal essence and responsibility of women and men to participate in attaining moral excellence.

Evidently close to her heart and mind, the khutbah in large part was delivered by Wadud from memory, after putting her notepad on the floor and demonstrating the vertical and horizontal lines of the tawhid paradigm with her hands during her speech. People in the congregation were listening intently, sitting on the carpet, some looking around. Ahmed Nassef's son can be seen sleeping in his lap. As the sermon continued, the journalists surrounding the prayer area became visibly restless and started to lose interest in its content.

Wadud then recited a *du'ah* (supplication), asking for God's mercy and forgiveness. She announced that she would sit down for one minute and ask silently for Allah's forgiveness. The camera follows her sitting down on her prayer mat, spread in front of her, facing Mecca, bowing her head, closing her eyes, and focusing on her prayer. After standing up again, Wadud continued the sermon with another supplication in Arabic and English. She ended with the sentence, "Please join me in reciting the Fatiha." The congregants, many with their hands open and palms facing upward, recited the opening chapter of the Qur'an together.

Delivered in a slow and careful voice, almost an hour long (a departure from established practice), and at least partially read from a script in her hand, the khutbah was intended, like the prayer following it, to adhere to traditional ritual protocol, except for the fact that both were offered by a woman. During the khutbah journalists to the right and left of Wadud were moving about, taking pictures and recording the speech, while clearly being more interested in the symbolic performance by a woman than the actual content. Wadud at several points had difficulty reading her script and struggled with holding her notes without a podium to rest them on. She apologized for not being able to read from her notes. The footage shows Abdul-Ghafur (in a purple headscarf) and Nomani (without headscarf) sitting in the front row, looking up and listening attentively to Wadud. At one point Nomani rose to leave, and the camera recorded her discussion with someone not visible about the sermon being too long and her concern about losing people's interest before the Friday prayer.

The Prayer

Immediately following the recitation of the Fatiha, the third call to prayer was sounded—the sign for the congregation to rise and follow Wadud in the ritual prayer movements and words. After being instructed by Wadud, participants moved to straighten and fill the rows of worshipers in the prayer area as is customary practice for Muslim congregational prayers. Wadud called on the congregants to make sure that the purpose of their prayer was their devotion to God and said, "Whether or not you can see Allah when you pray know that Allah can see you." Pronouncing "Allahu Akbar" Wadud started her performance of the two required *rakʿahs* (prayer units). Behind her, the congregation consisted of women and men. In many rows women stood to one side, men to the other, with a few intermingling in the middle of the row. Despite its symbolic significance, the praying of the two rakʿahs took only seven minutes to complete.

Wadud chose to recite Surah 94 (Surat ash-Sharh) for the first prayer unit and Surah 67 (Surat al-Mulk) for the second. At one point she got so distracted by the cameras in front of her, that is, between her and the qiblah, that she stumbled over one of the lines in the Surah. Someone in the congregation reminded her, and the prayer proceeded. The prayer movements included standing, bowing, and prostration, as prescribed in Islamic Law. Wadud then recited a duʿah asking God to accept the prayer and the intentions of the congregation: "Oh Allah, we have gathered here as Muslims, and people of faith all over the world have gathered in your name. Please accept the best intentions in our hearts, and please forgive any oversights on our parts."

Worshipers again, many with palms turned upward, engaged in a silent supplication. Slowly congregants started to stand up and leave the prayer area. Immediately after the prayer the camera followed Nomani as she exclaimed, "We did it!" and greeted and hugged women in the congregation, while Wadud can be seen performing an additional individual prayer.

The prayer was attended by more women than men and several children. As the camera moved over the group of worshipers, the diversity of American Muslims—ethnic background, choice of clothing, and perspective on Islam—became visible for a moment. What might have been going on in their minds as Wadud was speaking to them about gender equality, justice, and a new understanding of their sacred texts? How many of them had not attended a Friday prayer in years and now were praying under very different circumstances, in a very different space, following their convictions? How many had doubts about their participation in the prayer? How many were concerned with the protesters outside the building, shouting and carrying signs declaring that Amina Wadud was not a Muslim? How many, like me watching the footage in 2009, were wondering about the impact of the event but also about the different personal and political agendas of the organizers? How many were worried about the validity (in the eyes of God and their communities) of the ritual they were performing on that Friday? And how would they later remember the prayer and its significance?

Reflections and Memories

Several participants in the prayer, most notably Nomani and Wadud, have written about the event in narrative or memoir form. Published soon after or within a year, these reflections point us to the importance of personal perspective and the power of the mind to invest past events with meaning.

Asra Nomani: "I was proud to be in the front row"

Nomani has written extensively about herself, most notably in *Standing Alone in Mecca*, which details her journey and transformation as a Muslim woman—from the murder of her friend Daniel Pearl and her discovery that she is pregnant with her Pakistani boyfriend's child through her pilgrimage to Mecca with her family and baby to her reasserted Muslim identity and the subsequent activism aimed at greater mosque access for American Muslim women. Nomani has been vocal about her perspectives on the world and seemingly without any doubt about her agenda or methods or their implications. About the planning of the prayer event she wrote:

> While we challenge the status quo, we are busy creating a new reality. At Harvard University in March 2005, Muslim thinkers and activists planned to hold the first convention of the Progressive Muslim Union. . . . A possibility for the Muslim conference at Harvard: a Friday prayer led by a Muslim woman religious leader, who would also deliver the week's sermon. The woman: scholar Amina Wadud, who had been such an inspiration to me.[20]

On March 20, 2005, she wrote in the *Daily News*:

> Friday, March 18, 2005, will be remembered as the day when about 130 Muslim women and men stood shoulder-to-shoulder behind a woman on Manhattan's upper West Side and took their faith back from the extremists who had tried to define Islam on Sept. 11, 2001.
>
> I was proud to be in the front row.
>
> New York City has been a beacon to the world for its courage after 9/11. Our prayer makes New York a city of light to the Muslim world. As Wadud said her final blessings, I turned to Abdul-Ghafur, an Atlanta writer and activist who helped me organize the prayer, along with the sponsorship of MuslimWakeUp.com, and I exclaimed: "We did it!"
>
> I haven't been able to stop smiling ever since.[21]

Nomani also described Wadud's role in the prayer: "In the quiet of our sacred space, though, Amina Wadud, a scholar of Islam at Virginia Commonwealth University, took her place before me, the first woman in the modern day to lead women and men in a public Friday prayer."[22]

In Nomani's perspective on the event, it was at the center but not the end of her activist journey and agenda. It neatly followed her pilgrimage adventure with her son and family in 2003, her praying in the main hall of the Morgantown mosque in 2004, and her posting of the precepts in early 2005.

Amina Wadud: Defying Sensationalism

Wadud's recollections of the prayer and surrounding events are much more sober and at times even bitter.[23] In her book *Inside the Gender Jihad*, published in 2006, the story of the prayer as she recalled it is placed in the last chapter together with other controversies she has been embroiled in. The chapter, in reference to the jihad in the title of the book, is titled "Stories from the Trenches" and chronicles many of the instances in which Wadud found herself at the center of public debate, controversy, and personal attack.

Following Wadud's reflections on an earlier controversy at a mosque in Toronto, the prayer event appears in her recollection as a series of mediated misrepresentations and misunderstandings that she tried to balance through her performance during the event. Wadud insists that the prayer was not the only and certainly not the most important role she has played in her gender jihad and asks implicitly to not be reduced to her role as the leader of the prayer. She offers her recollections in part as an attempt to reclaim the prayer and its meaning and to rectify what she describes as sensationalist misrepresentations of her ideas.

In her narrative the prayer is directly linked to the creation of the Progressive Muslim Union. Wadud explains her original role as an advisory board member and her subsequent distancing from the organization and its goals. She describes how she was approached by Asra Nomani about the prayer on two occasions and eventually agreed to lead it, in part because she happened to have planned to be in New York during that week. According to her description, Nomani had secured funding from HarperCollins, publisher of *Standing Alone in Mecca*, and was thus able to organize the prayer. The impression that the prayer was at least in part a publicity event for Nomani is supported by the video footage, in which her agent, flown in from San Francisco, is prominently involved in the setup, discussions about security, and channeling reporters to Nomani to be interviewed.

Wadud describes her effort to follow established ritual protocol for the prayer itself based on concerns about the earlier controversy that erupted when she accepted "a similar invitation" in 1994 in South Africa.[24] She writes:

> Thus, I was especially keen that I concentrate on the nature of the public ritual as a performance directed toward Allah, rather than an act of defiance against those who created the necessity for a gender jihad by simply denying women the full human dignity with which Allah has created us. My conclusion was to keep the prayer service as close to the normative male privileged procedure, while contributing from my own female perspective, and encouraging greater gender parity in public ritual leadership.[25]

She accuses the organizers of intentionally hyping the event to the media by describing it as a "first" in modern history and then defends her own decision to avoid participation in the media circus by refusing interviews outside of the press conference that day.[26] In one interview she did grant later in the year, Wadud confessed that, contrary to Nomani's narrative in which she wholeheartedly and immediately agreed to lead the prayer, she in fact had reservations and from the beginning was concerned, among other things, about her own and her children's safety. In the video footage Wadud can be seen being whisked away by two bodyguards after the prayer, with journalists trying to follow her being told to leave her alone. After the controversy over the prayer and the threats, her employer, Virginia Commonwealth University, decided not to allow her to teach on campus but rather through teleconferencing in order to protect her and her students.[27] Wadud also criticizes the organizer for not entirely acceding to her requests for setting up the prayer space—including a podium for her—and her instructions for the formal schedule, which put her in the position of having to improvise several times during the event.

Overall, Wadud's account provides a sobering counterbalance to Nomani's proud and excited narrative assessment of the event. Even though Wadud includes a transcript of much of the khutbah in the chapter, she does not represent the event as central in her activist and academic Muslim trajectory. While Nomani received a considerable and wished-for amount of media attention, it was Wadud who stood at the center of the intra-Muslim debate about the Qur'anic and legal basis of women-led prayers and gender issues in Islam.

Michael Muhammad Knight: Huggable Islam

One other reflection on the prayer was written by the novelist and scholar Michael Muhammad Knight and published the day after on MuslimWakeUp. com.[28] Knight is of double significance to the woman-led prayer on March 18, 2005. He was the one man joining five Muslim women in prayer, led by one of the women, immediately before Nomani's march on the mosque in Morgantown in June 2004. And Nomani reports in her book that it was in his punk novel, *The Taqwacores*,[29] that she first encountered a scene of a woman leading men in prayer, which gave her the idea for the 2005 prayer event.[30]

Knight, famous for his provocative writing style,[31] opens his story with the acknowledgment that he did not drive to New York City to pray, despite the fact that he believed in "a woman's right to lead prayers," because he did not see progressive Muslims as spearheading American Muslims' return to the mosque and ritual prayer. After helping with the security checks at the gate and observing the protesters showing signs declaring, "Mixed Gender Prayer Today, Hellfire Tomorrow," which journalists gave the attention they desired, Knight briefly describes the scene of the prayer hall and contends that, to his surprise, "the jamaat was mostly segregated with women on the right and men on the left, kind of blurred in the middle." Assessing the possible reasons other Muslims attended the prayer and offering an apt and condensed critique of much of the Muslim "feminist" project, he writes, "I had the feeling that most of these people were coming from an innocent and optimistic place, where the core of Islam is good and the Prophet's life can be spun towards a proto-feminism."

Knight describes Wadud's khutbah as the brain of the event and Suhayla El-Attar's adhan as the heart. During the khutbah Knight lost interest for a while but was called back in by some of the things Wadud said. Right before the prayer he moved around the prayer rows, was called to fill a hole in one row, and ended up behind a woman in an orange hijab. His article closes with the following paragraph:

There was even a point during the prayer that I forgot I was being led by a woman. Then came the salams to the angels and we were done. Everyone seemed to know everyone, so it turned into the social event of the season. As we hugged and celebrated, I realized that we had no Muslim Martin Luther, no Muslim Rosa Parks, no lone voice crying beautifully in the desert. No cult of personality, no enshrined martyr. We were here for ourselves: progressives, culturals, heretics and the unsure.

2

Women Leading Prayers
Tracing the Debate

As a Muslim I am entitled to listen to various opinions of the Islamic
authorities, pray for guidance, and choose the view my conscience
tells me is right. My view—which is one of the several valid Islamic
viewpoints on this issue—is that we should follow the Prophet's
example, as well as the views of early and modern jurists, to allow
learned women (or learned men) to lead the prayer. . . . I would love
to be able to pray together with my husband and children, all standing
together, rather than in separate rooms or even separate groups. When
I first read of Professor Wadud's mixed prayer I felt a rush of sympathy
and hope.

Sumbul Ali-Karamali, *The Muslim Next Door*

Sympathy and hope, on one end of the spectrum, and rejection and condemnation, on the other, characterized the heated debate about the woman-led
Friday prayer and khutbah on March 18, 2005. Sumbul Ali-Karamali introduces several dimensions of the discussion of women's prayer leadership,
including authority, plurality of opinion, and her wish for a different kind
of personal prayer experience. Each of these dimensions were echoed in the
discussions before and after the prayer in March 2005.

This chapter traces the contours of this debate. It points to the significance of various forms of media in facilitating it; it highlights the local and
transnational dimensions of this mediated debate and its implications for
the roles of American Muslims in contemporary Muslim thought; and it describes in some detail the layers of argument emerging in the discussion.
Aside from engendering a broad spectrum of opinions on women's prayer
leadership and on this particular event, the debate was characterized by a
discursive disconnect. The organizers focused primarily on the symbolic

meaning of the prayer event and the values it signified, and at least some of their detractors acknowledged these concerns. However, the majority of opinions against the prayer were couched in legal terms and argued through Islamic legal and exegetical paradigms. The organizers and supporters of the event on the other hand were unable or unwilling to acknowledge these legal concerns and their implications for understanding authority and tradition. The ensuing debate, while on the surface engaging a large number of scholars and activists, essentially took place on irreconcilably different discursive levels but resulted in the development of several threads of conversation and debate on larger issues of gender and women's roles, especially in the American context. These include larger questions of authority, community, the contemporary role of Islamic Law, human rights discourses on women, women's leadership and mosque participation, and the impact of media representations on Muslim communities.

Precedent, History, and Media

The 2005 Friday prayer event was widely publicized in the global media and caused an equally global debate among Muslims, mediated through newspapers, television stations, and Internet sites and blogs. Opinion pieces, articles, and discussion threads appeared on websites; supporters, rejecters, and academic experts were quoted in newspaper articles and news items, and somewhat later the debate also found its way into other forms of media, such as documentary films and books. Hailed as "the first public Jum'ah prayer of its kind on record since Prophet Muhammad"[1] by the organizers in their March 7, 2005, announcement of the event, the prayer was in fact preceded by several events with similar symbolic significance.

In August 1994 Amina Wadud gave a Friday khutbah in the Claremont Main Road Mosque in Cape Town, South Africa. In her book *Inside the Gender Jihad*,[2] Wadud not only provides the text of the lecture but also states, "I gave this address as a khutbah."[3] She reflects on the politics of being invited to give the khutbah, as well as the role of Muslim activists and scholars and the media in shaping and/or distorting the contours of the debate.[4]

In 2000 Khaled Abou El Fadl, professor of Islamic Law at UCLA, issued a fatwa on women leading a mixed congregation in prayer.[5] The fatwa was prompted by a questioner who addressed a particular situation in a local Muslim Student Association, and Abou El Fadl concluded that while it was a complicated legal question, women could lead men in prayers if the community agreed to it and if the men in the congregation were not positioned directly behind the woman imam.[6]

On November 13, 2004, a York University student, Maryam Mirza, offered the second part of the Eid al-Fitr khutbah at the United Muslim Association mosque in Toronto, Canada. The mosque's imam, Jabar Ally, had invited her to do so, arguing that "women have the ability to be leaders—why not in prayer, why not in religion?" An article in the *Toronto Star* reporting the event cites a variety of opinions, both for and against the idea, and is remarkable in reflecting many of the parameters of the later debate on the 2005 prayer.[7] Haddad, Smith, and Moore refer to the event, based on the *Toronto Star* article, as the first time a woman gave a khutbah in America.[8]

In 1995 The Muslim Youth Movement (MYM) of South Africa formed an alternative prayer congregation and started meeting for Friday prayers in the MYM offices in Johannesburg. For two years the group alternated between male and female imams and khatibs and also met daily for *tarawih* prayers in Ramadan.[9] Anecdotal evidence from conversations and email listservers suggests that women leading mixed congregations in more private settings has been a more established practice than would be apparent from the public debates that emerged in 2005.

The major difference between these preceding events and the 2005 Friday prayer then was the degree of publicity. In announcing the prayer on MuslimWakeUp.com, publicizing it through interviews in various mainstream media outlets, and holding a press conference before the khutbah and prayer, the organizers demonstrated their intent to make their plans and motivations known worldwide. While less explicit, they also intended to create or catalyze intra-Muslim debates on women and gender issues, both in North America and worldwide. The outlines of the discussion and the involvement in if not reliance on various forms of media make this intention very clear. The organizers' insistence that the event was a "first" came to be recognized as a strategy to gain publicity and to emphasize its symbolic significance.

The use of media, in particular new media, for the advancement of intra-Muslim debates on questions of authority, interpretation, and politics is not new and has been widely studied in various historical and contemporary contexts.[10] Speaking specifically to the situation of Muslims in minority (or Western) contexts, Eickelman and Anderson assert that new forms of media and communication make interactions between Muslims in Muslim-majority countries and their "diaspora" counterparts "immediate and inter-

connected."[11] More broadly, they argue for the constitution of new Muslim
public spheres:

> As in earlier public spheres, challenges to authority revolve around
> rights to interpret. Consequently, Muslim politics is less an expansion
> of a unitary voice (although many would claim this as a goal) than an
> engagement to argue over correct interpretation. What is new today
> is that these engagements spill out of a few specialized channels into
> many generalized ones. They do not necessarily become more public
> than in the past[;] . . . they instead become public in different ways.
> Their characteristic is more, and new, interpreters and, from them,
> the engagement of a more diverse and wider public.[12]

The 2005 prayer event provides a clear illustration of this phenomenon.

The mediated prayer debate was transnational as well as American in
nature and connected Muslim scholars, activists, and communities in sometimes unexpected ways. While the available traces of the 2005 debate are
all textual or visual in nature, they provide a glimpse of other, less formal
layers of the discussion as it took place before and after the prayer. The
discussion here is focused on English-language materials, which limits the
picture to the debate and privileges of an English-speaking Muslim public
sphere. As Lehmann's study of discourses on women and gender issues in
the South African context (surrounding the 1994 and 2005 events) illustrates, the larger questions of women's leadership roles, participation, and
authority at the core of the prayer debate were translated into local contexts and conditions and reflected the needs and interests of local communities.[13] While no other study of such context is available, it is reasonable to
assume that an analysis of Turkish, Pakistani, or Indonesian news reports
and online discussions would confirm this thesis.[14] Expressions of opinions on the prayer in English connected North American scholars, activists,
and audiences with their counterparts elsewhere. The distinctions between
American and non-American Muslims became a part of the debate itself and
reflected local as well as shared global Muslim concerns about authority,
tradition, and community.

Progressive Muslims and Movements

The debate about the prayer cannot be understood without the overlapping
and parallel debate with, about, and between (self-identified) progressive

Muslims in and beyond the North American context. With the (North American) Progressive Muslim Union as an organizational sponsor, coorganized by Asra Nomani's Muslim Women's Freedom Tour and the progressive website MuslimWakeUp, the prayer event is intricately linked to the emergence of this group and the larger trend toward self-identified progressives among Muslims worldwide. In 2003 Omid Safi, then one of the cochairs of the PMU, argued that it would be a mistake to reduce progressive Islam to an American phenomenon and thus an expression of the emergence of a particular American form of Islam alone. Rather, he insisted, "progressive Muslims are found everywhere in the global Muslim umma."[15] In emphasizing the progressive critique of neocolonialism among progressive Muslims, Safi responded to criticism that the movement was exporting American Islam as a commodity to other parts of the world. The intellectual engagement of progressive Muslim scholars and the parameters of their debates were publicized in the 2003 volume *Progressive Muslims on Justice, Gender, and Pluralism*, edited by Safi. Among the contributors were many scholars discussed in this book, including Khaled Abou El Fadl, Saʿdiyya Shaikh, Kecia Ali, and Amina Wadud.[16] Safi described the goals of this group of scholars as beginning with

> a simple yet radical stance: that the Muslim community as a whole cannot achieve justice unless justice is guaranteed for Muslim women. . . . Gender justice is crucial, indispensable, and essential. . . . Gender equality is a measuring stick for the broader concerns of social justice and pluralism.[17]

The PMU itself, formed in 2004 after several years of conversations among activists, scholars, and community members, described itself as "a group of North American Muslims."[18] The MuslimWakeUp website played an especially important role in facilitating the debate about the 2005 prayer.

After 2006, following serious disagreements between its members, in part debated on the website, the PMU disintegrated. A newer organization with similar goals and values is Muslims for Progressive Values, formed in 2007. This organization describes its goals and principles as follows: "Muslims for Progressive Values is guided by ten principles rooted in Islam, including social equality, separation of religion and state, freedom of speech, women's rights, gay rights, and critical analysis and interpretation."[19] Claims to and accusations of being progressive or liberal became an integral part of the discussions about the prayer. Like any label, it needs to be interrogated as to its politics, power dynamics, and utility for self-identification and critique.[20]

Tracing the Debate: Women Leading Prayers

The following is a chronological account of the mediated debate surrounding the 2005 woman-led Friday prayer and khutbah, pointing to three important conclusions:

1. The intra-Muslim debate about the prayer event was public and carried out through a variety of media forms and outlets. Media sources, including occasional cross-postings between news media outlets and websites, are indicated in order to show their significance to the debate. Of special significance was the MuslimWakeUp website, which published a large number of opinion and discussion pieces over a period of several months.

2. A range of Muslims, proponents and detractors, in North America and other parts of the world participated in the debate, including Islamic legal scholars and Muslim academics, activists, and community members. The latter are mostly represented in responses to opinion polls and online articles.

3. Two major discursive levels emerge in the debate: one centered on the legal permissibility of women leading prayers with a range of legal intricacies and arguments; the other, on the symbolic meanings of the prayer and related arguments about liberal/progressive values and rights discourses.

The collected summaries of the contributions to the debate are necessarily brief and constitute a reduction of more complex arguments, some of which are explored later in the book.

Before the Prayer: Opening the Door for Debate

The original announcement of the prayer, posted on MuslimWakeUp on March 7, 2005, and listing several organizations and seventy-five individuals, including those of the organizers Asra Nomani, Sarah Eltantawi, and Saleemah Abdul-Ghafur, was met with immediate responses, many dating from before the actual prayer event.

One of the first was a statement posted by Aslam Abdullah, director of the Islamic Society of Nevada, Las Vegas, on Islamicity.com on March 9. In it he declared that the judgment of the legality of the event was in God's hand but warned that the prayer would not contribute to the improvement of the admittedly difficult status of Muslim women. Rather, the prayer would be the wrong kind of event in the wrong place; it would be imposing a controversy on Muslim communities to the detriment of real equality, and it would play into the hands of the Western media.[21]

On March 10, Nevin Reda, a student at the University of Toronto and a member of the Canadian Council of Muslim Women, published a lengthy document on MuslimWakeUp.com detailing the historical and textual evidence she had found in support of the permissibility of woman-led prayers, based on the historical precedent that at the time of the Prophet Muhammad a woman was commanded to lead a congregation.[22] The text cites a variety of Muslim scholars and opinions and responds in detail to many of the objections to viewing this event as historical precedent. It ends with a general appeal to contemporary Muslims to use their critical thinking skills and follow the most important divine command to follow only one God and not take the authority of scholars past and present more seriously than that command.

On March 12 Sarah Eltantawi published a spirited argument for the prayer and against its detractors on MuslimWakeUp.com and called on American Muslim organizations to take a stand on the issue, naming in particular the Muslim Women's League; the Muslim Public Affairs Council (MPAC), which she had previously worked for; the Council on American Islamic Relations (CAIR); and the Islamic Society of North America (ISNA), as well as the American Society for Muslim Advancement (ASMA) and *Azizah Magazine*. She also responded to Aslam Abdullah's opinion piece and rejected his argument, instead speaking in favor of empowering Muslim women.[23]

Also on March 12 the U.K.-based Shafi'i legal scholar Muhammad Afifi published his legal opinion on the issue, stating that a mixed congregational prayer led by a woman would make the prayer invalid for the men praying behind her. Citing the lack of historical precedent and the distinction between women's political and ritual leadership, he cautioned of the dangers of knowledge "that is useless . . . and that will become a proof against us in the Next World."[24]

On March 13 the prayer organizers issued "A Statement from the Organizers of the March 18th Woman-Led Jum'ah Prayer" on MuslimWakeUp.com.

The statement reiterated the plan to hold the prayer and acknowledged debates, threats, and security concerns. The statement asserted that the prayer was not about a specific person or hidden purpose but rather "about Muslim women reclaiming their rightful place in Islam." It continued:

> Those who will gather for the prayer later this week will do so as a result of deeply held convictions that are rooted in our faith. . . . We love and care deeply for our community, and we understand that good people will arrive at varying conclusions regarding the Islamic basis for female-led prayer. This is not an attempt to "change" Islam, nor to condemn others who interpret our religion differently than we do.[25]

Also on March 13, Amine Tais, a freelance writer and student based in Seattle, Washington, took issue with Aslam Abdullah's arguments against the significance of the prayer and argued that it was precisely the "abysmal situation of Muslim women in their societies" that had prompted the organizers. Rejecting his assertion that American Muslim women have legal and communal equality, she contended, echoing Nomani, that many American Muslim women did not even have a dignified space for their congregational prayers. In her eyes the prayer event would be "as heroic and important as any other struggle to make the world a better place for all."[26]

Sometime between the announcement and the event itself, Shaykh Abdullah bin Hamid Ali, an American Muslim scholar with Islamic training at al-Qarawiyyin University in Morocco and a teacher in alternative educational institutions in North America, published a legal opinion on the prayer on his website. Ali cited classical legal positions of the Sunni legal schools and strongly warned against overriding or even challenging the scholarly and community consensus on the issue of women-led prayers. He accused the organizers of following in the "footsteps of Satan." Ali first mentioned the possibility of the event being an act of apostasy: "I think that if people want to make up their own religion, let them do as they like. We just ask them to give us a little respect and not call it Islam, and don't call themselves Muslims. That's all."[27] His opinion was circulated on several blogs and became one of the key references for online Muslim debates.

March 15 saw the publication of a mock interview with an imaginary Saudi Arabian scientist, poking fun at the debate over women's intellectual ability to acquire religious knowledge and thus qualify for prayer leadership.[28]

On March 16 the English portal of IslamOnline published parts of a legal opinion and statement issued by the Assembly of Muslim Jurists of America, an organization consisting of Islamic legal scholars throughout the world but offering fatwas to American Muslims in particular. The statement described the plans for the prayer as misguided and an innovation in religion to be loathed. Citing Prophetic practice, classical legal positions on women's location during congregational prayer, and the fact that women are not legally required to attend Friday prayers, as well as rejecting the suggestion of historical precedent, the document warned that the *ummah* (Muslim community) would fall into *fitnah* (chaos) if Muslims followed the misguided call to attend and support the event.[29]

Also on March 16, IslamOnline published a fatwa by Yusuf al-Qaradawi, a prominent Qatar-based member of the Muslim Brotherhood of Egyptian origin and scholar of Islamic Law, in response to a fatwa question (the questioner requested al-Qaradawi's opinion). Al-Qaradawi's fatwa advanced several layers of opinion and included dissenting opinions as well as his own disagreement with some of the interpretations. He distinguished Friday prayers from the obligatory five daily prayers and particular settings, arguing that a woman cannot lead men in Friday prayers and that the purpose of this limitation is to avoid the sexual distraction of men. However, he agreed that women can lead male members of their own household or family in obligatory prayers and that, of course, women are permitted to lead other women in prayer. Al-Qaradawi rejected innovation or the introduction of new rulings and interpretations into Islamic tradition or practice and accused the organizers of causing dissent among the community. He also warned that they had to be careful not to get embroiled in U.S. conspiracies.[30]

On March 17 the Muslim Women's League (MWL), an American Muslim organization founded in the 1990s, as if in response to Eltantawi's challenge, discussed opinions and approaches to the woman-led prayer event and demonstrated considerable diversity of opinion within its ranks. The statement affirmed that "it is not forbidden (haram) for a woman to lead a mixed congregation in prayer." However, it also noted that at least some in the organization were not convinced that the prayer was the most appropriate way to advance the cause of Muslim women around the world but then congratulated Amina Wadud on her courage to follow through on her convictions. Importantly, MWL condemned the attempts to threaten and silence the organizers and supporters of the prayer.[31]

March 18, 2005: The Day of the Prayer

The day of the prayer saw a flurry of contributions to the discussion, most of them written before the event and published or posted in time for the prayer.

The renowned American Muslim poet Mohja Kahf expressed her support for the prayer in a poem, posted on MuslimWakeUp.com, teasing those who could not decide if they were for or against the event.[32] So did the journalist and PMU board member Mona Eltahawy in an opinion piece published in the *Washington Post* and on MuslimWakeUp.com titled "A Prayer toward Equality," in which she also celebrated Wadud's courage and recounted how hard it had been for her to preserve her faith in the face of "blatant misogyny." She also wrote: "It will be women who change Islam and bring it into the twenty-first century, because we have nothing to lose. But many men support our efforts, because our fight is their fight."[33]

Ahmed Nassef, coorganizer of the event, published a very short piece titled "Thank You Sheikh Gum'a,"[34] in which he referred to the opinion of a leading Islamic scholar in Egypt, ʿAli Jumʿah, who was quoted in a news report on the satellite news channel Al-Arabiyya as having stated that woman-led prayer is permissible if the community agrees to it.[35] Jumʿah later issued a formal fatwa to the contrary, in which he declared it against all existing schools of Islamic Law for a woman to lead men in prayer or give a khutbah to any congregation.[36]

A *New York Times* article by Andrea Elliott described the plans for the prayer and cited "community opinions," among them those of Khaled Abou El Fadl, who curiously did not repeat his earlier opinion, and Aisha al-Adawiya, executive director of Women in Islam in New York, who was planning to attend the prayer but not participate for fear of a community backlash and arguing that the initiative had not organically grown from within Muslim communities.[37] The imam of the Islamic Center of Mid-Manhattan, Ahmed Dewidar, was quoted as saying that the idea was strange to him but that he had urged his congregation to be "non-confrontational should they attend the prayer." Familiar arguments in support of the prayer were provided by Ahmed Nassef and Asra Nomani.[38]

Hesham Hassaballa, freelance writer and community activist from Chicago, offered his opinion on MuslimWakeUp.com under the title "What a Damn Shame!" In it he discussed the many faces of the oppression of Muslim women in history and many contemporary Muslim societies, and while critiquing the colonial enterprise of teaching Muslims about women's liberation he issued a call to Muslims:

> Armed with the model for true equality between men and women, we Muslims should be at the forefront of the struggle for women's rights, both here in America and around the world. Yet, before we can do this, we have to be credible in the eyes of the larger American society. That credibility will forever elude us if we continue to marginalize our sisters. This has to change.[39]

Louay Safi, executive director of the ISNA Leadership Development Center in Indianapolis and founding board member of the Center for the Study of Islam and Democracy (CSID), contributed a lengthy opinion piece on Islamicity.com. In addressing his remarks to the broader issues of women in American mosques, Safi contended that Muslim mosque communities had not done enough to affirm equal access for Muslim women to mosques, education, and leadership positions and that in abusing Islamic legal principles they had insisted on the seclusion of women in contradiction to Prophetic practice and instruction. In regard to the prayer plan he argued:

> It is unfortunate that Muslim feminists are following in the footsteps of their secularist precursors, breaking all traditions, and engaging in experimentations that break with formative principles and values. For individuals and movements interested in reforming attitudes and practices to take the opposite extreme can only hurt the reform agenda already underway throughout North America.[40]

Of the sixty-two comments posted on the website, more than half thought Safi's position on women's inclusion in the mosque was going too far and that Muslim women should be encouraged to pray and meet at home, while those who agreed welcomed his opinion and enlightened arguments. Several commentators rejected the idea of women leading men in prayers.

In response to Nevin Reda's opinion from March 10, Hina Azam, professor of Islamic studies at the University of Texas, Austin, and specialist in Islamic Law, published an article on another American Muslim site, www.altmuslim.com, in which she explained that although she supported the idea of women leading prayers as a contemporary principle, Reda's argument and methodology in working with the traditional sources was flawed, and thus there was no traditional legal support for the prayer event.

Drawing on classical Islamic legal principles and methodologies she concluded that the Umm Waraqa hadith was not a strong enough source to support the Friday prayer but that women could write khutbahs to be read by a male imam, they could offer pre-khutbah lectures, and they could be translators of khutbahs (presumably in Arabic) so that communities could get used to hearing women's voices in the mosque even if they did not express their own opinions or teachings.[41]

After the Prayer: Continuing the Debate

March 19 saw the publication of another article by Andrea Elliott in the *New York Times*. Now reporting on the prayer event the day before, Elliott again quoted Muslim opinions on the prayer and the larger issues. Samira Jaraba, a Palestinian American from Brooklyn, was described as traveling to the event out of curiosity but still in disagreement with the idea of women as imams. Khaled Abou El Fadl this time argued that separation and seclusion in mosques is a social tradition and not based on the Qur'an. Again he was not quoted as offering a legal argument, even though he had issued a fatwa on women's prayer leadership several years earlier. Nomani and Wadud were mentioned as the two central figures of the event.[42]

Muzammil Siddiqi, former president of ISNA and chairman of the Fiqh Council of North America, issued a fatwa-like statement on March 20 that was published on Islamicity.com. He argued that prayer leadership was restricted to men, both inside and outside the mosque and for obligatory daily prayers as well as Friday and Eid prayers. He based his argument on longstanding practice and thus community consensus and emphasized the danger of women distracting men during prayers. Thus women should at least be placed behind men in congregational prayers. Citing the Umm Waraqa hadith, he stated that it could not be applied outside of a woman's home and, according to some, also only to the leadership of other women.[43]

Also on March 20, *Arab News*, "the Middle East's Leading English Language Daily," published an article by Barbara Ferguson that described some of the worldwide reactions to the prayer. Ferguson quoted Shaykh Muhammad Tantawi of Cairo's al-Azhar Mosque[44] in support of women leading other women in prayer and Yusuf al-Qaradawi's opinion as mentioned above and focusing on his warning against the distraction a Muslim woman praying in front of men would be for the men and their prayers. Based on an Al-Arabiyya Television report, Ferguson also quoted ʿAli Jumʿah as in support of women leading mixed-gender congregation prayers "so long as the community agrees to it." Abdul Alim Mubarak (age fifty-three, African American) is quoted as saying that he was still not sure even after attending the prayer that women can be imams. Omar Haque (age twenty-five, Pakistani American) believed that the event made history and that he viewed it as important that Wadud is African American. Khabira Abdullah (age thirty, from New York City) thought the prayer event was "powerful and amazing" and long overdue.[45]

An Associated Press report from March 20 described reactions of "Mideast Muslims" as negative and quoted Suʿad Saleh, head of the Islamic studies department at Al-Azhar University's women's college, as calling the prayer "an act of apostasy." Saleh was the host of a popular Egyptian TV show, offering legal advice to viewers. She has also applied repeatedly to become a mufti, to be the first woman mufti in Egypt, arguing that the selection should be based on knowledge and training and not gender but was rejected.[46]

Anwar Iqbal of United Press International wrote two articles published on March 20 and 21. He reported ʿAli Jumʿah's legal support for the prayer as well but cited Rasheed Khalid, a professor in Islamabad, as cautioning that in light of the U.S.-led wars in Iraq and Afghanistan the event would be misinterpreted as sponsored by the United States and thus not gain followers despite being a worthy cause. Iqbal quoted a detractor, Mohammed Nazim, who frequently posted his opinion on MuslimWakeUp.com, arguing that the prayer organizers were forming a cult with Amina Wadud at its center and in reference to Elijah Muhammad, founder of the African American Nation of Islam in the 1930s. He also described Wadud as an outsider to Muslim communities who as a convert had not lived in Islamic culture enough. Wadud was quoted as defending herself and rejecting such claims. She was joined in the article by Asra Nomani, who rejected the "intimidation tactics" and reiterated that the purpose of the prayer event was to come together in worship of God. In the second installment several detractors with different arguments—no relevance outside the West, the movement coming from outside the mosques and communities—were situated vis-à-vis Nomani and Nassef. Both repeated their arguments *for* the prayer, including the Umm Waraqa hadith, classical legal sources as quoted in Nevin Reda's piece, and the rights discourse adopted by Nomani for her Muslim Women's Freedom Tour.

On March 21 an anonymous (female) author published a moving personal piece on MuslimWakeUp.com, describing how the prayer, which she did not attend, had convinced her to pray again after having given it up for years in response to the alienation and separation of women in mosques and communities. She had reportedly wanted a woman to lead prayers for a long time. The essay ends:

> I began with ghusl[47] this morning. Washed away the hardness I let cover the old wound. Dug out my big soft prayer scarf deep in the back of the linen closet. A few minutes before the salat was due to begin on the East Coast, I made wudu'.[48] I spread my prayer rug again. My knees have forgotten, in the intervening years, some of the suppleness that constant juloos[49] gave them, and they hurt. But not as much as my heart used to, before the woman-led prayer held by my Muslim heroes, and the angels who prayed beside them today.[50]

Also on March 21, IslamOnline published a fatwa by Shaykh ʿAli Jumʿah that contradicted his earlier (reported) statement in support of the prayer. Jumʿah asserted:

> As for a woman calling the Adhan, giving the Friday sermon, and leading the Friday Prayer, we do not know of a single difference of opinion between the Muslims—scholars and laymen alike—concerning its impermissibility; the fact is that should such a Prayer and Adhan be performed, they would be incorrect.[51]

Jumʿah dismissed the Umm Waraqa hadith as limited to supererogatory prayers, or other women, or Umm Waraqa. He also cautioned against confusing the issue of leading prayers with delivering the Friday sermon. He then made a broader and accusatory connection between prayer leadership and other attempts at reform:

> These confused people who adhere to schools of dissent are divided into various movements. Some deny the Sunnah and consensus, some tamper with the significance of words in the Arabic language, and others call for the permissibility of homosexuality, fornication, alcohol, abortion, and changing the prescribed portions on inheritance. These movements appear in almost every age, then they disappear and the Muslims follow the path Allah has made incumbent upon them, bearing the standard of felicity to all the worlds.[52]

Jordan Lite from the *New York Daily News*, in a short writeup published on March 23, juxtaposed Jum'ah's opinion with those of Nomani and Wadud and also reported on Nomani's own prayer leadership at Brandeis University.[53]

Imam Zaid Shakir of Zaytuna Institute in California published a lengthy response on March 23 to Nevin Reda's opinion from March 10. Shakir formulated another clear rejection of the scriptural and legal basis of the prayer as within the parameters of Islamic traditional interpretations. He responded to Reda's arguments one by one within a legal framework but refused to engage with her nonlegal arguments about justice as gender justice and women's discrimination in Muslim communities. However, he stated, "They are of importance in determining how existing rulings are to be understood and implemented. In this regard, Reda's passionate plea for greater compassion, justice, and understanding is appreciated." Shakir emphasized the importance of women in Muslim communities but rejected the necessity of women leading prayers as a symbolic act.[54]

On March 25 Hussein Ibish, vice-chair of the PMU, posted a scathing critique of Hina Azam's perspective in which he accused her of legal dogmatism and impeding the social and spiritual development of the Muslim community. He also claimed that Azam did not believe in her own conclusions.[55]

Also on March 25 the online magazine *Women's E News* ran an article by correspondent Rasha Elass titled "Islamic Women Break Custom, Lead Prayers," in which she took the Brandeis prayer follow-up as an occasion to report on the March 18 prayer, which she described as if she had been in attendance. Elass quoted detractors and supporters who attended the March 18 prayer in considerable detail, providing a broad spectrum of opinions. She quoted Omid Safi, then chair of the PMU: "At the heart of the issue is whether people are willing to accept men and women as beings created in the fullness of humanity, possessing fullness of emotional, spiritual and intellectual faculties." Elass also quoted from a telephone interview with a Syrian woman who described the event as a sign of the end of times. Leila Ahmed, professor at Harvard University, was quoted as saying: "This event is indeed the legacy of Islam in America."[56]

Elass also mentioned that Tayyibah Taylor, editor in chief of *Azizah Magazine*, an American Muslim women's magazine launched in 2001, had been swamped with questions about the prayer and was conducting an online survey over the course of the next week. The survey results were later reported in the magazine as follows: 82 percent felt that women should not lead mixed-gender congregation prayers; 85 percent felt that the woman-led prayer in March did not advance the cause of Muslim women; and 71 percent felt that there were more important issues facing Muslim women.[57]

On March 26 MuslimWakeUp.com republished a satirical essay by Siamack Baniameri titled "A Woman Leads Prayers? What's Left of Muslim Men's Dignity?" in which he made fun of the argument that a woman imam would be arousing to the male congregation behind her. In explicit sexual and sarcastic language, Baniameri deconstructs the arguments against the prayer and acknowledges Muslim women's unequal situation: "Maybe we'll see the day when women with their Gucci purses and Prada shoes walk in front and we follow two steps behind covered in thick dark sheets, pushing strollers and gasping for air."[58]

On March 28 *Time Magazine* ran an article by Jeff Chu and Nadia Mustafa titled "Her Turn to Pray." The article described parts of the prayer event and went on to discuss Nomani's life story as reflected in her book *Standing Alone in Mecca*. Daisy Khan of ASMA was quoted as defining the prayer as part of the American Muslim movement for gender equality based on a merging of Western values and Muslim teachings, continuing that there is nothing in the Qur'an speaking against "female leaders." Her husband, Feisal Abdul Rauf, director of the Cordoba Initiative and cofounder of ASMA, is quoted later as dismissing the event as a publicity stunt for Nomani's book and "less about worship and getting closer to God than about making a political statement." Finally, Khaled Abou El Fadl, described as "one of the most influential elders" and "a sheikh and professor" in the absence of a clerical hierarchy in Islam, was quoted as supporting prayer leadership based on merit and knowledge rather than gender.[59]

On March 29 Mona Eltahawy published another piece, this time in the *New York Times*, describing her positive and empowering experience of the prayer and condemning Libyan leader Muammar el-Qaddafi for alleging that the prayer event would create "a million bin Ladens."[60]

On March 31 Egyptian scholar of the Qur'an, Nasr Hamid Abu Zaid, joined the debate in a lecture delivered at Virginia Commonwealth University, where Amina Wadud was teaching at the time. A news piece in the *Richmond Times-Dispatch* by Alberta Lindsey reported that after his lecture Abu Zaid was asked several questions about the prayer event and responded that he would have attended the prayer had he been in the United States at the time and that he found nothing wrong with the concept. He commended Wadud for trying to bring together social space and divine space and demanding the equality of men and women promised in the Qur'an.[61]

Robert Crane, a prominent American convert to Islam, posted an opinion piece on his website on April 2. In it he discussed the "shock and awe" strategy of the prayer organizers and described the debate over the prayer as a conflict between legal and political arguments. He declared the question to be whether "the battle for women's rights can be carried out without splitting the Muslim umma still further" and argued that American Muslim women simply did not have the required knowledge and education to be leaders of their communities and that achieving prayer leadership was not important for gender equity.[62]

On April 4 Abdennur Prado, secretary of the Islamic Council of Spain, posted an opinion piece on altmuslim.com and on his own website. He took it upon himself to respond to many of the detracting opinions about the prayer and answer (i.e., refute) them one by one. He expressed bewilderment about the sexual distraction argument, supported a broad application of the Umm Waraqa hadith, and went on to discuss the question of scholarly and community consensus as the basis for rejecting any change in the Islamic legal regulations on ritual practice. In response to the al-Qaradawi and Assembly of Muslim Jurists of America fatwas, Prado remarked that the scholars were entitled to their opinion but simply not required to attend a woman-led prayer. However, their statements of reprimand and even hints at apostasy on the part of Wadud were far from established Prophetic practice.[63]

Also in April Laury Silvers, professor of religious studies at Skidmore College and PMU board member, offered a more nuanced contribution to the debate by arguing in response to Azam and Shakir that while the existing legal interpretations may seem to indicate that woman-led prayers are not permissible according to Islamic Law and historical practice, both also formulate room for doubt and, more important, open the door for a reassessment of the central question of justice in Muslim societies and communities as gender justice. She also called on Muslims to participate in women-led prayers as an act of "civil disobedience," that is, a symbolic act to further discussions in Muslim communities about leadership, authority, justice, and gender roles. Silvers refused to engage the argument about women imams as the source of sexual distraction as absurd and insulting to Muslim men but suggested several alternative prayer formations to accommodate various community needs, including one in which the prayer would be broadcast via loudspeaker to the men's section of the mosque.[64]

Sustaining a Movement?

While the intensity of the debate immediately before and after the event in March subsided somewhat, several more opinion contributions and newspaper pieces referred to it over the following months. These pieces document follow-up events to the March prayer and should be read as an attempt to turn the onetime event into a movement.

Asra Nomani continued her Muslim Women's Freedom Tour through the United States, covered by several articles including one in *Sojourners Magazine*[65] and one in the *Washington Post* in June 2005. In the second article Nomani received verbal support from Asma Gull Hasan, Pakistani American lawyer and author of *Why I Am a Muslim*, as well as verbal discouragement from Louay Safi and Gamal Fahmy, a professor at West Virginia University who had clashed with Nomani and her father in the past.[66]

Sarah Eltantawi and Zuriani Zonneveld reported on MuslimWakeUp.com about a town hall meeting with Khaled Abou El Fadl on woman-led prayers in which he discussed opinions on the sexual distraction argument, the intellectual capacity of women to lead prayers, and the politics of change in Muslim communities.[67]

After Nomani lead a small mixed-gender congregation in prayers at Brandeis University less than a week after the March 18 prayer,[68] Nakia Jackson reported on her own preparation and preaching of a Friday khutbah on MuslimWakeUp.com on April 29.[69] She also gave an Eid khutbah on January 20, 2006.[70]

Thomas Bartlett published a lengthy article in the *Chronicle of Higher Education* in August 2005, based on a rare interview with Amina Wadud. The article is an important example of media coverage of the prayer and its protagonists. It reprises arguments for and against the prayer and describes in some detail responses to the prayer event that had not been published elsewhere. A "wave of threats" emanated from the most ardent antiprayer faction. Those were threats of violence and death and accusations of apostasy and condemnation from various websites. Barrett cited Leila Ahmed as a supporter of the event, even though she thought it had been held at least partly to sell Nomani's book. But Ahmed also believed that it was "a good thing" and dismissed arguments that it was the wrong time, saying, "Every

time women demand something they say, 'Oh this isn't the right time.'"
Support also came from Duke professor and South African activist Ebrahim
Moosa, while Abdullahi An-Naʿim, professor of law at Emory University,
criticized the sensational nature of the event and argued that it would divert
attention from more important issues. Shaykh Ahmad Abdur-Rashid, identified as a Sufi teacher and one of Wadud's spiritual teachers, was quoted as
having cautioned her to take a step-by-step approach rather than a polariz-
ing onetime event.[71]

That Nomani's activism and the demands for mosque space and leadership are not tied to Nomani's person but rather a reflection of emerging
needs and debates in American Muslim communities is evident in a document that was developed over several years by members of Women in Islam,
a New York–based organization. The booklet, "Women Friendly Mosques
and Community Centers: Working Together to Reclaim Our Heritage," was
endorsed and distributed by the ISNA, CAIR, the Muslim American Society
(MAS), and the umbrella of the Muslim Student Organizations (MSA National) in summer 2005.[72]

Also in summer 2005, Omid Safi published an article in *Tikkun* summa-
rizing progressive positions on woman-led prayer, religious authority, interpretation, and gender equality. The final paragraph of the essay reads:

> The problem is not the Qurʾan, it is not God. It is patriarchy, a pro-
> found human error that must be addressed, resisted and corrected.
> Let us strive to create a society in which prayer, that most intimate
> of human acts toward God, can be a reflection of God's own mercy
> toward us, drawing us closer on the basis not of our race or gender,
> but of our piety and mindfulness of the Divine.[73]

THE RESPONSES AND OPINIONS assembled above constitute only a frac-
tion of those formulated and published during 2005, but they make clear
that the prayer event was recognized as profoundly symbolic and elicited a
great deal of commentary in the new media-generated public sphere. The
prayer debate was transnational and local at the same time and connected
allies, foes, and their supporters through news articles, online discussions,
blogs, and web articles.

Several underlying themes of the debate become evident in this chronological reading: the insistence of many on the preservation and integrity
of the Islamic legal tradition, with its methods and rulings on ritual and

worship of Muslims; the debated nature of religious authority and religious training; the evocation of universal values such as women's rights, gender equality, and justice; and the politicized perception of American and/or progressive Muslims as agents of the West, or the United States, and as dividers of the Muslim community, itself based on a particular understanding of community in global and local contexts.

3

Gender Justice and Qur'anic Exegesis

Many Islamic feminists approach the Divine Word as an active
and dynamic hermeneutical encounter. Revelation speaks to human
beings who are constantly striving to reach progressively deeper
understandings of God and the nature of human realities. Within
this view, *tafsir*, or Qur'anic exegesis, is woven intricately with ever
expanding human conceptions of justice and equality that sculpt the
living, emerging, social texts of Islam.

Sa'diyya Shaikh, "A *Tafsir* of Praxis"

The quotation above serves as a useful transition from the woman-led prayer
event and the surrounding controversy to the broader topic of American
Muslim women's exegetical projects.[1] In this chapter I argue that the prayer
event built on several decades of exegetical engagement with the Qur'an by
American Muslim women scholars and activists. It translated women's insistence on reading and discovering gender justice and equality in the sacred
text into a historical event that in turn affected the exegetical projects. The
significance of the prayer event and its connection to American Muslim
women's exegeses is emphasized through an analysis of Wadud's khutbahs,
one offered in 1994 in South Africa and the other on March 18, 2005.

Embodied Tafsir and Feminist Musings

To connect the prayer event to Qur'anic reinterpretation it is useful to introduce the concept "embodied tafsir" to argue that interpretive encounters
with the Qur'an can and do take place in many forms other than textual
engagement that produces new texts, namely, in shaping the understanding
and application of such understanding in ritual, social, and political acts.

Wadud's leading of the prayer was embodied tafsir, that is, the translation and enactment of her hermeneutical strategies into the bodily performance of a public, social, and religious ritual. This notion of activism as embodied tafsir is inspired by Saʿdiyya Shaikh's notion of a "tafsir of praxis" or "tafsir through praxis."[2] Shaikh, in examining the ethical and exegetical dilemmas of South African Muslim women confronted with spousal abuse, contends that the experiences of the women and their subsequent grappling with Qur'anic verses such as 4:34, constitute a form of tafsir that is separate from the textual and patriarchal approaches of men in that Muslim community. Drawing on feminist theory on experience and female subjectivity, Shaikh argues that Muslim feminist exegetes of the Qur'an can use this practical approach to challenge patriarchal interpretations. She writes:

> My approach explicitly foregrounds how a group of Muslim women think and speak in relation to the text and engage God, ethics, and religion through the realities of their suffering and oppression. What they often emerge with is an understanding of Islam that provides a very different ethical and existential vision than that of traditional male scholars, their husbands, and clerics around them.[3]

Her emphasis on ethical readings of the Qur'anic message, as well as her argument for an extension of the narrow and male boundaries for understanding tafsir, connects her to several of the American Muslim women at the center of this analysis. It is common to find Muslim women's exegetical projects described as feminist Qur'an interpretation. The use of the term *feminist* as equivalent to being carried out by a woman needs to be problematized and has been discussed by several scholars and writers.

Shaikh uses the term *Islamic feminists*, as do other scholars, including Margot Badran, whose book bears the title *Feminism in Islam*.[4] Shaikh mentions Amina Wadud and Asma Barlas in particular; thus we can assume that she would consider them Islamic feminists. Both Shaikh and Aysha Hidayatullah have offered useful overviews of the arguments for and against the use of the term *feminist* for the exegetical work of American Muslim women and Muslim women more generally.[5] Briefly, the argument against using the term is based on the rejection of feminism as a Western intellectual and political product, claiming that feminists and their discourses have been implicated in colonial and neocolonial projects.[6] This argument goes on to state that it is this implication in colonialism and imperialism as well as the display of intellectual hegemony that has discredited the notion for contemporary Muslims, thus decreasing the already embattled authority and legitimacy of Muslim women's discourses on gender. On the opposite end of the spectrum are those who argue, like Shaikh, that "the value of retaining the term 'feminism' is that it enables Muslim women to situate their praxis in a global political landscape." In taking up miriam cooke's notion of multiple critique and critiquing it at the same time, Shaikh goes on to describe the self-perception of "many Muslim feminists who see their feminism as emerging organically out of their faith commitment and whose contestation of gender injustice is more simply the result of a post-colonial power struggle."[7] cooke had earlier stated that "the term Islamic feminism invites us to consider what it means to have a difficult double commitment, on the one hand to a faith position, and on the other hand to women's rights both inside the home and outside."[8]

Drawing on Margot Badran's work again, Hidayatullah concludes her consideration of the term *Islamic feminism* by cautioning that an excessive focus on terminology can distract from the important and substantive goals of the scholars and exegetes in question. It is worth noting that many of the scholars at the center of this study tend to avoid the term or display significant discomfort in describing themselves as feminists. As Muslim women scholars both Shaikh and Hidayatullah themselves insist on using the term *Muslim feminist* or *Islamic feminist* to describe women exegetes and activists,[9] thus still applying their own perspective to the works and commitments of other women scholars and disregarding their epistemological and political concerns. In this book, I employ the term only for those women writers who identify themselves as feminists.

Beyond the politics of naming, this question is relevant for the content of Muslim women's exegeses and their drawing on various strands of feminist theory and thought. The dynamics of Muslim women scholars' involvement and investment in American feminist scholarship and possibly theological endeavors are complex. At least two generations of Muslim women have been involved in American academia and engaged in different levels of primary and secondary scholarship. In particular, in religious studies and in women's studies, they have encountered a range of challenges, theoretical and practical, because of their commitments to religious expression and/or exegetical/normative work in Islam. Muslim women, like other religiously engaged scholars in the academy, often face concerns about insider/outsider issues and/or tensions between analytical and exegetical scholarship.

As Muslims, they are moved to challenge colonial and postcolonial constructions of "the Muslim woman" while maintaining their commitments to religious intellectual projects and, equally important in many cases, their commitments to various forms of communal and global activism.

However, this discussion is relevant in another way. Whether Muslim women scholars perceive and describe their projects as feminist and whether they draw on feminist theory and method for their exegetical projects can also be linked to their construction and perception of the role of women exegetes in the (distant) Muslim past. Wadud has argued, in order to support her "rereading the Qur'an from a woman's perspective" (the subtitle of her 1992 book), that "women were nearly completely excluded from the foundational discourse that established the paradigmatic basis for what it means to be Muslim."[10] Drawing on Denise Spellberg's study of the life and significance of 'Aisha bint Abi Bakr (the Prophet Muhammad's favorite wife), Wadud quotes Spellberg's assessment that "women remained unable to participate in these most challenging intellectual undertakings."[11] Similarly, Riffat Hassan has asserted that "the Islamic tradition has, by and large, remained rigidly patriarchal till the present time, prohibiting growth of scholarship among women particularly in the realm of religious thought."[12] Hassan then connects this lack of women's perspective in scholarship by linking it, like Nimat Barazangi, to Muslim women's knowledge of their tradition and their rights within it.

Asma Sayeed has carried out an extensive study of the presence and significance of women as hadith transmitters from the first to the eighth Islamic centuries. She found a large number of women transmitters in the generation of the companions of the Prophet Muhammad, but their numbers and relevance declined for two hundred years before growing again in the fourth century. While no direct connection can be drawn between transmission of hadith and interpretation, Sayeed's work demonstrates the dynamics and changing fortunes of women as transmitters but also scholars more generally.[13] Even more recently, Aisha Geissinger has challenged this notion of the insignificance or even nonexistence of women exegetes in early Muslim history, notably in a study of the same 'Aisha bint Abi Bakr and her portrayal as an early exegetical authority in the canonical hadith collection of al-Bukhari (d. 870).[14] The justification of entirely new and unprecedented exegetical projects by contemporary Muslim women is balanced by the equally significant search for historical role models for the same contemporary Muslim women.[15] This quest for historical precedent is also intimately connected to questions of legitimacy and authority and the important task of interpretive community building.[16]

The question of whether women's Qur'an interpretation is new and innovative or in line with tradition and a question of recovering divine intent is at the heart of most reflections and debates. It often appears as a clash of progressive views of history with an equally powerful perception of a religious and communal golden age closest to the historical origin—for Muslims, the lifetime of the Prophet Muhammad. Muslim women are celebrated in the academy and the media for their innovative approaches and new perspectives while they themselves negotiate the notion of tradition and a noted tendency to essentialize Islam.[17]

The question of the historical existence of women interpreters of the Qur'an and their purported significance is also intrinsically linked to the significance of gender as a category of and for the continuous interpretation of the Qur'an. Even if women participated in Qur'anic exegesis in the past and even if they gained enough influence to have an impact on Muslim societies through their tafsir, they would still have been (like their male counterparts) products of their respective societies with particular histories, value systems, and perceptions of gender roles.[18] It is only an assumption that the mere existence of women's perspectives in tafsir would automatically and naturally change the nature of the interpretations. Wadud assumes as much when she states, "How could the Islamic intellectual ethos develop without giving clear and resounding attention to the female voice, both as part of the text and in response to it?"[19] Wadud's reading for gender in the Qur'an, however, as that for gender justice and equality carried out by other Muslim women, is clearly a product of our time and contested notions of gender roles, women's rights, and related societal values. That gender justice is not the only way even contemporary Muslim women read and understand the Qur'an is evident in secondary literature on "traditional" and "conservative" Muslim women, for example, the women's mosque movement in Cairo as described by Saba Mahmood;[20] the work of Nelly van Dorn-Haarder on Indonesia,[21] and those of Margot Badran and miriam cooke for Egypt and the larger Middle East.[22] These and other studies demonstrate the diversity of modern exegetical projects carried out by women and the ways in which they are shaped by particular historical, cultural, and political contexts. They also remind us not to overlook those approaches that do not fit liberal models of women's liberation and agency and instead posit alternative models of Muslim women's engagement with scripture and tradition.

The work of Muslim women exegetes has to be considered in light of recent theoretical and political developments and as part of landscapes of textual contestation, rights discourses, and debates about the roles of religion in the public sphere. Exegetical projects do not exist in a vacuum but are part of the discursive and political fabric of Muslim societies and communities. Thus the societal critiques leveled by Wadud and other scholars of the contemporary problems of Muslim women and possible remedies for unjust and unequal life conditions need to be recognized as not just inspiration but also the catalyst for their exegetical endeavors. Doing so allows for the recognition of possible avenues of critique, both of their underlying assumptions and politics and as an acknowledgment of the historical situatedness and debts to their times. It is thus anachronistic and unhelpful to level critiques of exegetical rethinking that express dissatisfaction with the breaks, fissures, and inconsistencies in exegetical works by Muslim women without seeing them as ongoing conversations and works in progress.

American Muslim Women and Qur'anic Exegesis

Among American Muslim women several shared characteristics can be observed: they have secular American educational degrees and they embarked on their exegetical projects with the intention of challenging and changing existing interpretations.[23] While not all of them actively engage with the term or category of gender, it is clear that their interpretations are based on the notion that gender distinctions exist and are of significance for any understanding of the Qur'an.

Reinterpretation projects with a focus on women and gender in the American context were pioneered by scholars such as Riffat Hassan and Azizah al-Hibri in the 1970s and 1980s. Hassan's work has focused on Qur'an interpretation, often in the context of women's rights as human rights, while al-Hibri's contribution lies in her passionate call to reform Islamic Law based on a different and more inclusive understanding of the Qur'an.[24] Many of their works first appeared in collections of writings by American religious feminists as part of the development of an ecumenical approach to women's religiosity and interpretation beyond Protestant Christianity and Judaism. Hassan and al-Hibri, who both still write but have focused their energies on various forms of activism, were followed in the 1990s by another group of women scholars, among them Amina Wadud,[25] Asma Barlas,[26] and Nimat Barazangi.[27] An even younger generation is emerging, larger in numbers, foremost among them Kecia Ali,[28] whose focus is also on the Islamic legal tradition and the need to reform Islamic Law. Others include Aysha Hidaya-tullah, Laury Silvers, and Hadia Mubarak.

The specific American context (and freedom) of these women inter-preters is acknowledged by Asma Barlas when she points out that the dis-tinctive feature of modern reinterpretations of the Qurʾan is direct involve-ment of the state "in defining the framework for the production of religious knowledge. . . . In such a milieu, rereading the Qurʾan in egalitarian modes is an exercise that has the potential to impinge on the hegemony of the state itself."[29] Thus Muslim women scholars in North America are afforded the freedom to develop their readings of the Qurʾan in an environment that is not free of coercion or pressures but is also not a threat to their well-being or personal safety. This position of relative freedom in correlation with read-ings of colonial and postcolonial history sometimes is the very reason to dis-miss them as agents of "the West" and colonialism and their interpretations as intent to destroy Muslim unity and societies. In epistemological terms, much of their work exhibits clear tensions over the use of "Western" her-meneutical methods and theories on the one hand and traditional Islamic terminology and concepts on the other.

Rather than describe the freedom to interpret as solely a political right, Hibba Abugideiri, in her 2001 article on women's interpretations of the Qurʾan, takes her conclusions further:

> That these female-inclusive Islamic formulations were created in America is related, in many ways, to postmodernist thought prevalent in this country that has allowed Muslims to be more critical of Islam and Muslims than may be possible in Muslim states. In fact, scholars such as Ali Mazrui argue that American secular society provides fer-tile ground for a brand of Islam that is unfettered by the cultural bag-gage originating in Muslim countries.[30]

This claim to a "culture free" and thus more authentic Islam has since been appropriated by many Muslim intellectuals and leaders. Often, especially after 9/11, this argument was used to assure the American public that Mus-lims supported American values and were loyal citizens, but it also led to the construct of a specifically American Islam, which curiously is usually not afflicted with cultural baggage of any (not even the American) kind but is constructed as a pure and unaltered version of Islam. This construction can be used for the creation of an American Muslim identity; however, it can also lead to a kind of Muslim Orientalism, in which traditions, interpretations, and practices in Muslim countries are not only perceived as different, but as less authentic and inferior. As Zareena Grewal has shown, this Orientalist practice is contradicted by the simultaneous quest for authenticity through traditional Islamic learning.[31] The focus on authenticity and the related concept of religious and interpretive authority is at the heart of debates about the woman-led prayer but also women's reinterpretations of the Qur'anic text more generally. What, then, is new about these women scholars' interpretations, and how do they differ from what might cautiously be called the classical tafsir tradition? Two dimensions of Muslim women's exegetical projects will be considered here before applying the insight from these considerations to Wadud's khutbah in 2005: the focus on content as expressed in various discussions and understandings of gender justice and equality and the hermeneutical methods applied by women exegetes.

Reading Gender Justice and Equality in the Qur'an

The exegetical projects of American Muslim women scholars in their broad outlines are significant for this book for a number of reasons. On the intellectual level they provide arguments and justification for various forms of activism; on the political level they supply academic and intellectual credentials to the organizers of events such as the woman-led prayer. Equally important, Muslim women scholars are often activists themselves and thus translate their own exegesis into activist projects and agendas. Events such as the prayer require at least temporary community and network building and should thus be read as attempts at building interpretive communities as well.

At the center of Muslim women's scholars exegesis is the search for gender equality or gender justice. Unlike for non-Muslim scholars, this search for an understanding of the Qur'an that allows for gender equality in society is existential for their personal faith, and like all exegetical projects it is conditioned by the exegetes' history, circumstances, and knowledge.[32] It is clear in the work of Wadud and Barlas that this gender equality as divine intent is a precondition for their exegetical work. In other words, they openly and intentionally bring their values, in this case the idea of gender equality or justice, to the text. The notion of justice, in Wadud's work, constitutes the central purpose of interpretation. The terminology of justice and equality has been a feature of her work since the publication of her first book, *Qur'an and Woman*, in the preface of which she writes, "Through reviewing the Qur'an itself—with its principles of social justice and human equality, and its objective of guidance—I hope to shed some new light on the role of woman."[33]

The idea of justice in the Qur'an is further developed in an article in 1999 where Wadud argues that "general discussions of social justice in Islam need to be clearly linked with specific discourses over the rights and wellbeing of women."[34] In her 2006 book, *Inside the Gender Jihad*, Wadud expands on this idea by insisting on the "egalitarian tendencies, principles, articulations, and implications" of Islam while acknowledging that the concepts of both Islam and justice "have always been relative to actual historical and cultural situations."[35] This acknowledgment seems to accept that her interpretations are relative to such contexts as well, which in turn raises the question of how they could become significant for interpretive community building and thus application to society. Wadud's and Barlas's work coincide when Wadud offers her "Tawhidic paradigm of horizontal reciprocity"[36] and Barlas contends that God cannot be perceived as a father figure to then be emulated by men without risking shirk, or the association of anything with God on the divine level.[37]

In connection with the woman-led prayer it is useful to point to another dimension of American Muslim women's exegesis: an emphasis on the spiritual/religious equality of women and men according to the Qur'an. This spiritual equality, as expressed in shared religious obligations and in the Qur'an's emphasis on individual responsibility for salvation, is then developed into a critique of societal inequality, for if women are equal in the eyes of God where would the argument for their inequality in human society be derived from?

Riffat Hassan has based her entire project as a Muslim feminist theologian (she describes herself as such) on the claim that the Qur'an asserts women's spiritual equality with men and that the glaring inequality of women in Muslim societies past and present is based on men's hegemonic interpretations of the text and on three faulty theological assumptions: that women were created out of and later than men (the Adam and Eve paradigm); that Eve on behalf of all women was responsible for the fall from paradise; and that women were created for men. Hassan rejects all three as patriarchal constructions, without basis in the Islamic sources, and influenced by equally misogynist assumptions in the Jewish and Christian tradi-tions.[38] She then develops her argument for equality based on the inalien-able rights the Qur'an has granted human beings regardless of gender, first among them the rights to life, respect, justice, and freedom. Hassan links these rights as an ethical framework directly to contemporary discussions of human rights, thereby deriving a Muslim theology of human rights as an-chored in the Qur'an as revelation.[39]

Wadud builds her argument on the basis of the concept of *taqwa*, which she translates as "piety" and which could also be rendered "God-consciousness." In citing part of Q 49:13, "Indeed the most noble of you from Allah's perspective is whosoever (he or she) has the most *taqwa*," Wadud offers the interpretation that human beings will be judged by God on the basis of their piety and that there is no gender discrimination in such judgment.[40] Spiritual or religious equality is understood to exceed social equality in significance. Thus social inequality would constitute a violation of God's command. This argument has been of particular significance for Muslim women in their debates on the Islamic source for their quest for equality, simultaneously defending Islam against "Western" critiques as mi-sogynist and oppressive for women and in asserting their own faith. The same argument of the distinction between spiritual and societal equality can also be employed against the quest for gender equality, precisely be-cause there need not be an organic connection between the two.

Wadud also advances an exegetical argument about the parallel and con-nected nature of the treatment of women and the issue of slavery in the Qur'an. According to her, slavery is mentioned and, importantly, not ex-plicitly abolished in the Qur'an, while elsewhere the concept of justice is advanced as a broad ethical goal of Muslim society in this world. Slavery was historically abandoned as a practice by Muslims; thus the same can be achieved through similar exegetical moves for gender equality. Wadud's par-allel argument also allows for a similar reformulation of Islamic legal pre-scriptions on issues of gender equality and women's mainstreaming.[41]

In a combined critique of Wadud and the Egyptian scholar Bint al-Shati', Nimat Barazangi affirms her own insistence on gender equality as derived from the Qur'an as the religio-moral framework for Muslim societies and accuses both scholars of conflating equity with equality, which in turn ce-ments women's inequality in Muslim societies.[42] Her reading of Wadud is based on *Qur'an and Woman*,[43] where Wadud had avoided or not yet reached her more radical conclusion that "gender justice is gender mainstreaming."[44] Barazangi's own understanding of equality (*al-musawah*)[45] is not further explained. Instead, she rejects complementarity in gender roles as unjust (like equity) and critiques al-Hibri's understandings of Islamic Law and its potential for change.[46] Barazangi's focus on education and knowledge as the central goal of her project results in a less refined exegetical argument and constantly blurs the boundaries between exegesis, legal understanding, and interpretations of Muslim history. It is thus more difficult to discern her exegetical methods in order to understand her reasoning. Her focus on what she calls "Islamic Higher Learning" for Muslim women is described as a precondition for justice as gender justice, and it is "limited access to Islamic higher learning" that is "the basis for the Muslim woman's inability to emancipate and self-identify as *khalifah*, a trustee—a Qur'anic mandate (or potential) of human existence."[47]

In conclusion, women's exegetical works share in common a concern with gender roles and dynamics as reflected in the Qur'anic text, an assumption of the Qur'an's intent to advocate justice including gender justice in human society as an ideal, and a critique of the existing inequality of Muslim women in society as the departure point for their respective authors. The contours of gender justice and equality are located in the text through a variety of hermeneutical strategies and methods.

Hermeneutical Strategies and Methods of Women's Interpretation

From the perspective of methodology, the exegetical works share a number of important characteristics,[48] namely, their thematic approach to the Qur'an, their arguments for a historical-critical approach to the text, and the idea of the necessity of a "conscientious pause."[49] All three of these exegetical moves are found in other modern interpretations of the Qur'an, and even the attention to gender issues cannot be called entirely new. In their appropriation of a thematic approach to the Qur'an as well as in their argument for the historical contextualization of the Qur'an as text, the women scholars follow in the footsteps of Fazlur Rahman, one of the first Muslim scholars active in the American secular academy.[50] Rahman developed what he called the "double movement" in approaching the Qur'anic text:

> Whereas the first movement has been from the specifics of the Qur'an to the eliciting and systematizing of its general principles, values, and long-range objectives, the second is to be from this general view to the

specific view that is to be formulated and realized now. That is, the general has to be embodied in the present concrete socio-historical context.[51]

Elsewhere he argued that the Qur'an is first and foremost a "book of religious and moral principles and exhortations," not a legal document. Regarding the legal injunctions contained in the Qur'anic text, Rahman states that the historical context of its revelation necessitated accepting the existing society as a frame of reference but that the legal passages in question were to be transcended in their interpretation when society changed. He thus distinguishes between those aspects of the Qur'an that are eternal and those that are bound by historical circumstances.[52]

In the words of Hidayatullah, the historical contextualization method includes several distinct subareas: "researching the occasion of a verse's revelation, . . . distinguishing between descriptive and prescriptive verses of the Qur'an, . . . distinguishing between universal and particular verses, . . . and identifying historical situations and assumptions that shaped the context of revelation in seventh century Arabia and subsequent exegesis of the Qur'an."[53] Each of these, except for the last, draws on and simultaneously challenges traditional modes of Qur'an interpretation.

The same is true when the hermeneutical strategies of contemporary women exegetes are described as "intra-textual."[54] Hidayatullah identifies two components of this method: "comparing verses and terms to one another instead of reading them in isolation" and reading Qur'anic verses in light of an overall ethic of justice as identified by women exegetes.[55] Both are part of the hermeneutical strategy of reading the Qur'an thematically rather than verse by verse. Hidayatullah correctly points out that neither of those strategies is unique to women exegetes but rather has precedents in "classical" and modern exegesis. In particular, thematic approaches to the text, as opposed to a verse-by-verse interpretation (as is common in traditional tafsir literature), and an interest in the historical context of revelation are shared features in many modernist interpretations. An even cursory reading of Suha Taji-Farouki's edited volume, *Modern Muslim Intellectuals and the Qur'an*, reveals that each of the modern exegetes introduced in the volume offered his or her perspective on women and gender issues, as if their perspectives on the issue functioned as proof of their ability or desire to be modern.[56]

While for Fazlur Rahman women and gender issues in the Qur'an were mostly a passing example in his reinterpretations (together with the issue of slavery),[57] Wadud and Barlas, as well as Shaikh and Barazangi, employ both exegetical moves to advance far-reaching conclusions about gender justice and gender equality. Karen Bauer has criticized (Muslim) scholars' work for treating "the Qur'an selectively and ahistorically, as it is brought to bear on current concerns such as the quest for justice and gender egalitarianism."[58] Bauer contends that the text treats women and men equally when it comes to religious obligations but that many other domains privilege men over women. Bauer concludes: "The level of discourse in the field of gender in Islam has been hampered by the reticence of modern scholars writing in English to confront the evidence that the Qur'an, on the whole, is not gender-egalitarian."[59] Bauer's critique of selective and ahistorical readings by scholars such as Wadud, Barlas, and, with somewhat more agreement, Kecia Ali points us to the complex investments of Muslim women scholars in their exegetical projects and the methodological as well as "theological" differences in approaching the text. Muslim women scholars do indeed bring their notions of justice and equality to the text. Equally important, the very notions of justice and equality need to be defined in order to have a meaningful conversation on this issue. Critiques of consistency and predetermined outcomes in the works of Muslim women exegetes have been voiced by scholars such as Bauer, Hidayatullah, and Chaudhry in their analyses of such projects. Kecia Ali, one of the exegetes, has also honestly engaged this question and comes to the conclusion that some tensions between different aspects and parts of the Qur'anic text can possibly not be resolved.[60]

The third exegetical move was developed in response to reaching an impasse in reading the Qur'an intratextually and contextualizing it historically. Developed by Khaled Abou El Fadl in his book on Islamic Law, authority, and women titled *Speaking in God's Name* and prominent in the work of Amina Wadud is the idea of a conscientious pause. Abou El Fadl states that this "pause" is necessitated by a conflict between the principles of one's faith and textual evidence.

> Having experienced this fundamental conflict between a conscientious conviction and a textual determination, a responsible and reflective person ought to pause. . . . I argue that as long as a person has exhausted all possible avenues toward resolving the conflict, in the final analysis, Islamic theology requires that a person abide by the dictates of his or her own conscience.[61]

Here, Abou El Fadl offers an approach to the Qurʾanic text that allows a Muslim to object to Qurʾanic injunctions under certain circumstances. But the idea of a conscientious pause can also be read to suggest that the Qurʾan does not carry absolute authority and is not the only source of religious and moral conviction. Wadud has even furthered the idea of the conscientious pause in opening up the possibility of saying no to certain passages in the Qurʾan. Clearly more controversial than pausing, this argument in relation to verse 4:34 and the question of marital violence against women sanctioned by the Qurʾan has earned her scorn and criticism from Muslims worldwide.[62]

Further research is needed to understand how Muslim women's exegeses are related to their conceptualization of the nature of the Qurʾanic text. Abou El Fadl has opened the door for a rethinking of the Islamic legal tradition and the Hadith corpus but does not apply the same standards of critical inquiry to the Qurʾanic text itself.[63] Fazlur Rahman contended over three decades ago that Muslim scholars needed to carry out a new investigation of the historical formation of the hadith collections in order to understand better the connection between the Prophet Muhammad, his early community, and the Qurʾan itself. Rahman opined that "the Qurʾan did not come in a vacuum, [hence] the well-known paradox that even the thorough-going skeptics about the Hadith cannot resist supporting their views by it whenever it suits them."[64]

Women scholars have largely rejected the hadith tradition as a viable source because of continuing debates about authenticity of the texts in question and the internal contradictions between even sound traditions.[65] If the compilation of the canonical Hadith collections is assumed to have been carried out by male scholars in the same time period (eighth to tenth centuries) as the development of the Islamic legal schools and classical tafsir works, then women scholars' suspicion of all three as essentially patriarchal projects and products of their own times is warranted. It follows logically that all three would need to be dismissed or at least very critically examined. Wadud and Barlas in particular can be criticized for a sweeping dismissal of the interpretive and legal traditions of many centuries. Other scholars, including al-Hibri, Ali, and Abou El Fadl, have called for and engaged in a critical rethinking of the Islamic legal tradition in particular. The works of younger scholars such as Chaudhry, Geissinger, and Hidayatullah mark the beginning of a scholarly engagement that provides us with a more thorough historical picture of discourses and attitudes to women and gender issues embedded in the classical tradition on the one hand and a thoughtful and forward-thinking engagement with contemporary exegetical scholarship on the other.

Muslim women exegetes have brought their values, their notions of justice and equality, and their quest for changes in the real-life situations of Muslim women to the Qur'an. Muslim women scholars have also pointed out that by definition all *tafasir* (pl. of *tafsir*) are a product of the backgrounds, values, and circumstances of the respective exegetes and their times.[66] A thorough chronological reading of the developments and arguments in women's exegeses is necessary and has not to date been carried out. To read and analyze the works of scholars like Wadud, Barlas, and Barazangi in their order of appearance and in conversation with each other, as well as in connection with changing historical circumstances and community developments, would facilitate recognition of hermeneutical traditions, political contexts, and theological limitations without leveling anachronistic critiques.

Imparting Knowledge: Two Khutbahs as Tafsir

A Friday khutbah is an orally delivered treatise on questions of religious (and political) significance to a congregation or community. As such, it can meaningfully contain elements of tafsir, provided tafsir is broadly understood as an elaboration on meanings of Qur'anic passages. Timur Yuskaev has analyzed the approaches to the Qur'an of four American Muslim intellectuals: Fazlur Rahman, Amina Wadud, Warith Deen Muhammad, and Hamza Yusuf. While he distinguishes between the largely written tafsir of Rahman and Wadud on the one hand and the largely orally delivered tafsir of Muhammad and Yusuf on the other, he introduces the concept of oral tafsir and analyzes their differences in rhetoric and approaches to the Qur'an as text. He argues that all four intellectuals have carried out a "double translation in language and time: in addition to translating the Qur'an into American idioms and placing it within the framework of American cultural references, they also guide their readers and listeners across epistemological rifts between seventh-century Arabia and [the] contemporary United States."[67] Yuskaev presents a brief analysis of Wadud's khutbahs in 1994 and 2005 but reserves the notion of oral tafsir for W. D. Muhammad and Hamza Yusuf. He approaches both khutbahs as reprinted in Wadud's *Inside the Gender Jihad* as her texts.[68] Extending Yuskaev's use of the term, Wadud, in her delivering her khutbahs in 1994 and 2005, produced two examples of oral tafsir. She delivered her thoughts on gender justice as contained in the Qur'an as a woman standing in front of the congregation and thus embodied the ideal of gender equality at the core of her exegesis, making the khutbahs at the same time examples of embodied tafsir.

As mentioned above, both "texts" were first delivered orally and in the process of debate and reconsideration turned into texts. Wadud has reproduced the text of the entire 1994 khutbah in *Inside the Gender Jihad* and has offered a shortened version of her 2005 khutbah in the last chapter of the same book.[69] The 2005 khutbah seems to be based on her notes prepared for delivering the khutbah and differs in places, although not significantly, from what she actually said in 2005 according to the video footage on which my transcription is based. The two khutbahs are different from each other in many significant ways, some formal and some content related. In addition, Wadud has also offered her own "interpretation" of the intentions, contexts, and resulting text for the 1994 khutbah to which she devoted an entire chapter of her book. I want to focus on the content and rhetorical devices Wadud employs. Both khutbahs reflect Wadud's particular hermeneutical and exegetical engagement with the Qur'an.

Wadud has described the 1994 khutbah as a deliberate attempt to "normalize" women's experiences by claiming them to be as universal as male experiences in order to challenge male claims to normativity, which are based on the exclusion of female voices and perspectives. Thus her 1994 khutbah focused on interconnected female experiences and their intimate connection to engaged surrender: pregnancy, childbirth, and marriage. Wadud describes the khutbah as one of her best presentations and contends that "the actual substance of the talk resulted from primal inspiration, not only from a source beyond my own conscious construction, but also from a place where I feel intuitively the greatest confidence through a unique, female place of experience: Islam as engaged surrender from the perspective of being female, mother and wife."[70]

The khutbah contains Wadud's formulation of "engaged surrender" as involving "an active consciousness in participation in our social lives, family lives, community lives, economic lives, and political lives, by the heart which is always open to the will of Allah, and which always gives precedent to Allah's will. The concept we have been inclined towards—submission— sometimes gives the idea that there is no will. But the one who willfully submits to the will of Allah is engaged in surrender."[71]

Wadud reflects on marriage as half of religion, but as only half, and a half that cannot and should not exist without engaged surrender and a constant appreciation for the agency, full humanity, and free will of one's spouse. Her thoughts on reciprocal relations between spouses, requiring "listening and hearing, respecting and honoring, loving and caring,"[72] anticipates her later formulated "tawhidic paradigm" and the associated idea of horizontal reciprocity of men and women in human society. While the sermon does not introduce justice or gender justice as terms, it does claim the full equality and full human dignity of women as well as men. As a sermon it calls Muslim men and women to respect each other as spouses and members of society, and it allows for human error, for trial and error, and for God's forgiveness of such errors. It also shares women's bodily and spiritual experiences as human and relevant not only to women but also to men, claiming to broaden Muslims' understanding of each other's humanity. Clear emphasis is put on God's mercy and God's willingness to forgive and understand the shortcomings of human behavior.

Stylistically, the khutbah includes three references to Qur'anic passages, two from Sura 94 and one from Sura 30. The passages from Sura 94 refer to questions of the alternation between hardship and ease in human life and the associated responsibility not to forget God when life becomes difficult but also when life becomes easier and more successful. In both states humans are called to remember God and their utter dependence on his will. The passage in Sura 30 (Q 30:21) reads, "And among His signs is that He has created from your own selves mates. And He has made between the two of you love and mercy."[73] This is an oft-quoted verse in Muslim discussions of marriage and one that is of significance for Muslim women exegetes in developing a nonhierarchical model of marital relations in which spouses are equal in rights and duties. It also emphasizes the importance of love and mercy over contractual and legally regulated relations.

Compared to many of Wadud's published writings, the khutbah appears subtle in its message and careful in its wording. Wadud has pointed out that while the khutbah was advertised by the (male) organizers of the event, she herself did not find out about her role in the service until forty-five minutes before it was to take place. Thus she had very little time to prepare more textually grounded or complex remarks.[74]

It is internally consistent with much of Wadud's work that the 2005 khutbah, while different in style, picks up and reasserts many of the themes developed in the 1994 sermon. The style differs in that the 2005 khutbah contains many more quotes from the Qur'an; that those passages as well as supplications formulated by Wadud were delivered in Arabic and then translated into English; and in that this khutbah was significantly longer. They share in common the surrounding debate, the media attention, and Wadud's concern that their form mattered more for the controversy than the content of her sermons. Wadud discusses her disappointment with this fact in much detail regarding the 1994 khutbah; however, these reflections were formulated more than a decade after the event and thus contain several layers of later analysis of the event, all informed by later exegetical, spiritual, and personal developments in Wadud's life. The account of her utilization for someone else's political and religious agenda echoes Wadud's frustrations but also reasserts her own agency in interpreting events in her life, thus claiming at least one possible reading of events. Parallel reflections on the 2005 event in her book seem less complex and may not have been far enough removed historically and in her memory to engage in a similarly deep analysis.

The 2005 khutbah is more formal and follows, by Wadud's intention, centuries of established ritual practice of Muslims except for the gender of the khatibah.[75] The Qur'anic passages selected are offered as an introduction and recited in Arabic and then translated into English, and they parallel Wadud's later exegetical argument: Q 62:9 calls Muslims to leave their daily business and heed the call for congregation prayer on Friday for remembrance of God as more important than any business or material gain. Here one could infer that Wadud reads this call as addressed to women as well as men, even though the particular passage addresses males grammatically (which in Arabic can include women in the collective). Q 2:255 emphasizes God's omnipotence and His knowledge of all things, beings, and parts of creation, a knowledge that human beings cannot claim to be able to attain. The passage could be linked to Wadud's insistence on engaged surrender, based on the realization that God's will has power over humans but that power can more meaningfully be actualized through willingly surrendering to it. Q 33:35 is one of the passages in the Qur'an that addresses men and women specifically through the use of masculine and feminine pronouns and verb forms. It enjoins both sexes to participate in Islamic rituals such as charity and fasting but also emphasizes their equal responsibility to speak and act truthfully and to guard their modesty. Aptly mirroring Wadud's tawhidic paradigm with God at the top and women and men on a line of "horizontal reciprocity," the passage is later in the khutbah connected to that same paradigm. Notably, the revelation of this passage is associated with the question posed to the Prophet Muhammad by one of his wives, Umm Salama, reportedly representing several other women in Medina, asking why the Qur'an did not mention women and their reward for faith and steadfastness. Ahmad van Denffer cites the authority of al-Tirmidhi (d. 892), an early hadith scholar, saying that the question prompted the revelation of this verse and two other passages addressing women (Q 3:195 and Q 4:23). We find here the intervention of a woman in the early Muslim community, which has been cited as a source for contemporary Muslim women to derive models for women's roles as recipients but also as interpreters of revelation.[76] Wadud interprets the verse to communicate that "moral excellence is a result of *iman*."[77] Wadud moves to connect Q 39:35 and Q 2:286 in order to develop her argument that God has outlined for men and women what they need to do in order to achieve moral excellence. God's expectations are not different, and it is ultimately trust in God and his wise distribution of burdens on particular individuals that proves His omnipotence. She then connects God's knowledge to His judgment and adds a sarcastic remark on the fortitude of being judged by God and not by other human beings.[78]

The khutbah continues by stringing together various thoughts, on human imperfection and the gift of creation as God's self-disclosure, on revelation as a mercy, and, quite surprisingly here, on plurality of religions. This thread continues to connect revelation to Muhammad to taqwa (piety) in order to emphasize the importance of appreciating the Qur'an as yet another form of self-disclosure. In recounting Q 4:1, Wadud then returns to questions of gender by indicating that God created men and women from a single soul— that is, they have a unified origin—which points back to tawhid (Oneness), but Wadud also argues for the unity of humanity as derived from their common origin. The argument then moves to everything other than God being in pairs, as created by God, which distinguishes creation from the creator, emphasizing the Oneness of God and the very different pairedness of the creation. This line of thinking leads into an exploration and explanation of Wadud's tawhidic paradigm, according to which men and women cannot be situated hierarchically because that would put those in power on par with God. As mentioned above, Wadud's tawhidic paradigm aligns itself with Asma Barlas's similar argument that patriarchy is in fact a form of shirk (associating something else on the level of God, and the greatest sin in Islam), claiming Godlike status for men, fathers, and husbands.

Wadud's paradigm is not confined to gender issues but can equally be applied to race, class, and other markers of hierarchical relations between humans. Thus her exegetical argument that the justice commanded in the Qur'an has to be gender justice is here reflected back onto other possible forms of social justice, linking gender struggles to other important struggles that Wadud feels strongly about, including racial and economic discrimination.

In a direct connection to the 1994 khutbah, Wadud then calls out the silencing of women's voices, perspectives, and experiences. She goes on to describe Islamic Law itself as developed and codified in early Muslim history as an innovation: one reflecting men's best intentions but excluding women's voices in error, an error that needs to be corrected in our time.

The remaining part of the khutbah consists of a variety of supplications, asking God for guidance in this and all other endeavors and for forgiveness of mistakes made with the best intentions. The khutbah ends with expressions of gratitude and awe for the power and presence of God and asking God for blessings for the Prophet Muhammad, his family, and his followers. Here Wadud pronounces passages in Arabic and then immediately offers a translation. In the middle of the last part, Wadud exclaims that she would engage in a silent supplication asking God's forgiveness.

Notable, as in the 1994 khutbah, is the clear attempt to use appropriate and subtle language to address the congregation. Wadud's preaching is not forceful and provocative but is delivered with no punch lines or other attempts to involve the congregation. This speaking to but not with the congregation is traditional Islamic practice. Compared to some male American Muslim preachers such as the late Warith Deen Muhammad or Zaid Shakir, Wadud is markedly subtle. Her thoughts and lines of argument are not always easy to follow and only open themselves to understanding on closer scrutiny. None of those attending the 2005 prayer event have reflected on the content, which raises the question of how effective the khutbah was in conveying Wadud's complicated argument and exegesis. In closer analysis of the text, which was not possible during the prayer, Wadud's exegetical arguments and strategies are clearly reflected in the khutbah, even though she has formulated many of them in stronger and in more critical words elsewhere. For the 1994 khutbah Wadud has reported that Farid Esack, one of the organizers of the event, was so excited about the symbolic significance of the event that he did not listen to the khutbah. Two women attending the event reportedly appreciated the content, albeit in different ways.[79] Esack's sentiment that the symbolism of a woman giving the khutbah was more important than what she actually said was likely paralleled by many of those in attendance at the 2005 prayer event. However, in publishing the text versions of both khutbahs Wadud has made her thoughts and arguments available to an audience beyond those attending the prayer, thus actively participating in the debate over gender justice and women's Qur'an interpretation but also over women's authority and leadership.

The application of the term *tafsir* to the exegetical projects of American Muslim women scholars and the inclusion of applied or broadened forms of exegesis as exemplified in Shaikh's tafsir of praxis and my notion of embodied tafsir make it possible to broaden our understanding of the ways in which Muslims, especially modern and contemporary, have approached their sacred text. Despite my focus on scholarly and gendered approaches to the Qur'an, these expanded notions of tafsir illustrate the "democratization" of access to the text and immediately raise questions about authority, authenticity, and legitimacy.

4
History, Women's Rights, and Islamic Law

Careful investigation of the legal tradition . . . demonstrates the ways
in which authorities have, from the earliest years of Islam, used their
own judgment and the customs of their societies to adapt Qur'anic and
prophetic dictates to changed circumstances. It illustrates that some of
the doctrines taken for granted as "Islamic" emerged at a particular time
and place as the result of human interpretive endeavor and need not be
binding for all time. Furthermore, the precedent of earlier jurists can
authorize a similar interpretive and adaptive process for Muslims today,
including bypassing (through a variety of interpretive devices) even
seemingly clear Qur'anic statements.

Kecia Ali, *Sexual Ethics and Islam*

Qur'anic exegesis (tafsir) and the systematic development of Islamic legal
rulings and regulations (fiqh) are distinct areas of the traditional Islamic sciences. They are also intricately linked with each other and with a third important component, hadith science. More specifically, both tafsir and hadith
science became important tools for the derivation of legal rulings, especially in the eighth through tenth centuries when the Islamic legal schools
(madhahib, sing. madhhab) emerged. Kecia Ali's statement above reminds
us not to take for granted the construction of an integrated, canonical, and
self-contained Islamic tradition, legal and otherwise, but rather to see the
negotiation of ethics, law, and interpretation as contextual, negotiated, and
part of a historical process. The debates about the permissibility of women's
prayer leadership indicate the differing vantage points and opinions put forward before and after the prayer in 2005 and especially the insistence on a
legal framework for such debate. How can the legal dimensions of the debate be understood, and how do they relate to the larger contributions of

American Muslim women to discussions of women's rights, Islamic Law, and historical role models?

This chapter focuses on contemporary connections between Islamic Law, women's rights discourses, and the investment in historical female role models for contemporary activism and change. Those participating in the debate about women's prayer leadership within a legal framework are part of a long-standing historical concern with this question rather than a new movement. Contemporary American Muslim contributions to Islamic legal interpretation and women's rights discourses can be read as an attempt to reconcile a constructed classical Islamic tradition with contemporary sensitivities, values, and ethical concerns. Drawing on the examples of Umm Waraqa, Hagar, Khadija, and 'Aisha,[1] this chapter also addresses the significance and difficulties of constructing historical women figures as role models for contemporary Muslim women in America and the ways in which these role models have informed American Muslim women's domestic and transnational activism beyond the prayer.

The Umm Waraqa Hadith

The hadith about Umm Waraqa was one of the most frequently quoted references in the debate about woman-led prayer, thus not only acquiring a central role in the argumentation but also illustrating the dynamics of textual and historical references in the debate. Simonetta Calderini rightly notes that "less than five years ago, very few scholars of Islam and Islamic Studies, and even fewer individuals outside academia, knew about Umm Waraqa (d. 641)."[2] So why the sudden attention to a female companion of the Prophet Muhammad and a Prophetic tradition about her? Calderini's exploration of the "permissibility of female Imams" and subsequent analysis of hadith traditions about Umm Waraqa was prompted by this new interest, and she has connected it to recent events such as the 1994 khutbah in South Africa and the 2005 woman-led prayer as well. Who was Umm Waraqa, and what does the hadith in question say?

Umm Waraqa was a companion of the Prophet Muhammad, reported to have asked the Prophet to participate in the Battle of Badr, in response to which he persuaded her to stay at home and assured her that she would achieve martyrdom by doing so. She is also reported to have been one of the Medinan followers of Muhammad (*ansar*) and that she knew the Qur'an by heart.[3] The hadith in question, in the version reported by Ahmad Ibn

Hanbal (d. 855) in his Musnad, states: "The Prophet ordered her to be the imam for the people of her house [or household, Arabic *dar*] and she has a *mu'adhdhin* [caller to prayer] and she used to be the imam for the people of her household."[4] In a slightly longer version, Abu Da'ud (d. 889) reports the text (*matn*) of the hadith as follows: "The Prophet used to visit her in her house and he appointed someone as a mu'adhdhin for her and he sounded the call to prayer for her, and he [the Prophet] ordered her to be an imam for the people of her household," and [says the narrator], 'I saw her mu'adhdhin and he was an old man.'"[5] Calderini also reports that in some versions of the hadith the Prophet is reported to have "allowed" (*adhana*), rather than "ordered" (*amara*), Umm Waraqa to be the imam of her household. Later versions replace the word *household* (dar) with "her women" (*nisa'aha*).

These changes in wording and, equally important, meaning, as Calderini argues, together with changes in and discussions about the chain of transmitters, are significant and can be read in several ways. In a detailed analysis of hadith texts and chains of transmissions, Calderini advances the argument that changes in both can be read as indicative of important developments in earlier Muslim communities, namely, the clarification and regulation of the prayer ritual (the call and caller to prayer, who can lead prayers, etc.) and the importance of the Medinan companions of Muhammad as part of the early Muslim community.[6] In later debates, and indeed in the contemporary ones as well, the hadith became more invested in the legal dimensions of prayer practice and eventually acquired a gendered life of its own. Interpreters of the hadith (legal scholars and others) argued for various meanings of the word *dar*: house, household, or neighborhood. The circumstances of the Prophet's order or permission to lead people in prayer were interpreted to apply only to her or to be a precedent for other women; those following her in prayer included free men, male slaves, or only women, depending on various readings of the context and different versions of the hadith; and not least, the status of the hadith based on its chain of transmission was debated and generally found weak.

Most participants in the debate about the 2005 Friday prayer who couched their contributions in legal and textual terminology and arguments used their readings of the Umm Waraqa hadith to dismiss or at least severely restrict the permissibility of women's leadership. The Assembly of Muslim Jurists in America states that if the hadith were deemed authentic (their statement does not say whether they consider it so), it would have no bearing on the debate about women leading Friday prayers because it clearly referred to prayers led in Umm Waraqa's house, and only the most "lenient explanations" would assume that men were present in that home congregation.[7] Muhammad al-Akiti quotes the Abu Daʿud version of the Umm Waraqa hadith but doubts its authority based on two weaknesses in the chain of transmission and thus dismisses its value for supporting women leading prayers.[8] Yusuf al-Qaradawi draws on the hadith, despite the weak chain of transmission, and argues (against another scholar he cites) that the permission to lead women and men in prayer within her house is not limited to the person of Umm Waraqa but can be extended to other women in similar circumstances, based on knowledge of the Qurʾan.[9] Hina Azam evaluates the evidentiary potential of the Umm Waraqa hadith as well and concludes that it can support the permission for women to lead women and men within a domestic setting in daily prayers but that it does not hold as support for woman-led Friday prayers.[10] Zaid Shakir emphasizes the more limited reading that Umm Waraqa was indeed encouraged to lead an all-female congregation, thus establishing support for women's prayer leadership of other women, which is also supported by other reports that the Prophet's wives ʿAisha and Umm Salama led other women in prayer during Muhammad's lifetime.[11]

Of the opinions built on the Umm Waraqa hadith, only Nevin Reda finds it in support of her argument for the permissibility of women-led Friday prayers. Reda reads the word *dar* to mean neighborhood rather than house or household and argues that the Prophet Muhammad appointed Umm Waraqa as imam for the second mosque in Medina after the first had turned out to be too small and far away for some community members to attend daily prayers. This appointment is a historical precedent that makes it possible to appoint women to religious leadership positions, including as imams and khatibs, for Friday prayers. Reda addresses the objections she anticipates from other scholars, which are exactly the objections later developed in responses to her statement by Hina Azam and Zaid Shakir.[12]

The larger legal dimensions of the contemporary debate cannot be understood without considering its extensive reliance on what is constructed as the "classical" Islamic legal tradition. To remind us that the claim to normativity espoused in contemporary legal opinions based on a self-contained, coherent, and "true" set of ethical precepts and theological convictions (the "classical" tradition) is indeed constructed, the legal positions of the past are refracted in the discussion that follows through their presence in con-temporary discourses. This strategy allows for a disruption of the conve-nient juxtaposition of the classical Islamic tradition to its rethinking since the early nineteenth century. As Ali points out, the legal tradition itself has a history and is always a product of its historical circumstances.

Women's Prayer Leadership as a Legal Issue

The historical circumstances of the juristic discourses on women's prayer leadership are not only significant; the very existence of such discourses from the ninth to the thirteenth century and beyond should give one pause. It is somewhat surprising that Muslim jurists in the formative period of Islamic jurisprudence would have been concerned with the question of whether women could or should lead prayers, have access to mosques, or participate in battle. While participation in battle can easily be traced as a product of Prophetic history, namely the military operations the early Muslim community under the leadership of the Prophet Muhammad was involved in, the question whether women can or should be able to attend mosques and whether they can be imams would be less expected in early texts. If one were to read juristic discourse and legal opinions as reflections of social realities, then it stands to reason that early Muslim communities and the women within them had questions about the very issues Muslims are discussing today, including those of gender, though they would not have been identified as such. Leila Ahmed has argued that discursive and legal texts can be read as reflections of differing social realities. For example, texts that repeatedly call for the prohibition of certain practices tell us that these were social practices that jurists and scholars deemed worthy of cri-tique without being able to end them.[13]

Women's activities such as participation in battle, Qur'an recitation, and even women's verbal challenging of the Prophet Muhammad himself are part of the traditionally accepted hadith literature, and the early collectors and evaluators of Prophetic traditions perceived them as valuable and in many cases authentic. Their existence, as we have seen in the Umm Waraqa hadith, does not necessarily translate into gender-inclusive interpretations and applications; however, their existence can be and has been taken as a starting point for challenging widely accepted and less gender-inclusive readings.

Ali's argument, echoed in Calderini's exploration of the transmission and application of the Umm Waraqa hadith, is clearly and extensively demonstrated by Behnam Sadeghi, who uses debates about women and prayer to demonstrate structures of reasoning in the development of canonical Hanafi positions on these issues. Hanafi jurists' rulings on women praying with women, women praying with men, and women leading women or men in prayer are diverse, changing, and part of an ongoing conversation about methodology and the purposes of Islamic Law. Sadeghi also finds that especially in earlier periods regional differences in ritual practice and the significance of localized schools of thought and opinion played an important role in the canonization process.[14] The complicated web of scholars, their positions, and their arguments within the Hanafi school from the eighth to the twentieth century, as explored by Sadeghi, is simplified in the 2005 debate, primarily for practical purposes.

However, the picture of widely accepted majority opinions on the issue of women leading prayers is still multilayered and somewhat more complicated than a dichotomy between those who support women leading prayers and those who do not. The debate itself also provides a case study for the much larger questions of the significance of Islamic Law for contemporary Muslims and the creation (or retention) of an integrated and applicable body of legal opinions. Three interrelated questions emerge in the debate about the 2005 prayer: *if* women can lead prayers, *who* they can lead in prayers, and *which kinds of prayers* they can lead if at all.

The legal answers to these questions are interconnected, and, as Elewa and Silvers rightfully point out, the initial concern was not one of permissibility but rather of the validity of prayers offered under certain conditions. Thus the legal debate needs to be understood as part of a larger concern about fulfilling the Islamic duty to worship God rather than primarily as social regulations. Strikingly, the contemporary debate seems to have focused on the question of permission, leaving that of validity aside and emphasizing the social dimensions of congregational prayers. Elewa and Silvers also identify the major concerns of many involved in the debate: the well-being of society (or community), modesty, consensus, and the default position of prohibition.[15]

As to the first question, whether women can lead prayers at all, according to Zaid Shakir, central figures in the four extant Sunni legal schools gave the following opinions. The Maliki school did not allow women to lead prayers, whereas the Hanafi, Shafi'i, and Hanbali schools allowed such leadership under certain conditions and for certain prayers.[16] This general answer is supported by many of the other scholars participating in the debate, including Yusuf al-Qaradawi and Muhammad al-Akiti.

As to the second question, Shakir states that the Hanbali, Shafi'i, and Hanafi schools permitted women to lead other women in prayers under certain circumstances. Hanafi jurists considered it permissible but disliked (*makruh*, one of the possible positions on a scale of legal rulings),[17] whereas the Shafi'i and Hanbali schools allowed the practice. All three schools stipulated that the woman imam should not stand in front of the congregation but rather among the women in the first row. Shakir also quotes a minority opinion of the Hanbali school that allows women to lead men in tarawih prayers.[18] The concern about validity is returned to in Shakir's mention of Imam an-Nawawi's opinion, "If a woman leads a man or men in prayer, the prayer for the men is invalid. As for her prayer, and the prayer of the women praying with her, it is sound."[19] Quoting "some modern scholars," Shakir states that it may be permissible for women to lead men of their household in prayer if the men are not qualified. Shakir, along with other scholars, also mentions that scholars of some of the extinct schools of jurisprudence in Islamic history had permitted unrestricted female prayer leadership but dismisses their significance because they are defunct and their rulings are not considered valid arguments in the extant schools. However, the knowledge of such permission in extinct schools is at least of historiographic interest, for one can then assume that women led prayers in those communities at that time. Al-Qaradawi only allows women to lead men of their household in prayer, provided they are more qualified, of older age, and lead the men from behind the congregation. He enthusiastically supports the revival of the Sunnah practice of women leading other women in prayer.[20]

As to the third question, Shakir concludes, "From what we have presented above, it should be clear that a woman leading a mixed gender, public congregational prayer is not something sanctioned by Islamic Law, in the Sunni tradition. Her leading the Friday congregational prayer is even more unfounded, as she would be required to do things that are forbidden or disliked in other prayers."[21] Muhammad al-Akiti, a U.K.-based Shafi'i jurist, offers the more particular position of his school in support of women leading prayers and opines that women can even lead Eid prayers but should preferably not give an Eid khutbah, or if they choose to do so, it should not be called a khutbah. He also declares that the prayers of all those attending a woman-led Friday prayer are invalid and that woman-led obligatory prayers are not valid for the men in attendance.[22]

Several scholars advance arguments as to the issues that arise if and when women lead men in prayer, chief among them the issue of modesty or temptation and thus distraction. Thus the issue of prayer leadership also becomes an opportunity to advance rulings about gender separation during prayers and the positioning of the women of the congregation behind the men.[23]

In a statement on the political participation of women, first formulated in 1995, the Muslim Women's League advanced the argument that women could act as imams based on qualifications as specified in ahadith that did not include explicit references to the gender of an imam, and referred to the Umm Waraqa hadith and later jurists' minority opinions that women could lead men in prayer.[24] The same line of argument is taken up in a fatwa by Khaled Abou El Fadl, who also opined that prayer leadership and thus religious guidance should be based on knowledge and qualifications, not on gender; however, in his opinion a woman imam should not pray directly in front of men so as to avoid distraction and temptation.[25]

Elewa and Silvers, in their most recent contribution to the debate that critically surveys the preceding arguments, both classical and contemporary, argue that contemporary scholars' concerns can be answered from within the tradition. They also conclude that unrestricted female prayer leadership is by default permissible. While Elewa and Silvers differ in their view on the prudence and priority of women insisting on leading prayers at this time, they both agree that the obligation to lead prayers was addressed to both men and women, as evident in the absence of any explicit or contextual evidence to the contrary.[26] They go on to refute the prohibitions based on the well-being of society as in the eye of the beholder, the modesty concern easily addressed by innovative special solutions during prayer, and the default understanding of Prophetic rulings as only addressed to and thus applicable to men. Most important, they challenge the authority of consensus rulings (*ijmaʿ*), that is, the argument for the prohibition to be valid because the majority of scholars agree on it.

The debate reflected on here has demonstrated that such consensus is not only relative but also based on a particular definition of who is able and qualified to participate in consensus building. Those assuming the authority to issue legal rulings on this matter are primarily male scholars with a claim to traditional Islamic training and the status of Islamic scholar. This narrow definition of where religious and legal authority needs to be situated allows these same scholars to dismiss not only the arguments of their detractors but also their qualifications for participating in the debate. This may be one reason the organizers of the prayer did not for the most part engage in the debate on the legal level.[27]

Other contributions to the debate broadened or altogether ignored the legal framework in favor of arguing from the Qur'an itself, for example, Amina Wadud and Jamal al-Banna, whose book *Jawaz imamat al-mar'a li-al-rijal* (The Permissibility of Female Prayer Leadership of Men) was published in June 2005.[28] Al-Banna offers a survey of "classical" and "contemporary" opinions on the issue of woman-led prayer and concludes that it is permissible for women to lead men in prayer because there is no evidence in the Qur'an to the contrary. He goes on to state that many contemporary scholars are vested in their emulation of the classical tradition without concern for changing circumstances and the need to develop opinions based on current circumstances. Al-Banna challenges contemporary Muslim scholars to admit that they are afraid of losing male privileges and asserts that the real issue is not prayer leadership but the status of Muslim women in society and law and that in a (future) gender-equitable society women's prayer leadership would not be an issue at all.

As is clearly demonstrated in the discussions of woman-led prayers, debates about gender roles and women's status in Muslim societies cannot neatly be divided according to their legal, exegetical, or other frameworks, as if those categories were hermetically sealed from each other and not in fact part of the same interpretive tradition with the same goal of trying to understand God's will for humanity in this world. The intersections of exegetical, ethical, and legal approaches are a product of centuries of engagement with this question, while the increasing participation of women in the conversation and the explicit focus on gender as a category have to be acknowledged as products of the more recent past.

Beyond the issue of prayer leadership, American Muslim women scholars and activists have taken several different routes in their engagement with questions of women's rights and legal gender equality. Two are explored here in more detail: the cross-genre, ethics-centered work of Kecia Ali on marriage and sexuality; and attempts to harmonize discourses on women's rights as human rights with an Islamic legal framework, as evident in the work of Riffat Hassan and Azizah al-Hibri.

Kecia Ali: Rethinking Islamic Sexual Ethics

The work of Kecia Ali, professor of Islamic studies at Boston University and author of *Sexual Ethics and Islam*,[29] is not easily categorized as only an engagement with the Islamic legal tradition (in its historical and contemporary expressions). By far the most (self-)critical and honest attempt to reconcile modern, feminist, and Western concepts of justice, equality, and rights with the long Muslim tradition of exegesis and jurisprudence, Ali's work brings together her readings of the Qur'an, ahadith, and legal works on sexuality and marriage in order to assess the potential relevance of the "tradition" for contemporary Muslims, especially in North America, through a careful rereading and, where necessary, construction of a new set of ethical and legal regulations. Her book addresses a set of the most contentious issues for Muslim women (and men), among them Muslim contractual marriage agreements, divorce, illicit sex as defined by Islamic Law, homosexuality, and female circumcision. The underlying concern of Ali's work is a sexual ethic based on human agency and consensus, that is, the right to make independent choices with regard to sexual practice, marriage, and divorce.

Ali reads and engages the Islamic legal corpus in its breadth instead of merely choosing rulings and interpretations that satisfy contemporary sensibilities; and rather than dismiss the entire legal tradition as misogynist, she offers a comprehensive overview of the internal logic and foundational assumptions of classical jurists. This is especially evident in her treatment of marriage and lawful sexual acts, where she argues that "there is a mismatch between views of marriage and sexual intimacy as based in mutual consent and reciprocal desire and the entire structure of classical jurisprudential doctrines surrounding lawful sexuality."[30] She explains that male ownership or control was considered the basis for licit sex, within both marriage and slavery. The legal tradition is replete with references to sexual acts in the context of slave-owner relations. Ali argues that although slavery is no longer practiced, the assumptions about women's agency and consent to sexual acts did not differ significantly within marriage and slavery and thus still inform those who claim to follow the Islamic legal tradition with regard to marriage. Restating an important and in her view obvious point, Ali points out that both early jurists and contemporary Muslim thinkers "could not help but be influenced by their own sense of what was right and wrong, natural and unnatural. In engaging with Muslim texts of the past, it is important to consider the ways in which their authors' base assumptions differ from those of the present."[31] She then stresses that "consent and mutuality" are not "fundamentally incompatible with an Islamic ethics of sex[;] these values were not prefigured in premodern Muslim texts in a way satisfactory for the twenty-first century."[32]

A more specific example of Ali's line of reasoning illustrates her approach to the Qur'an and jurisprudence more clearly. In a section on conceptions of sex within marriage Ali discusses the attention of classical texts to female sexual gratification and satisfaction as expressed in the work of the tenth-century theologian al-Ghazali. She points out that the mere existence of such attention has been celebrated by contemporary Muslims as a positive attitude to human sexuality and as an expression of Muslims' concerns for women's "rights." However, her discussion of legal texts from various schools demonstrates that

> the overwhelming weight of the Muslim legal and exegetical tradition is on women's obligations to make themselves sexually available to their husbands, rather than the reverse. This bias in the sources emerges even in contemporary discussions that attempt to discuss male and female sexual rights in parallel, highlighting the immensity of the task for those who would redefine sex within marriage as a fully mutual endeavor.[33]

Ali argues that the conception of marriage as based on dower as the husband's compensation for "exclusive legitimate sexual access to his wife"[34] and extending to the financial regulation of divorce has created "gender-differentiated marital claims" that men's ethical obligation to satisfy their wives sexually cannot override. She describes modern attempts to retain the classical concept of Muslim marriage and achieve spouses' mutual sexual rights as bound to fail.

In a 2009 article Ali develops her earlier reflections on the issue further and insists on returning to the Qur'an as the source for reformist and feminist thinking on the issue of sex within marriage but also proposes, based on her acknowledgment of a "reading" impasse of the Qur'anic text, that feminist Muslim scholars may have to look to the larger textual tradition, including Sufi writings and noncanonical texts, for inspiration on how to solve these issues. Returning to her concern with ethical reform, Ali argues that a larger conceptualization of a Muslim ethic of equality as derived from the Qur'an may be necessary to achieve change on particular questions. She concludes with a set of questions about reading egalitarianism in the Qur'an without distorting its meaning and calls for a new approach to the connection between God's relationship to humanity and equality, essentially advancing a theory of individual submission to God and its connection to freedom of choice. "The implications of *tawhid* for exegesis and ethics," she writes, "remain to be worked out in a comprehensive fashion. . . . [B]ut in thinking about the union of two selves in physical intimacy, remembering the separateness and Oneness of God to whom all Muslims must ultimately submit as individuals may serve as a place to begin."[35]

Ali consistently acknowledges her own values as a product of contemporary ethical sensibilities, which include freedom of choice, consensus, and individual rights. She at least occasionally draws on feminist theory and the works of other religious feminists.

The palpable tension between yearning for gender equality and commitment to Muslim identity is negotiated differently in the works of American Muslim women scholars and activists. Ali, a member of a younger generation, has critically engaged with the works of earlier scholars such as Azizah al-Hibri and has transcended their tendencies to develop more apologetic arguments about women's rights in Islamic Law and exegesis by acknowledging the tensions, fissures, and open-ended questions brought up by her work. The work of al-Hibri and Hassan in particular needs to be understood in its historical context but also as a product of the authors' activist commitments. Especially the latter demanded pragmatic and applicable solutions to such tensions in the face of the immense task to improve Muslim women's lives. Thus their exegetical and legal work on women's rights as human rights and as rooted within Islamic Law warrants closer attention.

Islamic Law and Women's Rights Discourses

Both Riffat Hassan and Azizah al-Hibri started publishing on women's rights and women's issues from Muslim theological and legal perspectives in the 1980s. Most of their writings have appeared in edited collections, notably on the subject of women in world religions, and neither scholar has to date published a book-length study of women or gender questions in Islam. Thus their formative years as Muslim women scholars (from Muslim-majority countries) within the American academy took place at a time when Muslim women were primarily spoken about rather than spoken to. The often quite explicit assumptions about Muslim women's oppression but also their lack of critical distance to their tradition as expressed in the views and projects of Western feminist scholars and activists made it difficult if not impossible to advance alternative discourses.[36] At the same time, it was difficult to find open ears within Muslim communities for activist agendas that challenged male privilege, especially definitions of (male) scholarly and religious authority and the status quo on women's issues. Frequently accused of being agents of Western attempts to destroy "Islam" from within, this generation of women scholars and activists was forced to walk a fine line to achieve intellectual and practical changes.

Azizah al-Hibri

Azizah al-Hibri's work has focused on a rethinking and creative application of the existing Islamic legal tradition based on the assumption that God's intent expressed in the Qur'an is equality between men and women in Muslim societies. Al-Hibri is keenly aware of the power of outside discourses on Muslim women and Islam and rejects colonial and neocolonial projects that interfere with reform and change in Muslim societies and communities. Her version of miriam cooke's "multiple critique"[37] combines the development of "an indigenous Muslim women's movement,"[38] without Western interference and hegemony, with the rejection of patriarchal interpretations of foundational texts based on a "Satanic logic"[39] that assumes male superiority over women in violation of tawhid.

Several key themes emerge in her work: the importance of *ijtihad* (independent legal reasoning), not only as an available tool of Islamic jurisprudential methodology, but also as a reflection of the principle of change inherent in God's creation; the distinction between religion and culture, which in turn allows her to construct an essentially gender-egalitarian Islam and detach it from patriarchal and culturally as well as historically bound interpretations as expressed in Islamic Law; the potential for and necessity of active involvement of American Muslims in the reform of Islamic Law; and an obligation to translate her interpretations into transnational as well as local activism.

Here an example of al-Hibri's reasoning is helpful. Al-Hibri's articles tend to be general: "Islamic Law and Muslim Women in America,"[40] "Redefining Muslim Women's Roles in the Next Century,"[41] and "An Introduction to Muslim Women's Rights."[42] In many of these texts she focuses on Muslim women's rights in marriage and divorce laws and the potential avenues for the improvement of women's status from within such laws. One specific topic that is addressed in several texts is the financial rights of Muslim women, especially within marriage. Al-Hibri asserts that women retain their financial independence after marriage, including control of property owned before marriage and the dower to be paid at the time of the wedding.[43] She describes the dower (*mahr*) as similar to an engagement ring—a material expression of the groom's commitment to the marriage—and argues that the dower is not a brideprice but part of a civil contract that ensures the protection of women both financially and otherwise by deterring husbands from easily declaring a divorce. "In short," she writes, "it is a vehicle for ensuring the continued well-being of women entering matrimonial life in a world of patriarchal injustices and inequalities."[44] Al-Hibri does not perceive the stipulation of the financial responsibility of the husband for the maintenance of the family as unequal and describes this obligation as expressed in Qur'anic terms[45] as "providing women with added security in a difficult patriarchal world."[46]

Kecia Ali has criticized al-Hibri for "sanitizing" the institution of Islamic marriage by emphasizing women's "rights" to sexual enjoyment at the expense of overlooking the connection between dower and sexual access as described in her own work. She has called for a more critical and detailed reading of the legal tradition while acknowledging that reform from within the system may still be possible.[47]

Al-Hibri on the other hand has always insisted on a direct connection between her ideas and their translation into activism on the ground. As her founding of and work within Karamah (Muslim Women Lawyers for Human Rights) demonstrates, she has chosen to approach and mine the Islamic legal and interpretive tradition selectively in order to support her activist goals. She assumes that Muslim women's rights are human rights, which is implied in her adoption of women's rights language even where it is not expressed in direct support for the declaration of human rights. In addition to changes in existing laws in Muslim-majority countries and in legal practice, al-Hibri has advocated education of Muslim women, arguing that Muslim women can achieve their rightful place in Muslim societies only if they are informed and educated about their rights.[48]

She has also hailed the United States as a place where Muslims can carry out important reform work under democratic conditions and "unburdened by patriarchal assumptions," rereading the Qur'an "with fresh, liberated eyes." However, Hidayatullah notes al-Hibri's emerging and more recent critique of U.S. foreign policy in regard to the Muslim world, in contrast to her previous celebration of it as espousing democratic principles and offering freedom of expression.[49]

In 1993 Azizah al-Hibri founded Karamah. Its mission statement reflects al-Hibri's intellectual and activist commitments:

> KARAMAH believes in the empowerment of Muslim women within their own spiritual and cultural contexts. In its judgment, only this approach will enable women to address and successfully eradicate the social ills in their communities. For this reason, KARAMAH is to develop a comprehensive, just, and thoughtful Islamic jurisprudence, which takes into account the current concerns of Muslim women worldwide. To this end, KARAMAH has rooted its work in the best of the classical Islamic jurisprudential tradition.[50]

Al-Hibri is still directly involved in many of the activities of the organization, both domestically and internationally, and serves as its chairperson. Karamah's work is focused on women's leadership and jurisprudence training and on specialized programs, among them prevention of domestic violence in Muslim communities, especially in North America and Europe.[51]

Riffat Hassan

In numerous articles over the past decades, Riffat Hassan has produced a discourse on Muslim women's rights with a focus on two areas: the status of women in God's creation and patriarchal distortions of God's justice on the one hand and the discussion of women's (and men's) human rights as derived from the Qur'an, including women's practical rights to sexual fulfillment and family planning, on the other. The former has been discussed earlier; thus the focus here is on Hassan's discourse on women's rights. In contrast to Ali and al-Hibri, Hassan engages directly with the Qur'an to produce a justice and rights discourse that only rarely connects with the Islamic legal tradition. Hassan also largely rejects the Islamic textual tradition and its interpretation based on ahadith because such interpretation was carried out almost exclusively by men.[52]

Hassan has directly acknowledged her support for the Universal Declaration of Human Rights[53] while also pointing out the cognitive dissonance produced by an activist commitment to Muslim women's rights as human rights because it often causes alienation from Muslim communities and societies and because it is a product of the secular West. Hassan is careful to place God's law and intent far above such human legal concepts, however steeped her writings are in the language of human rights.[54] Rather she asserts:

> On the basis of my research and reflection, as well as my deepest faith, I believe that the Qur'an is the Magna Carta of human rights and that a large part of its concern is to free human beings from the bondage of traditionalism, authoritarianism, tribalism, racism, sexism, slavery or anything else that prohibits or inhibits human beings from actualizing the Qur'anic vision of human destiny embodied in the classic proclamation: Towards Allah is thy limit.[55]

Her extensive list of rights includes the rights to life, respect, justice, freedom, privacy; the right to protection from slander, backbiting, and ridicule; the right to acquire knowledge; the right to leave one's homeland under oppressive conditions; the right to develop one's aesthetic sensibilities and enjoy the bounties created by God; and the rights to sustenance, work, and "the good life."[56]

Like al-Hibri, she addresses the discrepancy between Islamic foundations and Muslim practice, or religion and culture, as the core problem of Muslim women's lack of rights in Muslim societies and communities. Also like al-Hibri, her writings in English are addressed to American and international audiences, thus frequently repeating the same arguments for different audiences and framing all discussions by distancing herself from the "Western" demonization of Islam and positioning herself as an informant and link to Muslim women and communities.[57]

Hassan's activist work has focused on family planning and violence against women. She participated in the 1994 United Nations Conference on Population and Development in Cairo and the 1995 United Nations Fourth World Conference on Women in Beijing. Her views on family planning are based on her assertion that women have the right to control their bodies and their sexuality, including contraception and abortion. While the Qur'an does not address family planning directly and male jurists have assumed control over women's bodies by regulating their sexuality and family planning, the Qur'an does contain a set of principles of justice and rights that in turn should be the basis of family planning and development work in the Muslim world. In 1995 Hassan prepared a document to this effect for the Family Planning Association of Pakistan.[58] In 1999 she founded the International Network for the Rights of Female Victims of Violence in Pakistan whose primary purpose was the political and activist struggle against "honor killings" in that country.[59] More recently, Hassan has written and published several more articles but she seems to have withdrawn to some extent from public debates and community settings.

Her work has to be assessed in its historical context. The women scholar activists of her generation, among them Azizah al-Hibri, were trailblazers for more recent intellectual and activist developments. It was due to the persistence of Hassan, al-Hibri, and others that discussions of women's rights became part of mainstream Muslim conversations, even among those who disagreed with their conclusions. Hassan's and al-Hibri's, as well as Amina Wadud's, participation in the development of religious women's discourses on women's rights and in feminist discussions and debates also opened the door for the conversations with—instead of about—Muslim women that have been taking place since the 1990s in American and international feminist circles.

A direct engagement with international (and secular) conceptions of human rights is also evident in the work of other scholars, including Amina Wadud and Zoharah Simmons.[60] The connection of women's rights to human rights and perhaps equally important to an American framework of civil rights and civil rights struggles is evident in several contributions to the debate about woman-led prayer. Wadud has frequently made connections between her history and identity as an African American and as a woman, thus connecting racial and gendered discrimination.[61] Nomani has used civil rights rhetoric, for example, in advocating women's access to mosques by likening women's moves from the back of the mosque to the front of the mosque to the civil rights era demand for African Americans' access to the front of the bus.[62] Silvers, in her 2005 contribution to the woman-led prayer debate, called for women to lead prayers as acts of civil disobedience.[63] While Wadud organically connects civil rights struggles (the era of her coming of age) with her struggles for gender justice, the use of civil rights rhetoric in the writings of Asra Nomani can also be read as a commodification of the experiences of and struggles against discrimination of African Americans. The appeal to the power of such references primarily rests in the expected reactions of the American public rather than in successfully arguing for greater rights for Muslim women within Muslim communities. American Muslim women's engagement with the Islamic tradition on the one hand and the contemporary situations of Muslim women on the other are braided together in many strands of Muslim women's activism.

Intellectuals and activists alike have reflected on the importance and construction of historical models for contemporary Muslim women.

Constructing Historical Role Models: "Hagar on My Mind"

The "recovery" of women's religious historiography and of their erased voices has played an important role in the development of (monotheistic) feminist religious theologies. In addition to rereading sacred texts and rethinking their possible interpretations on the one hand and discussing possibilities for gaining religious authority on the other, religious women have searched for historical models to emulate through an understanding of their paradigmatic roles within God's creation. Judith Plaskow writes, "On the one side, while the activities of women leaders tell us little about the lives of ordinary women during the same historical periods, accounts of exceptional women indicate the accessibility to women of charismatic leadership roles." Equally important, "the stories of exceptional women also allow us to glimpse the process of textual editing through which the roles of women are downplayed and obscured.[64]

Many Muslim women scholars have for several decades engaged in scholarship that attempts to recover the stories and histories of earlier Muslim women, from the companions and wives of the Prophet Muhammad to female hadith transmitters, scholars, Sufis, and rulers.[65] Of particular importance have been the women surrounding the Prophet Muhammad, including his wives Khadija, 'Aisha, and Umm Salama and other women such as Umm Waraqa.

Leila Ahmed, implicitly critiquing nostalgic or romanticizing attempts at such recovery, has argued that if one wanted to take one wife of Muhammad as a role model for Muslim women it should not be Khadija, Muhammad's first wife and the first Muslim woman, but rather 'Aisha, one of his later wives whom he married after Khadija's death. Ahmed argues that most of Khadija's lifetime predated the advent of Islam, thus her independent wealth, her widowhood and remarriage, and her general autonomy were typical for the *jahiliyyah* (ignorance; applied to pre-Islamic history) period but not for Islam. 'Aisha on the other hand became Muhammad's wife after the migration from Mecca to Medina in 622, where Muhammad established a Muslim community/state based on Qur'anic revelations and with early forms of legal interpretation. Thus 'Aisha's life as one of several wives, within the compound of the Prophet's household and adhering to the high standards of a "mother of the believers," enjoyed far less autonomy and control.[66]

One other historical woman who interestingly is not Muslim but part of Islamic sacred history is Hagar.[67] She is discussed in the works of Wadud, al-Hibri,[68] and Hassan and is central to the story told by Nomani in *Standing Alone in Mecca*. Nomani also referenced Hajar in an interview before the 2005 prayer:

> I tell them think of the story of Bibi Hajar who was a mother of Islam, who stood alone in Mecca, who is the source of our strength. It is from her courage that we have the tribe from which the Prophet Muhammad was born. It is because of the strength of a woman that Islam exists today. If she had been devastated and destroyed we would never have existed.

Al-Hibri opens her autobiographical essay with her ancestral connection to Hagar, the Egyptian princess alone in the desert, running to find water for her starving child. Hagar's persistence and her faith in the face of obstacles become the guiding principle for al-Hibri's transformation from secular (and socialist) Lebanese daughter to American Muslim woman lawyer for human rights. She writes, "Hagar is very important to me. She is the mother of my whole family, the mother of my mostly unknown mothers." It was "Hagar's faithful determination" that "drove this immigrant female to study religion, logic, law, and feminist theory, to fight for other women around the world."[69]

Hassan contributed the Muslim perspective to a collection of essays on Sarah and Hagar.[70] She outlines the stories of Hagar, Sarah, Abraham, and Ishmael and their basis in the Islamic textual sources. In deeply engaged and programmatic words, she writes in the conclusion:

> The story of Hagar is important not only for the Muslim daughters of Hagar but for all women who are oppressed by systems of thought or structures based on ideas of gender, class, or racial inequality. Like her, women must have the faith and courage to venture out of the security of the known into the insecurity of the unknown and to carve out, with their own hands, a new world from which the injustices and inequities that separate men from women, class from class, and race from race, have been eliminated.[71]

Hibba Abugideiri develops her discussion of contemporary American Muslim women's examples of leadership around the model of Hagar, not to argue that Hagar as a model is all that important for contemporary women, but rather in an attempt to revive her potential as an example of "female agency." Abugideiri notes the near-absence of Hagar in exegetical commentaries of the classical period and sets out to reconstruct her as a historical example of a "female reformer" with much to offer contemporary Muslim women in terms of her taqwa, or God-consciousness, and her strength in carrying out God's command under difficult circumstances and as one of God's chosen "messengers." Abugideiri writes:

> Her maternal strength, her courage, constancy, and self-initiative as messenger—all derived from her taqwa—provided her with the necessary qualities not only to fulfill her sacred mission, but also to become an aspect of the mission itself. In her suffering for God's cause, Hagar had to endure the distress and danger that have typically marked the careers of God's chosen historical agents. Like God's prophets, moreover, Hagar persevered, and thus her name and memory came to be part of Islam's sacred history and ritual.[72]

Mohja Kahf has written more than one poem on Hagar. One is titled "The Water of Hajar" and reflects on the earth as the source of water. Another poem, "Hagar Writes a Cathartic Letter to Sarah as an Exercise Suggested by Her Therapist," satirically explores the relationship between Hagar and Sarah in contemporary terms.[73] Another one of Kahf's poems describes Hagar and her actions from the perspective of Abraham. Hagar appears more strong-willed than Abraham, surrendering to the will of God and determined to persist in her new and dangerous environment.[74] Wadud cites this poem as the introduction to her own reflections on Hagar in relation to motherhood and family. Deeply critical of the academic trend to reread the stories of Sarah and Hagar from primarily Judeo-Christian sources and perspectives, Wadud takes Hagar's status as a slave as the entry point for her reflections on slavery, childbirth, responsibility, and the confines of traditional models for Muslim women as mothers and child-bearers. Braiding together women's histories (and her own) as heirs of African slaves, generations of Muslim women, and an Islamic legal tradition that has no place for single mothers and those excluded from the idealized family model, Wadud concludes that the patriarchal structure of the family needs to be questioned and transformed in order to allow for the inclusion and leadership of women on all levels, social, political, cultural, and economic, and for their basis in an egalitarian family model. She concludes, "The Hajar paradigm is the reality of Muslim women heads of household whose legal category in *shari'ah* deviates from the patriarchal, man centered norm. Yet it is through the law they expect their honor and dignity to be upheld."[75]

Wadud calls for a rethinking of Islamic family law to create legal structures that can accommodate changed societal conditions and the need for egalitarian structures within Muslim families and hopes that such legal changes would in turn affect Muslim attitudes toward egalitarian family models (or vice versa).[76] For Wadud, then, Hagar is not so much a role model as a reflection of the shortcomings of patriarchal Muslim constructions of family and motherhood. In stark contrast to the celebration of Hagar as a model of engaged surrender (Wadud's term) and strength in the writings of Hassan, al-Hibri, and Kahf, for Wadud Hagar embodies the struggles and predicaments of poor, single (and often black) mothers and their attempts at survival for themselves and their children.

Wadud's activist commitment can be traced at least to her first teaching position in Malaysia in the early 1990s. She started her involvement with a Malaysian women's organization, Sisters in Islam, while she taught at the International Islamic University in Kuala Lumpur. She credits the group with teaching her the connection between the theory and the practice of justice.[77] Wadud's ideas and her rereading of the Qur'an in turn were important for the organization's formulations of specific reform goals. She describes the organization's accomplishments as affirming an egalitarian and women-friendly rereading of the Qur'an, which in turn empowered Malaysian women to question patriarchal and oppressive systems of law and interpretation.[78] In 2007 Sisters in Islam initiated a global Muslim women's movement called Musawah (Equality), specifically aimed at the formulation and implementation of an egalitarian Muslim family law. The movement's principles are formulated as follows:

> The universal and Islamic values of equality, non-discrimination, justice and dignity as the basis of all human relations; full and equal citizenship, including full participation in all aspects of society, as the right of every individual; and marriage and family relations based on equality and justice, with men and women sharing equal rights and responsibilities.[79]

Wadud has contributed to this new organization at least through one position paper, "Islam beyond Patriarchy through Gender Inclusive Qur'anic Analysis."[80] The organization seems to reflect exactly the reforms to Islamic law and its application that Wadud had formulated in her reflections on the Hagar paradigm.

Hagar is also central to the story of Asra Nomani, herself a single mother. Nomani's Hagar has courage and strength as well and is Nomani's role model.

> She had the courage to raise her son by herself and to experience the wonderful love between a mother and a child. Her life story had special meaning to me, abandoned by my baby's father. She gave me courage in my own decision to raise my son alone. She didn't even have water. I had Wal-Mart. Her story is timeless and universal and gives strength to all women and men who make lonely choices in life and face alienation for those choices.[81]

Nomani deeply resents Hagar's erasure from Muslim history. While telling Hagar's story, Nomani traces her steps during her pilgrimage to Mecca and declares Hagar's story the most significant one in the Qur'an for women.[82] Her later decision to call her group Daughters of Hajar is explained as part of her pilgrimage experience and transformation.

> That moment meant so much to me. I was in Mecca, a criminal in this land for having given birth without a wedding ring on my finger. And I was nursing my son at the holy mosque of Mecca, overlooking the sacred Ka'bah. This was nature's law expressing itself, more powerfully than man's law. I drank the sacred water called zamzam. From me, it flowed into Shibli. I recognized then the great lineage I had in Islam. I was a daughter of Hajar. I looked up to the sky with one thought: blessed are the daughters of Hajar.[83]

Nomani has published two documents, a "Bill of Rights for Women in the Mosque" and a "Bill of Rights for Women in the Bedroom."[84] Both are modeled and named after the amendments to the U.S. Constitution and draw directly on Nomani's conception of women's rights as natural rights of modern (American) citizens and human beings, thus implicitly absorbing human rights discourses and conceptions.

Critique and Praise

It is easy to dismiss the search for historical models as nostalgia and naïveté, even when carried out in sophisticated ways and with tremendous insight into and knowledge of historical sources and documents. But the same could be said for feminist thought in general or for the endeavors of African American scholars and communities to recover African roots and diasporic histories and cultures. The past as a source of lessons for the present is not peculiar to Muslims or Muslim women. The questioning of male-centered historiographies has not only unearthed alternative readings of the past and enabled a reconstruction of collective memory; it may also have provided the motivation and energy for changes in the present. Similarly, the rethinking of Islamic Law, the mining of the legal tradition for a coherent yet gender-inclusive methodology to support new legal models of family, marriage, and sexual conduct, and the negotiation of Muslim women's rights as part of human rights have all fueled the undertaking of a plethora of activist projects, both in North America and in the transnational activist engagement of American Muslim women.

Whether one perceives Islamic Law as a coherent legal system or as a set of ethical guidelines, and whether its application to Muslims' lives has been transformed by modernity, nation building, and globalization, Islamic legal and ethical constructs of Muslim womanhood, marriage, sexuality, and rights influence the lives of Muslim women and men in multifaceted ways. Like reinterpretation of the Qur'an, so too any rethinking of Islamic Law has to start with a careful evaluation of the sources and methodologies available. The complicated status of Islamic Law in the modern world and the pervasiveness of liberal and secular human rights discourses have forced Muslims into debates and conversations about God's intent and law as expressed through ethics and practice. American Muslim women, through the debate about woman-led prayers, through their quest for historical models, and through their multifaceted participation in transnational women's rights activism have taken up the challenges of Muslim women's rights and status. Their work in these fields is directly linked to reinterpretation and re-reading of the Qur'an on the one hand and questions of religious authority, constructions of the Islamic knowledge tradition, and multilayered community building on the other.

5

Authority, Tradition, and Community

> Every adult Muslim, man or woman, is obligated to understand and
> implement the *Shari'ah*. Accountability is personal and individual,
> and no single person or institution may or can represent the Divine
> Will. . . . God wishes human beings to search and seek for the Divine
> Will. Truth adheres to the search—the search itself is the ultimate
> truth. Consequently, correctness is measured according to the
> sincerity of the individual's search.
>
> Khaled Abou El Fadl, *Speaking in God's Name*

Here shari'ah is understood as Islamic Law applied by and to Muslim individuals and societies, which is more correctly the science of fiqh. It is a path
to God, with emphasis on its individual dimension. However, as an Islamic
legal scholar Abou El Fadl has focused on the collective interpretations and
negotiations of shari'ah in Muslim societies and communities through the
complex methodologies and schools of fiqh. His aptly titled book, *Speaking in God's Name: Islamic Law, Authority, and Women*, points to the significance of those who have historically assumed the role of interpreters of
the Divine Will, the *'ulama*.[1] If Muslim religious scholars, specifically those
dealing with Islamic Law, were indeed speaking in God's name, they carried
significant religious authority.

The question of who has the authority to interpret and judge actions
according to Islamic Law is the underlying theme not only of the debates
about woman-led prayers but also of larger questions of gender and interpretation. Thus this chapter focuses directly on the issue of authority as reflected in the woman-led prayer and gender debates among American Muslims. Muslim women scholars and activists have stepped into positions of

authority opened up by the "democratization of authority," which in turn was triggered by the multifaceted encounters of Muslims with modernity. Furthermore, the authority to interpret is directly linked to conceptualizations of textual authority, more specifically, of the Qur'an and the sunnah. The nature and significance of these sources is connected to the definition of the boundaries of Islamic knowledge and the Islamic tradition as understood by a wide range of Muslim scholars. For new and gender-conscious interpretations to be relevant, women scholars and activists have to translate their exegetical projects into efforts at interpretive community building, a process that has taken place with differing success, including through the woman-led prayer itself.

Muslims, Authority, and Modernity

The question of authority is at the center of many intellectual debates about the role of religions in modern societies and the impact of modernity and its product, secularism, on religious interpretation and practice. No attempt can be made to survey the existing literature on the topic of modernity, Muslims, and authority, although several relevant discourses should be considered in their inherently contradictory perspective on the historical and contemporary aspects of the question of authority.

In the absence of ordained clergy in Islam, religious authority came to be defined in a variety of ways. The emergence of a class of scholars, trained in one or more of the traditional Islamic sciences—tafsir, fiqh, or hadith—in the ninth century marked a gradual departure from the previous model of authority and interpretation (based on the Divine inspiration of the Prophet Muhammad and his companions' proximity to him) in that these scholars, the 'ulama, developed discipline-specific methods for approaching texts, deriving interpretations, and building interpretive communities. Islamic (legal) knowledge was transmitted from teacher to student, and formal institutions of Islamic learning when they developed did not have standardized curricula. Thus conceptions of Islamic knowledge stayed open to a variety of interpretations in the premodern period. The authority to interpret was derived from a chain of knowledge transmission, ideally going back to the Prophet Muhammad, and from the number of followers and students a particular scholar or teacher could assemble. The traditional roles of the 'ulama, depending on their geographic and historical context, ranged from open opposition to local rulers to equally open support of the ruling elite through legal interpretations.[2]

Suha Taji-Farouki and others have linked the "breaking of the monopoly" of the ʿulama to the introduction of print culture to Muslim societies, which in turn democratized access to traditional texts, including the Qurʾan itself, but also increasingly the texts that the ʿulama had produced and transmitted over the centuries. This democratization of textual access went hand in hand with mass education, which weakened the exclusive knowledge base of the ʿulama. Taji-Farouki writes somewhat pessimistically:

> Increasingly today, those without formal training in the Islamic disciplines claim direct interpretive rights over the Islamic texts as equals with the ulama, and in direct competition with them. Any possibility of uniformity or continuity of interpretation, or of a controlled diversity of readings, has been lost.[3]

In her view, the impact of modernity needs to be described as a break from the classical tradition and its integrity.

Similarly, in *The Great Theft*, Abou El Fadl claims that contemporary "Muslims have suffered a crisis of authority that has deteriorated to the point of full-fledged chaos."[4] Abou El Fadl traces the roots of this crisis of authority to the impact of colonialism on Muslim societies from the eighteenth century onward and proclaims that the crisis went into full effect in the twentieth century. His definition of the ʿulama is limited to *fuqaha* (jurists or legal scholars), and he describes the premodern application of Islamic Law as based on a diversity of opinion but not a limitless chaos of opinions with no authority attached. In Abou El Fadl's view, the crisis of authority is at least in part a crisis of the traditional institutions of Islamic learning that were destroyed or greatly limited by the Western colonial powers. In connection with the destruction of the Islamic legal system and its postcolonial replacement with European models of nation-state laws, this destruction of institutions of learning led to the decline, first in importance and then in the existence, of the ʿulama.[5] In his view, these developments led directly to the rise of what he calls "puritan" or Wahhabi Islam. More generally, he remarks:

> The vacuum in authority meant not so much that *no one* could authoritatively speak for Islam, but that virtually *every* Muslim with a

modest knowledge of the Qur'an and the traditions of the Prophet was suddenly considered qualified to speak for the Islamic tradition and Shari'a law—even Muslims unfamiliar with the precedents and accomplishments of past generations.[6]

Abou El Fadl has also written extensively on the emergence of authoritarianism from the same "crisis of authority." He warns that the simplification of the complex and vast Islamic legal tradition feeds into authoritarian positions that do not allow for dissent.

Some contemporary Muslims take great pride in the idea of Islam being "the simple religion." This often manifests itself in a rabid anti-intellectualism reminiscent of certain forms of evangelical Christianity. Simplicity is seen as the key for unity and, therefore, there is a strong demand to limit the range of disagreements and promote intellectual homogeneity.[7]

In contrast to the views of Abou Fadl, Muhammad Qasim Zaman, in his *The Ulama in Contemporary Islam*, argues that the 'ulama have weathered the challenges of the colonial and postcolonial period better than is often appreciated and that they have in fact proven rather adaptable in their strategies. Zaman also makes the claim that while the 'ulama compete with "new religious intellectuals," both use various media, from print to the Internet, to market their positions and opinions. These developments have certainly created a shift in or democratization of Islamic knowledge and interpretations but have in his view not led to a vacuum of authority.[8]

If we agree with Abou El Fadl's view of a declining role of the 'ulama and a vacuum in interpretive authority, it is possible to argue that this vacuum created new spaces to claim authority for those previously not represented in circles of authority, especially women. Even Zaman's perspective could be appropriated here to argue that the new religious intellectuals the traditional 'ulama are now competing with may include women intellectuals. In reality, those identified as new religious intellectuals have been predominantly male. It is in the North American context that some women have risen to the ranks of prominent Muslim intellectuals. This development can in part be explained through different economic, social, and political opportunities for women, even though gender equality is an ideal more than a reality. It may also be explained by an Orientalist obsession with supporting purportedly oppressed Muslim women in their quest for "liberation," though this liberation may more often take the form of expecting women to shed their religious convictions altogether.[9]

As members of Muslim-minority communities, Muslim women scholars are embedded in a societal and religious context that has privileged secular laws and the privatization of religious practice, which in turn make the application of Islamic Law to one's life and practice almost entirely voluntary. Olivier Roy has described this development as "religious consumerism" that is evident in religions other than Islam but linked to the crisis of authority, the minimalization of religious knowledge, and the rise of charismatic authority as a replacement for traditional authority structures.[10]

Remarkable in the discussions of the crisis of or challenge to traditional religious authority is the tendency of authors to interpret the trends in one of two directions: as the destruction of something historically important and thus pessimistic, like Abou El Fadl and Taji-Farouki, or as an opportunity for new interpretations and interpreters. While those scholars who take up the challenge to offer new (gender-conscious) interpretations certainly do not lament the democratization of religious authority, they still have to grapple with the question itself. Ironically, they are competing with the other end of the new interpreter spectrum: Salafi or "puritan" exegetes and preachers. They may have diametrically opposed goals in their exegetical enterprises, but they often have the same approach to the definition of textual authority.

Authority and Text

In *Speaking in God's Name*, Abou El Fadl walks readers through the complex process of explaining the nature of authority in Islam, its relation to sacred texts, and the possibilities for working with and assessing the Islamic tradition of jurisprudence for its contemporary relevance. At the outset Abou El Fadl presents the traditionally accepted approach to God's revelation of His will through the Qur'an and through the actions and utterances of the Prophet Muhammad (sunnah).

> God is the ultimate authority in the sense that if God wants one thing and not another, any person who wants the contrary does so in defiance of God. . . . This is assumed as a matter of faith or conviction, and therefore is the starting point for the analysis. Having made this faith

based assumption, we still need to deal with understanding what God wants as well as the means for understanding what God wants. For a Muslim, the most obvious ways of knowing what God wants are the Qur'an and Sunnah.[11]

He also shares his own faith-based assumption that "the Qur'an is the immutable and uncorrupted Word of God. This is tantamount to assuming that God is the author of the Qur'an and that the competence of the Qur'an is not subject to reproach. As far as the Qur'an is concerned, the only pertinent issue is to determine its meaning."[12]

Abou El Fadl then presents his more complicated perspective on the sunnah. Drawing on the historical compilation of the texts that comprise the sunnah, Abou El Fadl argues that contrary to the Qur'an, the sunnah does not stand above human influence. In positing that almost every text is part of a triangle consisting of text, author, and reader mutually influenced and influenceable, Abou El Fadl excludes the Qur'an from being influenced by the community or communities that interpret the text. In other words, the communities of Muslims who follow the Qur'an in their attempts to understand the Divine Will had and have no impact on the text and through that on God Himself. However, the sunnah can meaningfully be perceived, according to Abou El Fadl, as produced, through selection, evaluation, and interpretation, by the interpretive community surrounding it.[13]

> The interpretive community is bound to take account of the authorial enterprise with all its historical permutations in order to understand the appropriate balance between the historical author (the Prophet) and the various authorial voices that provided the context for the historical author.[14]

Abou El Fadl's approach to the Qur'an and the sunnah is important for his later considerations of the Islamic legal tradition and his exploration of traditional, modern, and new authoritarian discourses on women, gender issues, and Islamic Law. It is also significant because it reflects one of the prominent approaches of Muslim women scholars to the textual authority of the Qur'an and the sunnah.

None of the women authors discussed here has doubted the nature of the Qur'an as revelation or the Word of God, for doing so could lead a Muslim outside the boundaries of Muslim communities. This is not to say that women scholars (and modern scholars generally) have not debated the nature of the Qur'anic text or have at least made general assumptions about its nature before proceeding to offer their own exegeses. Notable again here is Abou El Fadl's idea of the "conscientious pause" or Amina Wadud's pronouncement that one might sometimes have to say no to certain passages in the Qur'an without rejecting the text in its entirety or the primacy of its author.[15]

The varying approaches of Muslim women scholars to the sunnah and its most important component, the hadith tradition, can meaningfully be understood only as part of the longer history of modern interpretation. Hidayatullah has traced the existence of two (in her view) distinct camps in determining the status of the sunnah as authoritative text to early modernist thinkers. She asserts that Muhammad ʿAbduh (d. 1905) and Sayyid Ahmad Khan (d. 1898) shared with the later thinker Fazlur Rahman (d. 1988) a "noted skepticism toward the Hadith," if not its outright rejection based on issues of verification and possible fabrication.[16] Modernist approaches to Qur'anic exegesis, including historical contingency, ethical rather than legal guidance, and thematic approaches, have been discussed above, so my concern here is to connect such hermeneutical methods to the thinkers' assessment of the authority of the texts in question. Hidayatullah goes on to describe the "revivalist" camp as the other end of the spectrum and a reaction to modernist ideas and asserts that "revivalists tend to 'emphasize the absolute character' of the Qur'an and Sunnah as the ultimate sources of Islamic authority."[17] Revivalists include figures such as Abu-l ʿAla al-Maududi (d. 1979) and Sayyid Qutb (d. 1966).

Among American Muslim women scholars, two tendencies rather than camps should be noted, with the caveat that within both tendencies significant variation and disagreements are possible. The two tendencies follow roughly the division into those who have focused their efforts on tafsir and thus on the Qur'anic text and those who are interested in rethinking the Islamic legal tradition in both its methods and its rulings for contemporary circumstances.

Among those whose primary focus is the Qur'an are Wadud, Barlas, and Barazangi.[18] Wadud writes in the preface to *Qur'an and Woman*, "While I accept the role of the prophet both with regards to revelation, as understood in Islam, and to the development of Islamic law on the basis of his *sunnah* or normative practice, I place greater significance on the Qur'an. This is congruent with the orthodox understanding of the inerrancy of Qur'anic preservation versus historical contradictions within the hadith literature."[19] In

Inside the Gender Jihad, Wadud occasionally cites ahadith to support her argument, apparently having reconsidered her earlier suspicion of the validity of ahadith.[20]

Barlas, in her project of "unreading patriarchal interpretations of the Qur'an," claims that "inequality and discrimination derive not from the teachings of the Qur'an but from the secondary religious texts, the Tafsir (Qur'anic exegesis) and the Ahadith (s. hadith) (narratives purportedly detailing the life and praxis of the Prophet Muhammad)."[21]

Barazangi rarely quotes hadith sources to support her argument and explains her exclusive focus on the Qur'an and its "proper" reading by women by declaring, "I mainly focus on the Qur'an because it is the divine text of Islam and because the results of my scholarly activist work suggest that the central issue for Muslim women is their lack of participation in the interpretation of the Qur'an."[22] Her use of ahadith traditions tends to treat them as history, that is, as reflections of what Muhammad did and said, which she in turn can be critical of. An example is her discussion of a hadith on inheritance involving Muhammad's wife 'Aisha, which Barazangi interprets to indicate the Prophet's position on inheriting leadership positions. She criticizes the Prophet Muhammad for not announcing said rule to the community more explicitly but only in response to a problem.[23] Hassan has approached the hadith tradition with skepticism as to its compilation and interpretation while acknowledging its emotive and historical significance for Muslims. She cautions that contrary to the Qur'an, hadith collections are surrounded by controversy and that both sources have been interpreted by men to the exclusion of women's interests and perspectives. However, echoing Rahman, she also contends that rejecting the hadith literature entirely would remove the basis for the historical situating process of the Qur'an.[24]

Wadud reminds us that "the text is silent" and "needs interpretation, and has always historically and currently been subjected to interpretation." She also contextualizes her own encounter with the Qur'an as historically contingent and relative in its truth claim and attempts a broad understanding of the nature of the text:

The Qur'an is, as it were, a window to look through. A doorway with a threshold one must pass over toward the infinite possibilities that point humanity toward a continuum of spiritual and social development. . . . I am not afraid of my efforts to understand the text, to act upon my understanding, and to share each stage of development in that understanding as part of the human love, belief, and surrender to the Author of the text, however I might encounter Allah from one moment to the next. The substance of the Qur'an cannot be constrained by its particular utterances, let alone by the narrowness of its readers.[25]

In what might constitute the end of the spectrum outside scholarly circles, Saleemah Abdul-Ghafur writes about the Qur'an and its interpretation:

Through reading and prayer, I began to realize that by following others' interpretations of Islam, I had constructed my own prison and relinquished the rights God granted to me. I now have a profound understanding of taqwa (God-consciousness). I understand that taqwa has always been within me. What that means practically is that now, after years of surrendering my own will and voice to follow another's, if something doesn't resonate with me, I don't do it. I don't need to find proof in sacred text, because I already know it.[26]

The second tendency in approaching the question of textual authority is represented by those women scholars who have chosen to engage the historical interpretive tradition rather than return to the Qur'an as the ultimate source of authority. Because this interpretive tradition draws on sources beyond the Qur'an, in particular, the hadith and sunnah, and eventually on its own production of exegetical and legal sources, its approach to textual authority has to be more inclusive, albeit critical. For the same reason, these scholars tend not to directly discuss the validity and significance of the sunnah, except where such discussion pertains to the utility and reliability of hadith for existing interpretations and legal rulings, or conversely for challenging such interpretations and offering alternatives.

Islam and Tradition

Several scholars have addressed the emergence of a concept of "Islam" that is all but alien to the historical tradition of Muslim interpretation of texts and the derivation of legal guidelines and rules. Eickelman and Piscatori speak of the "objectification of Islam,"[27] that is, the process by which "Islam" becomes a definable and defined entity rather than a continually changing product of Muslims' engagement with sources, ethics, and circumstances. Olivier Roy remarks on discussions about what Islam is: "This is a novel development: I know of no classical works of theology with such formulations, and to my knowledge the word Islam does not appear in the titles of key religious works. Islam has become an object that must be apprehended as such."[28] More important, this new focus on "Islam" replaces earlier references to God and the Prophet Muhammad as sources of authority. Kevin Reinhardt has argued that this shift limits the possibility of ethical discourses because it assumes a self-referential search for solutions to ethical questions from within the construct, by way of excluding or even considering other perspectives. But, according to Reinhardt, it also allows a shift from rules to principles, or, to speak with Fazlur Rahman, from a legal to an ethical framework for Muslim behavior and practice.[29]

This shift to the recognition of Islam as "a thing" that can be studied, discussed, and applied is evident in the work of many contemporary Muslim scholars and not limited to those identified as involved in authoritarian discourses. It is very common to find scholars, both Muslim and non-Muslim, use formulations such as "Islam says," implying a claim to normativity and homogeneity that can be become a powerful tool for discursive debates.

Barazangi constructs Islam through her curriculum for Muslim women's Islamic higher learning, which includes an introduction to Islamic principles. In her view, Islam is an integrated system of beliefs and practices to be taught to Muslim women so that they may realize their full human potential, which in turn presupposes that there is a system of "Islamic knowledge" or principles that can be defined and taught. However, through her simultaneous critique of the idealization of early Muslim women as role models and the total exclusion of women from the process of interpretation, she questions the very framework of her curriculum. Her writings do not solve this issue but exhibit the inherent tension between an assumed normative framework and gender-critical reflections on its limitations.[30]

Wadud has struggled with her own conceptualization of Islam. In 1999 she wrote that she once thought Islam and Muslims were one and the same.[31] In *Inside the Gender Jihad* she devotes an entire chapter to the question of "what Islam means" and concludes that "to define Islam is to have power over it." She recognizes the power of this definition when she writes:

Despite numerous definitions, historical and current, whether explained or not, knowingly or unknowingly, each user assumes some authority to justify him or her to determine when others would be

considered adherents to their understanding, practice and limitations of "Islam," the discussions with diverse presumptions, the socio-
cultural climate, and the positions of authority, others could be accused of heresy, deviance, or even blasphemy or kufr, disbelief or
infidelity to Islam.[32]

Wadud does not recognize the defining of Islam and thus the boundaries of
tradition and community as a modern phenomenon but rather perceives it
as a perennial problem.

The power to include or exclude on the basis of agreement or disagreement on what "Islam" is, is evident for example in the charge of apostasy
leveled against Wadud by demonstrators outside the 2005 prayer event and
in at least two opinions of scholars.[33] Here the decision to either ignore
what had been defined as the "Islamic" approach to woman-led prayer as
expressed in a set of legal opinions or to counter it with an alternative interpretation primarily based on the Qur'an, as Wadud did, was read as a transgression of the "boundaries of Islam" or "the tradition."

More broadly, the power of the construct of a unified "classical Islamic
tradition" is evident in the entire legal dimension of the debate on women-
led prayers, as seen in the previous chapter. Those who argued against the
prayer event on the basis of its "prohibition" in the legal opinions of the four
Sunni legal schools, while sometimes including dissenting opinions, sub-
scribed to a simplified or flattened conception of the Islamic legal tradition.
Those who supported the woman-led prayer by means of legal arguments,
such as Nevin Reda, Khaled Abou El Fadl, and more recently Ahmed Elewa
and Laury Silvers, while employing the same set of sources, have accounted
differently for the diversity of legal perspectives embedded in it.

The two strands of approaches to the Qur'an and sunnah identified above
are intertwined with the same scholars' approaches to the "classical Islamic
tradition," especially in its juristic dimension. While more nuanced within
the group, the first strand would include those who focus primarily on the
Qur'an, arguing that it is the primary source for Muslim guidance and interpretation, among them Wadud, Barlas, and Barazangi. We have seen the
ambivalent use of hadith sources in their work. However, the same scholars
tend to reject the historical interpretive tradition, comprising tafsir, hadith
science, and fiqh, as male dominated, sometimes misogynist, and in the ex-
treme as of no relevance for contemporary exegetical projects.

The second strand advocates a critical yet inclusive approach to the interpretive tradition, arguing that its methodologies and principles if not its conclusions can be of value for contemporary Muslims. Abou El Fadl advocates a return to the nuanced and complex juristic methods of the past (he speaks of the "classical Muslim jurists") in order to combat modern tendencies toward simplification and authoritarianism. In passing, he also criticizes what he calls Muslim apologists for similarly citing Qurʾanic verses, hadith reports, and juristic opinions when "their treatment of these sources often lacks critical evaluation and is generally used to bolster their conclusions established at the outset."[34]

Kecia Ali has acknowledged her own positionality as a contemporary and progressive Muslim but argues that a deep and honest study of the "Islamic intellectual tradition" is necessary because of the scholars' "methodological sophistication, acceptance of divergent perspectives, and their diligence in pursuit of understanding the divine will." And "they are worth analyzing because their frameworks and assumptions often undergird modern views in ways that are not fully recognized or understood."[35] Later she contends:

> The scholarly tradition is one significant source of knowledge and wisdom; much is lost when Muslims—Qurʾan-only feminists or pro-hadith Salafis—choose to bypass it for a literalist approach to source texts. . . . The precedent of earlier jurists can authorize similar interpretive and adaptive processes for Muslims today, including bypassing (through a variety of interpretive devices) even seemingly clear Qurʾanic statements. A legal methodology offers legitimacy for a flexible approach to the Qurʾan and the Prophet's sunnah as revelation that emerged in a historical context.[36]

Here, too, we find a methodological appreciation for the historical tradition of interpretation, and in drawing on Abou El Fadl, Ali adopts his critique of both feminist apologetics and authoritarian reduction.[37]

Azizah al-Hibri and Riffat Hassan, as discussed in the previous chapter, both employ a selective approach to the intellectual history of Muslim interpretation by treating it as a depository for various opinions and perspectives that they choose from to advance their arguments, both in the cause of theoretical gender equality and in the improvement of Muslim women's status and lives.

Amira Sonbol, whose work is primarily historiographic, has argued that for Muslim women the advent of modernity, the experience of colonialism, and the subsequent development of nation-states, which came with significant legal reforms and transformations, have all contributed to a deterioration of the legal situation and status of women in society. Far from idealizing premodern conditions and gender dynamics, Sonbol attempts to rescue women's historiography from triumphant progress narratives by pointing out, based on extensive archival and historiographic work, that in many instances women had more choices, freedom of negotiation of their rights, and indeed rights when variations of Islamic Law were applied to them outside the control of the state, as was the case in most premodern Muslim societies.[38]

Those who incorporate the Muslim interpretive tradition and its texts in their deliberations on gender issues and Muslim women, more than those who reject that tradition, are forced to deal with the limitations of possible gender-conscious interpretations, whether they are directly drawn from the traditions or constitute new answers to equally new questions. In the context of female genital cutting (FGC), Kecia Ali has argued that it may be necessary to reject certain practices and interpretations even if they were approved by classical jurists or the Prophet Muhammad according to hadith.[39] She prefers such conscious rejection over what she identifies as "well-meaning but deceitful manipulation of the texts," to advance certain interpretations but not distance oneself from the interpretive tradition as a whole or a particular ruling.[40]

However, scholars in both strands face their most formidable challenge when their values and ethical assumptions clash with the Qur'anic text itself. It may be possible to reject all or parts of the Islamic legal and interpretive tradition; however, rejection of the Qur'an would place the scholar(s) in question on the edge of or outside the boundaries of Muslim communities even with the broadest understanding of such. Wadud has formulated her concern thus:

> I reclaim the right for all Muslims to accept their own identity as Muslim while holding a vast diversity of opinions and experiences. While I accept their identification as Muslim, I also expect their acceptance of others who identify as Muslims. . . . The patriarchal norms of seventh-century Arabia left its mark upon the nature of the Qur'anic articulation and continued to do so for centuries with interpretation and implementation. . . . Hopefully, reformists will not only point to more liberative and egalitarian references, they will also elaborate on these references to free the text from the potential snares in some of its

own particular utterances. This fortunately lends support to accepting human agency as a critical resource for establishing and maintaining dynamism between linguistically articulated text, of divine origin, addressed at a fixed time while simultaneously intending to provide eternal guidance.[41]

Ali, like Barlas and others, has honestly acknowledged her own position and investment in alternative interpretations but has also argued for the need to reflect on value commitments rather than take them as normative or the only acceptable ethical standard:

> One must debunk and counter aggressively patriarchal and indeed misogynist interpretations, but also justify the project of egalitarian interpretation. . . . Feminist exegetes must take care not to be as blinded by the commitment to equality, and the presumption that equality is necessary for justice, as classical exegetes were by their assumptions about the naturalness of male superiority and dominance in family and society.[42]

Ayesha Chaudhry has framed the clash between the Qur'anic text and modern values as a problem of "hermeneutics and conscience." In her analysis of contemporary interpretations of Q 4:34 ("the beating verse"), Chaudhry identifies three distinct approaches to the cognitive dissonance produced by the explicit formulation that husbands should/could/might beat their wives in cases of disobedient behavior as a last choice. In contesting the translation of the verb *daraba* and connecting its meaning to different understandings of disobedience, the commentators follow one of the following routes: *traditionalists* absolve "the Qur'an, deemed to be the literal word of God, of all blame for any perceived injustice,"[43] blaming the tension on limitations of human understanding; *idealists* blame the exegetical (rather than the juristic) tradition for patriarchal and/or misogynist biases and thus argue for a new, more egalitarian interpretation of the verse; and *reformists* advocate emphasizing gender justice elsewhere in the Qur'an, which in turn would allow for deemphasizing or even calling for a "conscientious pause." Chaudhry argues that saying no to the Qur'an is much more final than allowing for a pause that is open to different possibilities.[44] This classification is helpful for understanding gender-conscious approaches to the Qur'anic text more generally as well. Chaudhry also ventures that the boundaries are fluid and that particular scholars (she mentions Wadud) have moved from one into another category as they advanced their interpretations and ideas over time. In the end, the different approaches to hermeneutics and exegesis are redefining the absolute authority of the Qur'an as sacred text by qualifying which themes, aspects, and passages carry such absolute authority. This process of exegesis and the inherent interpretive choices are not new per se; however, in the context of gender discourses, more than in any other context, they acquire a new political and communal dynamic, both on the theoretical and practical levels. This specific dynamic of gender-conscious Muslim discourses is reflected not only in discussions of content but also in the overlapping debate over the link between interpretive authority and knowledge/training in "Islamic sciences."

Authority and Knowledge/Training

When the plans for the prayer event were announced in early 2005, varied responses started to be formulated, and the positions outlined above evolved over a period of several months (and in some cases years). The insistence on a legal framework has already been discussed. However, in this context the concern over the correlation between interpretive positions and qualifications to make such pronouncements became significant as well. Challenges to interpretive authority were primarily addressed to Amina Wadud, the scholar who agreed to lead the prayer and deliver the khutbah. Her qualifications, which had been challenged on previous occasions,[45] became a discussion point for detractors and critics in particular. Robert Crane argued that American Muslim women lacked the training necessary to reinterpret Islamic laws pertaining to women: "To my knowledge, there is not a single American woman with dual degrees, one in American law and one in the shari'ah from a recognized university like Al Azhar."[46] Until women achieved such dual education, their efforts were premature, he said. Abou El Fadl and the Muslim Women's League agreed in their assessment that prayer leadership and the khatib position, like other leadership positions, should be assigned and assumed on the basis of knowledge, regardless of gender.[47]

American Muslim women scholars, including Wadud, Barlas, Barazangi, and Ali, have typically studied at American universities, and of these four only Wadud and Ali hold degrees in Islamic studies.[48] Abou El Fadl has supported women's exegetical projects;[49] however, elsewhere he has lamented the reduction of the rich Islamic intellectual and legal tradition to the "extracurricular hobby of pamphlet readers and writers." While this comment and the implied lack of training of those offering legal and other interpretations is directed against authoritarian "puritans" among Muslims, the critique inherent in these words applies equally to Muslim women scholars in North America. Abou El Fadl himself holds the dual degrees advocated by Robert Crane and thus amply qualifies for his interpretive projects.

The irony in the critiques of the purported lack of qualifications and traditional Islamic training of Muslim women scholars lies in the fact that the institutions of higher Islamic learning and their products, the ʿulama, have undergone transformations and a decrease in significance over the past two centuries, resulting in the challenge to traditional religious authority. Zareena Grewal has identified the trend toward seeking Islamic education or training in the Muslim world as a quest for authenticity. American Muslims of different backgrounds travel to and live in various Muslim countries in search of such authenticity. The legitimacy, and in fact authority, acquired through this process is evident in the success of charismatic "traditional" teachers such as Hamza Yusuf and Zaid Shakir, founders of the Zaytuna Institute in California. Grewal's ethnographic study also demonstrates the frustration that authenticity seekers experience when they arrive in their countries of destination and realize the complications of defining and evaluating who traditional teachers and institutions might be and how their instructional methods are applied.[50] Other recently founded institutions and organizations that facilitate higher Islamic learning and dissemination of knowledge, including sunnipath.com and Al-Maghrib Institute, emphasize the traditional training and thus authenticity of their teachers on their respective Internet sites.[51]

The debate about the woman-led prayer, too, demonstrates the significance of legal training in particular, as legal opinions by scholars with authentic Islamic pedigree were circulated, creating a set of "orthodox" positions on the issue. In several Muslim-majority countries (Turkey, Morocco) the state has initiated training projects for Muslim women preachers and in some cases even legal scholars and has developed programs for their placement and employment in the service of state-defined religious interpretations and doctrines. Here the celebration of women's advancement becomes ironic in that women preachers usually receive very little training (contrary to the decade or more that traditional education required), which qualifies them only to disseminate existing interpretations and a codified (or simplified) system of regulations.[52]

The women scholars, challenged and questioned in different venues, are keenly aware of these challenges, which often take the form of personal attacks, and tend to explain their need to engage in exegesis in two ways: as a personal voyage of faith and their struggle to preserve their faith as Muslim women or as a direct challenge to the classical Islamic interpretive tradition and the educational structures associated with it. As Muslim women they have no choice but to challenge the traditional system of knowledge transmission and preservation, for there has historically been little space for them within such a system. And while women could historically acquire Islamic knowledge, their ability to build interpretive communities was hampered by their social and legal status in Muslim societies.[53]

In an uncharacteristically self-effacing tone, Kecia Ali writes about her position: "I am not a jurist, a Qur'an scholar, or an ethicist, and I certainly do not 'do' jurisprudence here."[54] Her disclaimer might be read as an acknowledgment of her "lack" of traditional training; however, it could also situate her project in the opened space created by the challenge to traditional religious authority. Many of the male modernist Muslim scholars of the past century or so did not possess such training either and entered the competition arena armed with new (often "Western") perspectives and methodologies. The same can be said for American Muslim women scholars who draw at least in part on this modernist Muslim legacy and its methods.

Barlas writes more openly about rejection by non-Muslims based on expectations of the Muslim woman "other" as silent or conforming to preconceived notions of "proper" feminist expression.[55] However, implicit in her writing is a deep reflection about the potential of her own and other women's rereading of the Qur'an and the obstacles that patriarchal Muslim societies pose to such rereading because only a male scholarly elite, according to her, claims "to speak authoritatively in God's name,"[56] which effectively suppresses women's ideas and voices. In the postscript to her book she contends:

That is the end toward which I undertook this work: in the hope that it will be among those egalitarian and antipatriarchal readings of Islam that will, in time, come to replace misogynist and patriarchal understandings of it. Yet, I remain aware that such a possibility is remote, at least in my lifetime. . . . As for me, I belong to no sanctioned interpretive community, nor am I a male, or even a recognized scholar of

Islam (the chances of being accepted as a scholar by most Muslims if one is not a man are slim to begin with). However, as a Muslim woman, I have a great deal at stake in combating repressive readings of the Qur'an and also in affirming that Islam is not based in the idea of male epistemic privilege, or in a formally ordained interpretive community.[57]

One specific critique leveled against Wadud and Barlas relates to the role of Arabic as the sacred language of the Qur'an. Barazangi is a native speaker of Arabic—which does not make her an expert in Qur'anic Arabic—and her work addresses the role of Arabic in several ways. Her initial concern is with the role of translation (by various individuals and into English) in creating confusion over the meaning(s) of words and terms in the Qur'an. Later in her book she writes:

> Understanding Qur'anic guidance and the Islamic worldview, relying mainly on the oral recitation of the Qur'an, is as simple as the ability to recite perceptually . . . and to know the meaning of the article of faith stripped of many layers of translations and meanings that might be class, ethnic, or gender-biased.[58]

Her hermeneutic arguments are based on her appropriation (and translation) of Arabic terms and the argument that if different tafsir scholars understood them differently, they are not binding meanings.

Wadud has extensive training in classical Arabic, and her earlier hermeneutical work is dependent on arguments based on language and meaning. She rejects the construction of Arabic as a sacred language and contends that the Qur'an was revealed in Arabic in a particular place and time to make it comprehensible to those initially receiving it. However, "it is unfathomable that the Lord of all worlds is not potentially multilingual."[59] According to her, "Each term should therefore be examined on the basis of its language act, syntactical structures, and textual contexts in order to more fully determine the parameters of meaning."[60]

Barlas has devoted a significant amount of writing to the role of Arabic for understanding and interpreting the Qur'an, primarily in the form of a defense against the centrality of Arabic. Her conclusion differs significantly in that she ultimately argues against the importance of "mastering Arabic" as a precondition for exegesis: "While the Qur'an lends itself to language analysis, interpreting does not necessarily require a mastery of Arabic since interpretation is not an exercise in philology." But it "seems reasonable to argue that if we can read the Qur'an in translation, we can also interpret it in translation."[61] This constitutes a radical departure from the approaches to Arabic taken by Wadud and Barazangi. Ali works with original Arabic sources but has not addressed the issue in her writings.

Laleh Bakhtiar has produced a gender-inclusive translation (or rendering) of the entire Qur'an without being fluent in Arabic. Her translation is based on other translations and was prompted by her unwillingness to accept the translation of the word *daraba* as "beat."[62]

To mention that women's approaches to the Qur'an, Islamic Law, and religious authority do not emerge from or exist in a vacuum or in a female space alone would be stating the obvious. However, in the study of Muslim women we still find a tendency to focus exclusively on women as women because this is after all the object of our study. Such a gender-centered perspective runs the risk of excluding important connections, influences, and lifeworlds of Muslim women. One important male scholar who actively participated in the conversation on new perspectives on gender in Islam is Khaled Abou El Fadl. He has offered significant support to egalitarian readings of the Qur'an and to more egalitarian reformulations of Islamic Law in many of his works. He has supported the work of Amina Wadud and has been an inspiration for Asra Nomani. Nomani describes him as the "pope of tolerant Islam" and credits him with supporting her in difficult times.[63] Abou El Fadl also offered a fatwa in which he argues that women should be allowed to lead mixed-gender congregations in prayer if the community of worshipers agree to it.[64] The significance of another male scholar, Fazlur Rahman, for women's exegetical projects, though he would probably not have supported them, was discussed earlier. Timur Yuskaev describes Fazlur Rahman's methodology as foundational for the work of Wadud and Barlas as well.[65] The reliance of Muslim women scholars on male Muslim intellectuals and their ideas can also be read as a problem. Do women need male authority and support in order to advance their projects? Do they draw on such scholarship for its utility or to gain religious and scholarly authority? Or, alternatively, is the gender of these scholars of no concern to them?

The textual production of American Muslim women scholars analyzed here, in its quantity and quality, attests to the conviction of the scholars that their work is important and necessary and that their perspectives need to be expressed. More study is necessary to understand the dynamics of American

Muslim women's knowledge production in the context of a secular academic system with its own history of secular liberalism and feminist theory.[66]

However, more than two decades of scholarly writings convincingly argue that the women scholars see value and indeed urgency in their exegetical work. At the core of the "crisis of authority," and a parallel democratization of knowledge, they have demonstrated their conviction that ultimately it is their arguments, and not someone else's definition of qualification, that matter for their projects. Having put forward such arguments for gender justice and equality within a Muslim framework, Muslim women scholars and exegetes are now faced with the challenge to build interpretive communities. Ironically, the greatest obstacle is the very crisis of authority that provided an opening for their exegetical participation in the first place.

Ali has suggested that the transformations in Islamic Law and its application and the particular conditions of Muslim-minority communities have largely obliterated the possibility of establishing religious authority similar to that enjoyed by classical Muslim jurists and scholars in their time. Her own thoughts and arguments presuppose "that Muslims will undertake this process of reflection primarily as individuals, for ourselves and in dialogue with those close to us."[67] Other Muslim women scholars and activists would likely not agree with this view and advocate collective attempts at challenge and change.

More important for my reflections here, Ali has also observed, "Many Muslim thinkers and authors who are perceived as authorities, and who write and speak from a position of authenticity, are not themselves fully grounded in the classical tradition; they have a selective and often incoherent relationship to law and scriptural interpretation."[68] Ali continues by arguing that such thinkers are accepted as authoritative voices because their views are congruent with their listeners' expectations and "because their maleness and ethnic background give them an air of authority."[69] I would argue that some examples show that it is primarily the congruency of their views, in this case their attitude to gender issues and reforms, that bolster their authority, more than their gender or ethnic backgrounds. Ingrid Mattson, Hamza Yusuf, and Zaid Shakir are prominent examples.[70]

Muslim women scholars' convictions that their ideas and interpretations matter are challenged by divergent perspectives on their authority as scholars and exegetes. The crisis of authority has made it possible for women to assume the authority to rethink, and reinterpret, but their interpretations can only become relevant beyond the world of academia and publishing in

North America if they succeed in their efforts at interpretive community building: only when they convince others of their arguments will they gain the authority they claim.

Building and Rethinking Communities

Muslim women scholars have striven for community building since they began to write and publish in the early 1980s. The women's rights projects discussed in the previous chapter are a case in point. Ali writes:

> Reinterpretation is not only an individual project, for application in our own lives; it must also be a collective enterprise of scholars thinking, talking, and writing jointly and in counter-point. Muslim feminists have become part of the Islamic intellectual tradition and, in doing so, have begun to push at its boundaries and shape its contours.[71]

When these words were written in 1995, several such intellectual projects were already taking place. The volume *Windows of Faith: Muslim Women Scholar Activists in North America,* edited by Gisela Webb and published in 2000, illustrates this development. The volume grew out of two conference panels, at the Middle East Studies Association and the American Academy of Religions meetings in 2005. The conversations at these meetings and the subsequent exchange of ideas and eventually writings constituted the formation of a community of scholars and activists with diverse methodological and activist commitments and a shared interest in gender issues and Muslim women, as well as a shared American Muslim scholar activist identity.[72] It asserted the need for Muslim women's engagement with the study of Islam and Muslims in the academy on the one hand and their participation in intracommunal debates and activism on the other.

Sonbol has described her observation of and participation in collective scholarly efforts and the connections between challenging academic historiographies of "what has been done to women" rather than histories of women "trying to achieve greater rights for women,"[73] chronicling several such projects. She writes, "The important thing about this effort is that it is communal, with academics interacting with colleagues interested in the same issue and with activists and women's groups."[74]

Many such scholarly and activist community building efforts have taken place over the past two decades. However, in reading the texts produced by American Muslim women scholars over the same period, it is striking and rather surprising how limited the intellectual engagement among this group of scholars has been, at least in writing. For the most part, women scholars quote each other in order to disagree and advance their own interpretation. This strategy, while true to their own perspectives, methodologies, and value commitments, seems counterproductive to the task of community building, especially considering the enormous external pressures from within the secular academy, feminist circles, media, and public opinion and not least from dissenting Muslims within their communities. Asma Barlas has written about Amina Wadud. Most prominently, she is the author of the essay on Wadud in Suha Taji-Farouki's *Modern Muslim Intellectuals and the Qur'an*, where Wadud is the only woman and the only American Muslim scholar included for analysis.[75] In another essay on women's Qur'an interpretations, in the *Cambridge Companion to the Qur'an*, Barlas presents many of Wadud's ideas but adds her own perspective and directly critiques Wadud's.[76] In her book *Believing Women in Islam*, Barlas draws extensively on Wadud, several times on Riffat Hassan, mostly in agreement, and once on Azizah al-Hibri. Nimat Barazangi engages with works by Wadud and al-Hibri but almost exclusively in a critical manner.[77] Kecia Ali mentions Wadud and Barlas once in the text of her book and refers to their work in several footnotes throughout. Ali has most critically engaged with the work of al-Hibri in her contribution to the volume *Progressive Muslims*.[78] Aysha Hidayatullah makes the same observations in her study of American Muslim women's exegetical projects and notes that her study does not imply or reveal conformity or consensus and certainly not much cooperation. Her use of the word *fragmentation* to describe these works adequately expresses my impression after reading them. One reason for this fragmentation may be the precarious and complex situation of Muslim women in the academy, who have a great deal at stake as they carve out individualized spaces for their interpretive work.

In the long run, and with the increasing complexity of Muslim gender debates and the growing number of texts and authors, collaborative academic intellectual projects, in which women scholars combine their respective fields, ideas, and methodologies, will become more important and indeed urgent. Only then can interpretive community building start at the very beginning of the interpretive process. Many of the critiques formulated by Hidayatullah in the conclusion of her dissertation, including the issue of privilege, economic and ethnic exclusion, insistence on heterosexual gender normativity on the structural side, the internal inconsistencies in exegesis and legal interpretation, and the ultimate complexity of the nature of the Qur'anic text can only be resolved in a collective effort.[79] The fact that Muslim women now carry out studies of other Muslim women scholars, including myself, raises new questions about ethical dilemmas, personal relationships, and shared activist commitments.[80]

While the debate about the 2005 prayer event seems to point primarily to the divisiveness of the issue, which was frequently brought up by its critics, one could also argue that the prayer event indeed demonstrated an effort in and the possibility of interpretive community building. Those attending and those supporting the prayer event, for a variety of reasons, all constituted a community in their agreement on the significance and acceptability of woman-led Friday prayer and a woman giving the Friday khutbah. One could also argue that those who rejected the prayer as significant or permissible formed an interpretive community while simultaneously drawing and guarding the boundaries of the "Islamic tradition" and Muslim communities.

It is useful in this context to question the definitions of community often employed in discourses on American Muslims. If our understanding of Muslim communities and their boundaries is limited to groups of American Muslims who are associated with the same mosque or community centers, or those affiliated with Muslim institutions and organizations, we as scholars tend to erase the presence of all those who are not involved in these kinds of communities. It makes sense, then, to push the boundaries of communities to include virtual networks, informal groups (including women-led prayer congregations that meet in private spaces), and temporary formations of community such as those associated with the 2005 prayer.

Women scholars and activists have not only built their own gender-specific networks and communities, addressing issues and concerns from specifically "female" perspectives, but they have also participated in gender-inclusive or gender-neutral projects for and with Muslim women and men. Hanadi al-Samman describes such projects in her analysis of women's networks and what she calls "Islamic feminine hermeneutics," which includes organizations such as the above as well as textual production. She writes:

> The geographical spaces conquered, due to the enactment of these religious and legal journeys, do claim more than personal and private spaces for these Muslim women. Indeed they forge political and cultural bridges of understanding for the entire Muslim ummah as well.

Virtual and real "networks" are created in the process of reclaiming the religious feminine voice from the androcentric exclusionary tradition of erasure, and of re-inscribing it onto the body of contemporary Islamic jurisprudence.[81]

From the quest for gender justice in the Qur'an through the legal dimensions of the debate about woman-led prayers and women's rights, American Muslim women's scholarly writings have contributed in myriad ways to gender debates in American Muslim communities. While some stay in the realm of ideas and theory, others dedicate and indeed shape their scholarly work through their activist commitments. Larger developments in Muslim structures of interpretation and authority in the wake of modernity have affected American Muslims in significant ways and need to be taken into account, while processes of globalization have allowed for transnational networks of activism as well as the global dissemination of American Muslim women's ideas, writings, and activist projects.

6

Space, Leadership, and Voice

Muslims always seem to be talking about the injustices done to them by the outside world. But I rarely hear Muslims talk about the unfairness that exists within our own communities. I pray in a room where there is a one-way mirror, so the men cannot see me. I am told we are a distraction. I look out and I see them but they just see a mirror. The presence of women in my mosque has been erased.

Zarqa Nawaz, *Me and the Mosque*

The opening narration of the 2005 documentary *Me and Mosque*, directed by Zarqa Nawaz, serves as an introduction to several issues associated with the presence, participation, and significance of Muslim women for and in North American mosques and communities. Her statement assumes that women once had a significant presence, at least in her mosque, and that this presence would be a reflection of fairness and ultimately justice. Nawaz claims that women are treated unfairly by being excluded from the main space of the mosque and by extension from leadership positions within mosques and communities. The film goes on to chronicle recent developments in North American mosques regarding the establishment of physical barriers between men and women in prayer spaces. She laments these developments and nostalgically remembers her childhood when she and her female family members felt included and valued in the community. The film features the journalist and activist Asra Nomani who in the same period initiated the Muslim Women's Freedom Tour and the woman-led Friday prayer in New York City. The film and tour coincided in their timing as well as their discursive goals and should be read as part of the same community dynamics and developments.[1]

The goal of Nomani's Muslim Women's Freedom Tour was to reclaim physical and metaphorical spaces for Muslim women in the main part of American mosques. This chapter begins with reflections on gendered and mixed-gender spaces in mosques to then connect the issue of space to questions of leadership, ritual, exegetical, and social/political. It links space and leadership to the issue of women's voices (as formulated several times during the prayer),[2] by reflecting on the direct and symbolic significance of women assuming, acquiring, and using their voices. The prayer engendered discussions about ritual and other forms of women's leadership. It significantly altered American Muslim discourses on women's spaces and presence in mosques. Conversations about women's spaces, leadership, and voices are also implicitly concerned with questions of female sexuality.

Spaces for Women: Mosques and Communities

The documentary *Me and the Mosque* opens with the following skit by the American Muslim comedian Azhar Usman.

> You know, there is this hot issue: women in the mosques. What exactly is the issue here? I just don't get it, I mean, women, they need to pray, this is a mosque, a house of worship. Maybe, the women should be in the mosque. And when the women are in the mosque, they talk about it like it is some special mosque feature, you know: Mashallah, we have intizam[3] for ladies, we have a dungeon. It is a very nice dungeon. And Mashallah we have an excellent sound system, but it is not working. And we have a wonderful cooling system during the hot summer months, we have two fans. When it is 116 degrees outside, it is only 99 downstairs.[4]

The audience visible in the clip consists of Muslim men and women, sitting in gender-separated sections on the floor in a large room. The women find this much more entertaining than the men and are visibly animated by the jokes about their spaces in American mosques.

In the epigraph Nawaz laments that women's presence was erased from her mosque and many others in North America by the installation of barriers to separate men and women during prayer and by the construction of completely separate and invisible spaces for women in new mosques. Asra Nomani's march on her own mosque and the subsequent Muslim Women's Freedom Tour aimed to highlight this issue of exclusion and erasure by walking into the main prayer space of several mosques and praying there, despite rejection and hostility on the part of mosque officials and community members.

Women in American Mosques

Some features of the debate about women's prayer space are unique to the American context. While women's participation in prayer and their architectural expression vary by historical period and geographic context, mosques in the Muslim world share the key function of being spaces for congregational prayers. Muslims in America started rededicating and eventually also designing mosque buildings in the early twentieth century. While there is an ongoing debate about which mosque was truly the first one in America, scholars agree that the appropriation of spaces as mosques first took place in the 1910s and 1920s. The first purposefully built mosque, according to Sally Howell, was the Moslem Mosque in Highland Park, Michigan, which celebrated its grand opening in 1921. Howell's account points to two important features of early American mosques: they were built by and for particular, usually immigrant communities, and immigrant communities consisted mainly of men, because U.S. law limited immigration from Asian countries and with that large-scale immigration of Muslims until the passage of the Immigration and Naturalization Act in 1965.[5] Thus spaces for women did not become an issue until there were a sizable number of women to attend prayers in mosques.

Equally important is the fact that in a minority context such as North America, mosques quickly became much more than spaces for communal prayer. They provided Muslims with physical spaces for community and identity building and helped provide an environment for worship, education, and celebration of religious holidays. After 1965 especially, mosques became centers of religious education for Muslim children and instruction in Arabic.[6]

Haddad, Smith, and Moore claim that the lack of prayer spaces for women may have been related to the fact that many mosques in the 1970s and 1980s were built with financial support from "oil-rich Islamic countries." While earlier mosques were often used for activities such as weddings and sometimes even community dances, more recent immigrants were critical of such practices and demanded conformity with their "Islamic" norms. However, the authors also state that "mosques in the United States function in ways that are more like churches and synagogues than mosques abroad."[7] Women's spaces have been and are being constructed and used in mosques throughout the Muslim world with particular historical, cultural, and political dynamics at work in each context. Immigrants from different countries and regions of the Muslim world have brought their experiences, norms, and expectations to North America, where they continue to be shaped and negotiated in American Muslim community contexts.

Haddad, Smith, and Moore point out that "national figures" from 2005 suggest that at least two-thirds of women who attend mosques pray in spaces separated from those of men.[8] The historical trajectory is of interest here. Early Muslim communities in North America tended to be organized along ethnic community lines and countries of origin. Thus it would be reasonable to expect that such immigrant communities replicated traditional spatial arrangements for women (or the lack thereof) while at the same time negotiating issues of access to space and economic challenges. If early communities used mosques as integrated community spaces and only when they could afford to designated separate spaces for women, the question needs to be asked, what exegetical or discursive forces would have been at work in such transformations of space? Did communities become more aware of traditional norms of segregation? Is this one expression of a worldwide religious revival, often expressed in a search for the fundamentals or roots of the religion? Did American Muslim communities become more conservative, or protective, or confident over time? More research is necessary to assess the histories and trajectories of particular mosques and communities in North America.

Gendered versus Mixed-Gender Spaces

A discussion aired on PBS radio in November 2004 and centered on Nomani's mosque tour illustrates the parameters of the conversation. It highlights the fact that opinions on joint prayer spaces and mixed-gender congregations are divided but not along gender lines. The program features women in support of separated spaces while men criticize them and vice versa. Nawaz's documentary, too, points to the fact that men as well as women argue for the need to separate prayer spaces for reasons of modesty and comfort. In the PBS program, those in favor of separation of the sexes during prayer do not provide authoritative support for their opinions from religious texts or scholars. Rather, unspecified reference to religious norms or practices of segregation is made. One female community member states, "We don't mingle with the brothers. That's the way it's stated."[9]

In discussions on online lists and forums women have argued for the comfort and privacy of separate women's spaces where they can chat, nurse, and let down their guard about modesty and propriety in ways that would not be possible if they were sharing the space with men. Women's spaces would thus function as protective outward frames for women's fellowship and community building. This argument is reminiscent of Leila Ahmed's distinction between women's and men's Islam,[10] whereby separate women's spaces in mosques become an embodiment of the positive difference between the two. Those arguing against separate spaces also employ access arguments, namely, women's access to knowledge during lectures and discussions and women's audiovisual access to the imam in order to correctly follow his prayer movements.

The imam of an African American congregation explains that his community is too poor to provide adequate spaces for women, only to exclaim later, "I am living a tradition that is 1,400 years old, nothing is going to change from it."[11] This economic argument, with its implications for the participation of men and women, is placed together with the construction of an immutable tradition that cannot and should not be debated. The second part of the argument holds less power considering that even conservative exegetes acknowledge that separate spaces for men and women did not exist in the Prophet Muhammad's time. Such special separation is still not observed in the central mosque in Mecca (surrounding the Ka'bah), a practice that is traced back to the Prophet's time as well. In many of the arguments about the necessity or legal permissibility of physical barriers or separations, the practice of the Prophet Muhammad is weighed against the danger of sexual temptation, which in turn would result in fitnah in the community.[12] Those who reject the demand for joint prayer spaces cite arguments that revolve around conceptions of women's sexuality. To claim that men will be distracted by the presence of women is to describe women, as Nawaz pointed, as a sexual temptation. The inability of those demanding gender egalitarianism in the mosque to engage the underlying argument has been criticized more broadly by Kecia Ali, who contends that "sexuality must be integral to the broader reformist quest for gender justice."[13] She sees in contemporary reformist contributions to Qur'anic exegesis a lack of emphasis on sex and sexuality. The reason for this absence may, according to Ali, lie in the "androcentric nature of the Qur'anic guidance on sex."[14]

The PBS debate, however, is also interestingly nuanced, in that it features Ingrid Mattson arguing for more inclusion of women in American mosques but not directly for or against joint prayer spaces. Muqtedar Khan accuses Nomani of not speaking for or coming from the community and describes the "movement" for women's access to mosques as very American and as a clash between "progressiveness" and "conservatism." Khan also expresses his own concern about getting distracted by a woman praying close to him, the same sexuality-driven argument we have encountered in the debate over women leading prayers.[15]

Jerrilynn Dodds offers a noteworthy window on our consideration of women's space and participation in American mosques. In her book, *New York Masjid*, a photographic and ethnographic portrait of mosques in New York City, Dodds discusses separation of the sexes and describes the range of physical and architectural arrangements in New York City mosques, ranging from side-by-side areas to separate rooms and floors.[16] Dodds identifies exigencies of space as well as "cultural" factors as determinants for the spacial arrangements and offers a sensitive discussion of the most common arguments on the issue. She quotes Aisha Al-Adawiya, who would later become the chief author of the pamphlet on women's participation in mosques, endorsed by major Muslim American organizations: "I assure you this is not a question of hierarchy or dominance. We simply should not be regarded from behind while at prayer."[17]

How, then, did the prayer organizers come from concerns about women's spaces and inclusion in mosques to performance of a woman-led Friday prayer? Nomani's experience in her mosque illustrates that the connection between religious space and religious leadership was obvious to her. Mosques are not required for the performance or attendance of Friday prayers, but the majority of American Muslims who attend Friday prayers do so in mosques around the country. Friday prayers have to be performed in a public setting in order to be considered valid, thus making them by their very nature a public performance. It was then quite logical for the organizers of the prayer event to select the most public prayer ritual for their performance of gender justice. The issue of space can also be addressed specifically with regard to Friday prayer. Anecdotal evidence suggests that not only have American mosques faced significant space problems in the past (due to growth of communities as well as attendance at prayers), but that one of the possible responses to this space shortage has often been to discourage women from attending Friday prayers so as not to take up space needed for male worshipers.[18] As pointed out earlier, according to Islamic legal regulations attending Friday prayers is required only of free male Muslims. Women are allowed but not required to attend Friday prayers. In his critical study of American mosque architecture and its connections to gender, space, and aesthetics, Akel Kahera has argued that "in America, Muslim women frequent the mosque with the same regularity as men and therefore cannot be excluded from the literal or practical meaning of the term 'jama'a,' or public gathering."[19] Kahera makes the compelling argument that mosque structures and requirements in the American context should be modeled after early Prophetic practice in which women participated in mosque activities, including prayers, and cautions that later developments in Islamic Law and community perception need to be understood as bound by their respective historical contexts.[20] In following this line of argument, Kahera, with a focus on architecture, replicates arguments about which traditions to follow and where to selectively apply historical criticism as offered by Nomani, Wadud, and Barlas.

Nomani had initiated her quest for space in the main prayer hall earlier in 2003, inspired by her experiences during her pilgrimage to Mecca where men and women pray side by side.[21] Her book chronicles the lessons of her pilgrimage and frames her activism after her return as a sequence of logically necessary steps to achieve her goal, "the struggle for the soul of Islam." When during Ramadan 2003 the new building of her mosque was dedicated she was shocked to find that while there was now a space for women, it was completely separated from the men's space and even had a "back entrance." Nomani writes, "I hadn't attached much significance to the moment when I had stood before the Ka'bah with my family, unhindered by gender segregation, but in a lesson I was slowly learning, I realized there really were no moments from the hajj that were without meaning."[22] Encouraged by the experience of praying with men in the same space in the mosque surrounding the Ka'bah in Mecca, Nomani set out to find scholarly support for her instinctive insistence on the right to pray in the same spaces as men. She discovered scholars such as Asma Afsaruddin at the University of Notre Dame, who wrote to her that "women's present marginalization in the mosque is a betrayal of what Islam had promised women," adding that women in the Prophet Muhammad's time were not relegated to the back of the mosque and that no physical separation existed between male and female worshipers.[23] Nomani also mentions Alan Godlas of the University of Georgia, Daisy Khan of ASMA in New York, and Ingrid Mattson, professor at Hartford Seminary and the first woman president of ISNA (2006–2010). Starting a relationship that in her narrative would come full circle with the woman-led prayer in 2005, Nomani contacted Amina Wadud and found her supportive of her quest. Nomani writes, "It was time that we took back our religion. The systematic elimination of women's rights was starting to make sense to me. I was relieved. It was about power and control. It wasn't about Islam."[24] Here again gender equality is equated with joint (and equal) access to space. The argument also parallels the exegetical and historical argument that women's issues are primarily issues of Muslim men's interpretation and not "Islam" itself. Only Wadud has clearly transcended this discursive move to separate Islam from Muslims.[25] Nomani, however, has frequently labeled the perspective of those who might advocate an alternative vision of gender relations as well as spatial arrangements in mosques as backward and un-enlightened. Consistent with her vision of gender reform, changes in practices are new, innovative, and a sign of progress while simultaneously constituting a return to the sources and intent of "true Islam."

Nomani's and Wadud's visions of equality as egalitarianism has been countered by an alternative gender model, one that argues for the complementarity of the sexes rather than their equality in all aspects of life. Jamal Badawi, a Canadian Muslim scholar and community leader uses the term *gender equity* and explains that "from an Islamic perspective, the roles of men and women are *complementary* and *cooperative,* rather than competitive."[26] A very different form of such complementarity can be derived from the work of Leila Ahmed.[27] In Western scholarship on Muslim women, both positions, the one asserting that women's rights and gender egalitarianism are universal and the other that there are indeed different gender models and that Muslim societies and in them Muslim women and men need to be understood on their own terms, can be found. They are variations on the long debate over universalist versus relativist arguments in approaching other people, "cultures," and contexts. If applied to the context of women's spaces in American mosques, the complementarity approach would support the creation of gendered spaces as an expression of women's agency and the inherent differences in cultural and religious approaches to gender. Relativist arguments on gender have in the past functioned to counter hegemonic discourses on gender as evident in the long debates among third wave feminists over the representation and perspectives of women of color and of different ethnic as well as economic backgrounds.

In the universalist argument that lies at the root of Nomani's, Nawaz's, and other Muslim women's demand for equal access and thus symbolic visibility, women's demands for separate spaces for women must be read as an expression of "false consciousness."[28] Nomani, in her contribution to the PBS debate, also repeated her opinion that space is not all that is at stake in the discussion: "Ultimately, barriers that are placed in front of women are barriers to full participation and leadership in our communities. They're symbolic of this greater denial of women's rights that we have to confront in the Muslim world."[29] To those American Muslim women who demanded equal access to their mosques the lack of space and visibility of women was symbolic of the exclusion of women from communities generally. Thus achieving connected, accessible, and nonsegregated prayer spaces would, in their understanding, recognize their equal rights with men and provide women with equal access to community leadership. Space becomes a metaphor for rights, which need to be actualized through women's leadership.

When Nomani entered her mosque through the main door in Ramadan 2003 and again when she marched with her supporters on the same mosque in June 2004 and then went to other mosques around North America, she actively demanded that women become leaders of American Muslim communities based on a discourse of equal rights. The issue of community leadership is discursively linked to ritual leadership as represented in Wadud leading the Friday prayer in 2005 and the concept of exegetical leadership as represented in women's interpretive activities in North America. These different forms of leadership need to be understood as contingent and as part of the same projects for gender justice and equality. While it is tempting to isolate religious or ritual and exegetical leadership from other forms, they are intimately connected in the lives of the Muslim women who demand and assume them.

Women and Mosque Leadership

Nomani's quest for space was also a quest for the inclusion of women in mosque leadership. A study of American mosques and mosque leadership, conducted by the Council on American Islamic Relations in 2001, was the first of its kind.[30] In an article based on the data collected in the study, Ihsan Bagby offers an analysis of mosque leadership by basing his assessment on an American model of congregations and their leadership.[31] Bagby's focus is on two different models of mosque leadership, by an imam and by a board (*majlis*). In the first, the imam holds considerable power and authority over all aspects of the mosque, which constitutes a departure from an imam's traditional role as prayer leader and religious guide. While being a prayer leader has been professionalized in the Muslim world as well, traditional imams would not engage in other types of community activity, education, or counseling. In the second type, the mosque is run by a *majlis ash-shura*, or a governing board, which appoints an imam as prayer leader but has control over all other aspects of community life. Bagby contends that statistically the majority of African American mosques follow the imam model, while the majority of immigrant mosques follow the majlis model. In the imam model, based on a form of charismatic leadership and, in Bagby's view, on the tradition of black preachers, the imam is a religious as well as social authority with wide-ranging influence over interpretations. In the majlis model an imam can be appointed and replaced easily, provided the board can reach consensus. Membership on the board is based on elections but often also on financial contributions to the mosque building and sustenance.

Bagby reflects on the qualifications an imam should bring and the varied expectations of such qualifications in American Muslim communities. Imam training programs are still rare in North America. Some institutions, first and foremost Hartford Seminary, have developed chaplain and imam training programs, primarily to train prison and military chaplains according to government standards. Increasingly, chaplains are also being hired by universities with large Muslim populations. Absent from Bagby's discussion is the participation of women in mosque leadership.

Haddad et al. contend that "until recently women have seldom played institutional leadership roles in their place of worship," thereby reducing the mosque yet again to a place of prayer, even though it serves many other functions, but acknowledging that small signs of change have begun to appear in American Muslim mosque communities.[32] Women have played an important role in raising and educating the next generation of Muslims, a task that has exerted considerable pressure on Muslim mothers to succeed. Women have also participated in gender-specific aspects of Muslim community life, such as preparing food for functions and events, organizing activities for children, occasionally participating in educational events, and, very important, raising money for the community.[33] This participation without direct or formal leadership responsibility has reinforced traditional roles for women in mosque communities while also providing social networks and activities outside the home, especially for those Muslim women who do not work outside the home.

Nomani's narrative of her encounters and struggles with her community tells of her exclusion from the mosque, a decision taken by the all-male board members. Later one woman was elected to the board, which Nomani perceives as one result of her struggles and interprets it as that woman's attempt to change the system from within. The same woman then resigned from the board and agreed that the mosque leadership had displayed their intolerance toward women in general by banning Nomani from attending prayers.[34] Nomani's attempt to change things in her mosque is a tale of struggle and eventual exclusion. Despite her focus on mosques, it is important to consider that scholars and observers estimate that only a quarter of American Muslims regularly attend a mosque. This means that 75 percent of American Muslims do not attend congregational prayers in mosques or community events other than Eid prayers twice a year, and some do not even do that. Scholarly discussions of secular and cultural Muslims have provided blueprints for understanding different kinds of community building, networking, and identity negotiations.

Discourses on Women's Leadership

American Muslim women have recognized that discourses on the leadership of women have to be part and parcel of their efforts to attain gender equality in their communities. Nomani, in her very personal style, offers insight into her development as a leader in an essay titled "Being the Leader I Want to See in the World."[35] She describes her lifelong expectations of others in her community, family, and larger society to be leaders, until she realized that all of them had failed her in her quest for women's rights and equality. It was then, after painful and disappointing personal experiences, that she realized for herself that determination to lead has to come from within and cannot be assigned from the outside. Encouraged by other women's example but also their support for her, Nomani decided to "be the leader she wanted to see in the world." Her essay chronicles her search for meaning in leadership but also the most common strategies used to discourage and discredit her. Like Wadud, she realized that women's leadership and authority are often questioned by assuming the right to decide which woman is Muslim enough, pious enough, or dressed properly enough to be accepted as a leader. She writes, "One of the most intimidating strategies used to deter women from working openly on reform within an Islamic framework is the powerful force of techniques that accuse others of denying or going against 'Islam.'"[36]

Nomani's "Islamic Bill of Rights for Women in the Mosque" contains this statement: "Women have an Islamic right to hold leadership positions as prayer leaders, or imams, and as members of the board of directors and management committees."[37]

Noteworthy because it was formulated in response to the 2005 prayer is an essay by Ingrid Mattson on women's leadership. Mattson attempts to shift the conversation from prayer or ritual leadership to larger questions of women's leadership roles and concerns.[38] She argues that when Muslim religious institutions do not take Muslim women seriously they defeat the very purpose of their existence, which is to bring their congregations closer to God. Mosques and communities that turn away women, or frustrate their aspirations as leaders and participants, effectively turn away half of their potential membership. Women in leadership positions are necessary to represent the specific needs and perspectives of women, which Mattson contends are different from those of men. Muslim women need Islamic knowledge and increased societal authority in order to help bring other Muslims closer to God. She writes:

> It is my observation that when religious leadership does not include women, their experiences, concerns, and priorities will not be well represented. There are those who are convinced that men are capable of guiding and leading the Muslim community in a just manner without female peers. I would argue that common sense tells us that even the most compassionate and insightful group of men will overlook some of the needs and concerns of the women of their community.[39]

In the final analysis, Mattson rejects women's prayer leadership of men but supports women's prayer leadership of other women (her example is women's mosques in China). Her argument is based on adherence to sunnah and established legal principles in the Islamic tradition. She then advocates more inclusion of women in mosque leadership and in another move away from the mosque contends that in American society women as well as men have other opportunities to build communities and to lead them.

The contribution of Imam Zaid Shakir, a founder of the Zaytuna Institute in California, goes in a similar direction. Shakir, in his essay "An Examination of the Issue of Female Prayer Leadership," rejects women as imams based on his understanding of the Islamic legal tradition. He critiques the prayer and its organizers for creating disunity in the community and for allowing non-Muslims to exploit the controversy over the prayer to taint Islam. The body of the essay, as discussed earlier, is a legal and historical refutation of the arguments made by the organizers to justify their decisions and the event. However, at the end, Shakir acknowledges, like Mattson, that there are problems with the treatment and status of Muslim women in American Muslim communities: "Saying this, we should not lose sight of the fact that there are many issues in our community involving the neglect, oppression, and in some instances, the degradation of our women. . . . Perhaps, if the men of our community had more humility, we would behave in ways that do not alienate, frustrate, or outright oppress our women."[40] Laury Silvers, a member of the Progressive Muslim Union and an avid supporter of the prayer, responded to Shakir's essay by advocating Muslim women's and men's civil disobedience in matters of religious practice and established rulings. She took serious issue with Shakir's use of the word *our* in speaking about American Muslim women. She writes, "The marginalization of women is so deep-rooted that even Imam Zaid, whom I know to be a long-time supporter of women's rights in Islam, demonstrates a habituated paternalism when he uses the phrase 'our women' in the passage above."[41]

Hibba Abugideiri offers a more complex argument for women's leadership by problematizing the very notion of female Islamic leadership. She argues that adopting such terminology assumes on the theoretical level that Islamic leadership is in fact gendered, that is, that leadership tasks and areas are distinguished by gender. On the historical level, she contends, traditional leadership roles have been assigned to men and women, with men being responsible for issues "of Islam" and women being responsible for issues relating to women. "In fact, 'Islamic leadership' comes to represent the invisible construct, certainly assumed to be masculine, to which the qualifier 'female' must be added in order to shift the focus from the larger issues to issues exclusive to women."[42] This argument is a version of the feminist critique leveled against defining the masculine as normative and the feminine as a derivation or more often an aberration. It also implicitly critiques women's leadership efforts addressed only to women or women's issues.

Abugideiri then argues that the intellectual, religious, and social leadership of Amina Wadud, Amira Sonbol, and Sharifa Alkhateeb, respectively, have provided American Muslim women with alternative and diverse leadership models. By taking possession of exegesis (Wadud), reformulations of Islamic Law (Sonbol), and women's organizations (Alkhateeb), these new Muslim women leaders have changed the rules of leadership by adopting Wadud's formulation of "gender jihad."

> "Gender jihad" seeks greater complementarity between the sexes, and is based on the Qur'an. In short, it is a struggle for gender parity in Muslim society in the name of divine justice; it is a struggle to end a long-standing gender regime that has paralyzed Muslim women, preventing them from being leaders without having to add the qualifier 'female' or 'woman.'"[43]

Abugideiri does not adopt the egalitarian language employed by scholars such as Barlas or Nomani. For Abugideiri, Muslim women's leadership is religious by virtue of its reference to the Qur'an and its (often critical and sometimes reluctant) engagement with the Islamic interpretive tradition. She does not make a distinction between community leadership and spiritual or religious leadership. Abugideiri's leadership model might be reflected in the real-life example of one American Muslim woman leader, Ingrid Mattson, who does not seem to fit the model(s) embodied by women leaders such as Wadud and Nomani.[44]

Just a Leader: Ingrid Mattson

What is so different about Ingrid Mattson? Mattson, a professor of Islamic studies at Hartford Seminary, has made her mark as a leader of American Muslim communities within the folds of an established American Muslim organization. She was elected vice president of the Islamic Society of North America in 2001 and president of the same organization in 2006.[45] Her academic work, with very few exceptions, has not explicitly been focused on gender issues or women in Islam. Rather, her focus is on the Qur'an in its historical and contemporary significance (not in an exegetical capacity) and the life example of the Prophet Muhammad. The above mentioned essay on women's leadership is a rare exception. Mattson, who was hailed as the first female president of ISNA and (mistakenly) as the first female leader of a Muslim organization in North America,[46] has consistently downplayed the significance of gender in her role as community leader and has espoused positions that would contradict the egalitarian stances of women such as Nomani and Wadud, by emphasizing the importance of tradition and community over potentially contentious calls for change. However, as seen above, she has criticized Muslim communities and organizations for their unwillingness or inability to accommodate women's demands and needs. Her approach is more subtle and less confrontational and sees value in community cohesion and peace. While celebrated by some as an important woman leader (she was selected to participate in the prayer following Barack Obama's inauguration), Mattson has also garnered criticism and indeed assault from neoconservative media outlets and policy circles, which 'treat' her in the same way any male leader would be treated. One other interesting connection to Barack Obama is the fact that just as Obama's election as president was hailed as symbolic for the inclusion of African Americans regardless of his promised or actualized policies on race and discrimination issues, so, too, Mattson's election can be read primarily as symbolic.[47] To put Mattson in a different category of woman leader may be a reflection of what Saba Mahmood warns of when she discusses Western feminist notions of agency and resistance among Muslim women.[48] Just because Mattson does not engage in publicized and provocative events or movements does not mean that she does not espouse a critical perspective on women's issues and a desire for changes in Muslim communities, and even if she did not embrace such agendas her potential desire to protect the status quo could not necessarily be criticized within such a framework without forcing particular understandings of agency and women's roles on her and other Muslim women within the ideological and interpretive spectrum found in Muslim communities.

Zahra Ayubi has described Mattson's emergence as an American Muslim leader of note and her work for training other American Muslim women to become leaders in their own right. Mattson advocated full participation of women in all affairs of Muslim communities except leading prayers. Ayubi quotes Mattson's statement about women's training to become chaplains: "Increasing numbers of Muslim women have found new confidence and acceptance in the field of Islamic scholarship. . . . Confidence springs from the knowledge that it is not an innovation to have women authoritatively and publicly interpreting and teaching Islamic texts; rather, this is a renewal of the spirit of the early Islamic community."[49] Mattson here draws in familiar ways on historical precedent to construct authenticity for projects that are reformist and "traditional" at the same time.

In the end, it was precisely the alienation and frustration women and men such as Asra Nomani, Saleemah Abdul-Ghafur, and Ahmed Nassef felt in dealing with their mosques and communities that led them to stage the woman-led prayer as a symbolic act of religious protest and civil disobedience. Amina Wadud agreed to lead the prayer after being approached by Nomani as a religious scholar with the knowledge of ritual practice to carry out the task. Wadud has described how she first encountered the idea of "a woman as imamah and khatibah" during her tour in South Africa in 1994. In meetings and lectures in different South African Muslim communities, she was repeatedly asked her opinion on the issue. "This was the first time I had ever given the matter consideration," she writes. "I admit a naive excitement about the idea although I had given little or no strategic thought to its impact or rationale."[50] Out of this excitement would develop her ethical model of reciprocal relations between men and women, as expressed in all realms, including the spiritual and religious.

Religious/Ritual/Exegetical Leadership

Nomani wrote in 2005 that "it was important for us to assume leadership in all aspects of our lives, from the spiritual to the intellectual. We challenged one of the deepest denials of women's full expression: her ability to lead prayer."[51] Why would Muslim women's ritual leadership be so much more controversial than the many other ways in which women have assumed authority and inhabited leadership positions throughout Muslim history and in qualitatively new ways in the twentieth and twenty-first centuries? Why, more than in other realms where women have challenged male privilege and domination, would Muslim communities collectively demand conformity to legal doctrines and ritual practices established more than thirteen hundred years ago?

When Wadud decided to stand in front of a mixed-gender congregation, she, according to the organizers of the event, was repeating history, not changing it.[52] Their insistence on the grounding of the prayer event in early Muslim history and Prophetic practice was intended to legitimize the event and provide "textual" support for their position.

Wadud perceived her acceptance of the invitation to lead the prayer as an expression of her conviction that "the gender jihad is a struggle to establish gender justice in Muslim thought and praxis. At the simplest level, gender justice is gender mainstreaming—the inclusion of women in *all* aspects of Muslim practice, performance, policy construction, and in both political and religious leadership."[53] Her emphasis on praxis, practice, and religious leadership makes explicit her conviction that ritual leadership is an integral part of attaining gender justice.

Whether leading Friday prayers is primarily an act of religious or ritual leadership or significantly more than that needs to be considered here in more detail. The most important reason that Islamic legal regulations are so specific with regard to the acceptable performance of and attendance at Friday prayers lies in the historical and communal significance of the Friday prayer. Research on the emergence of the Friday prayer in early Islamic history—when the Prophet Muhammad lived in Medina late in his life—emphasizes the sociopolitical nature of a gathering of Muslims for congregational worship and political rather than religious instruction. The institution of congregational prayers at midday every Friday brought together the small but growing Muslim community for a show of political allegiance to the Prophet Muhammad, which in turn explains the later legally defined duty of free and resident Muslim males to attend the prayer while such attendance was permissible but not required for women, slaves, and travelers. Oleg Grabar, in a study of early mosque architecture, describes Friday prayers as a religious act but, more important, as an opportunity to demonstrate allegiance to the political leader (first the Prophet Muhammad and then his successors), to communicate news, and to make collective decisions.[54] The limitations on who was required to attend Friday prayers to free male Muslims does imply a very particular understanding of community membership that effectively excluded women at least from political community membership and by extension leadership as well. It would also have meant exclusion from the emerging concept of community consensus.

One could also argue that assuming ritual leadership by leading prayers is simply an embodiment of the oft-stated spiritual equality of the sexes in Islam. Prayer leadership could be described as a reflection of such equality and thus in the realm of the spiritual or religious. On the other hand, congregational prayer clearly has a very social and therefore public dimension and would thus be expected to reflect social norms of Muslim societies as well. Muslim women scholars such as Wadud and Barlas have argued for extending spiritual equality to all other realms of Muslim life and experience, assuming that ritual leadership would bring their argument full circle while knowingly challenging the status quo.

One especially salient question is why Wadud decided to follow established ritual practice in leading the Friday prayer despite the fact that she is not a male. The Jewish feminist Judith Plaskow has argued in her work on Jewish feminism and feminist Judaism that addressing particular inequalities or injustices in Jewish ritual and textual understanding will not redress the larger problem but rather perpetuate the system. With regard to ritual leadership, she writes:

> Thus, as feminists demand that women be allowed to lead public prayer, the issue of language is often set aside. Traditional modes of liturgical expression are assumed to be adequate; the only issue is who has access to them. But women's leadership in synagogue ritual then leaves untouched the deeper contradictions between formal equality and the fundamental symbols of the service, contradictions that can be addressed only through the transformation of religious language.[55]

In the case of Muslim women in North America, a significant body of exegetical work on changing the "language" has been carried out by Wadud, Barlas, and others. Wadud explains that she focused on "proper" practice in order to minimize if not entirely avoid the controversy following her 1994 pre-khutbah lecture:

> I had not forgotten the extent of the controversy that had followed the previous public announcement and participation in a similar invitation in South Africa more than a decade before. Thus, I was especially keen that I concentrate on the nature of the public ritual as a performance toward Allah, rather than an act of defiance against those who have created the necessity for a gender jihad by simply denying women the full human dignity with which Allah has created us. My conclusion was to keep the prayer service to the normative male privileged procedure, while contributing from my own female perspective, and encouraging greater gender parity in public ritual leadership.[56]

Wadud's emphasis on conformity with established ritual was intended to increase the legitimacy of the prayer while also demonstrating her knowledge of the tradition and authority/leadership role in embodying the same tradition she was simultaneously following and challenging.

Equally significant in light of the established sequence of the prayer (which she describes as male-centered and not gender-neutral), Wadud emphasizes the content of her khutbah, in 2005 as in 1994, not to fight off criticism but to direct meaningful criticism and debate where she considers them most useful. While the form of the khutbah, too, followed established Muslim practice, it was indeed the content that designated Wadud as an exegetical leader of the Muslim community she led in prayer and preached to. Regarding the content of her khutbahs, it is useful to remember that Wadud had interpreted Qur'anic passages as pointing toward her tawhidic paradigm and the fundamental spiritual as well as social equality of human beings regardless of their sex. She also insisted on translating the Arabic noun *Huwa* as "He," "She," and even "It" in order to drive home her point that God is not male other than in grammatical terms and that consequently men cannot derive any sense of superiority from their likeness to God as male.

Another example of a woman assuming ritual leadership is of significance here. Despite its ritual nature, no controversy ensued when in early 2004 Kecia Ali officiated at a Muslim marriage. Ali, an expert in Islamic Law on marriage, was invited to be the imam for a wedding. After consulting with several scholars she decided that nothing in the Islamic legal tradition explicitly prevented her from performing the ceremony.[57] Those at the wedding appreciated her sermon on the significance of marriage. Ali later reflected on her thoughts and consideration of form as well as content and in line with her academic and exegetical work attempted to find a balance between the Qur'anic text and principles as she perceived them.[58]

Beyond the Mosque: Women's Activism and Leadership

In a study of American Muslim women's writings it makes sense to turn to those texts that women have produced about their activism and leadership and to include texts that are expressions of activism and that pronounce their authors to be leaders. Three collections of texts by (mostly) American Muslim women are considered here as examples of some of the many ways in which women have assumed leadership positions in Muslim communities and within American society at large. Part of a wave of narrative, personal, and activist accounts by Muslim women to appear in the wake of September 11, 2001,[59] the three volumes offer the "voices" of Muslim women, discussing their experiences, sharing their stories, and explaining their perspectives on faith, sexuality, and war. Katherine Bullock's edited collection, *Muslim Women Activists in North America: Speaking for Ourselves*, brings together the stories of seventeen women activists from a range of backgrounds.[60] Bullock frames the volume as having three purposes: to challenge stereotypes in mainstream society of Muslim women as oppressed, to challenge the exclusion of Muslim women from public roles within their own Muslim communities by claiming the legacy of the first Muslim women in history who were leaders and role models, and to use autobiographical writings as a tool to achieve authenticity without claiming representativeness.[61] The stories in the volume speak of various forms of activist work, for and by women, leading communities in matters of social improvement, education, and charitable organizing. Some of the women tell of their political engagement in demonstrations against war and conflict and of their roles as public representatives of Muslim communities and Islam. Very few employ the feminist language found in the works and activism of Nomani and others.

Two other volumes, *Shattering the Stereotypes: Muslim Women Speak Out*, edited by Fawzia Afzal-Khan,[62] and *Voices of Resistance: Muslim Women on War, Faith, and Sexuality*, edited by Sarah Husain,[63] much more directly reflect Muslim women's engagement with war, imperialism, and U.S. involvement in the Muslim world. The stories, essays, poems, and plays also directly and critically take on debates on women's sexuality in Muslim communities and offer insight into matters of faith, interpretation, and religious practice. Taken together, the three volumes offer a glimpse of the manifold ways in which Muslim women in North America (and beyond) have assumed leadership positions. They also show that the sometimes conflicted but never rejected commitment to being Muslim and woman are based on a tafsir of praxis. The presence of women scholar activists in two of the volumes, among them Hassan, al-Hibri, and Barazangi, points us back to the close connection between exegetical and activist leadership. The titles of two of the volumes also connect us to the question of voices, raised in the title of this chapter and in several statements by the organizers of the 2005 prayer. Women's voices are said to rise and be in need of being heard. The women in many of the texts are "speaking out," and during the prayer event it was Nomani who exclaimed, "When we listen to the voice of a woman call to the heavens and for prayer we will be hearing a sound that is not heard in the Muslim world today. The voices of women have been silenced through centuries of man-made traditions, and we are saying no more, enough is enough."[64]

Women's Voices

> Hear our song, and when the words become familiar, sing along, for ours has too often been the silence that sustained and nurtured the background.[65]

Thus writes Amina Wadud in the introduction to *Inside the Gender Jihad* after describing her book as joining "a concert of resounding voices creating and learning songs about what 'Islam' means with full inclusion of real Muslim women."[66] Women metaphorically and physically made their voices heard during the prayer event, by pronouncing the call for prayer, by speaking to journalists and congregants, and by offering the khutbah and leading the prayer. Muslim women's voices in this understanding have been silenced both by Muslim men and communities and by mainstream society. This assumption too easily buys into the stereotype of women's oppression without the willingness to listen to alternative examples. Having a voice or voices, raising one's voice, and speaking for oneself is an issue of representation but also an issue of ritual, sexuality, and gender.

Discussions on women's voices as part of her *'awrah* (nakedness or private parts)[67] abound on Muslim online forums.[68] The discourse revolves around the understanding that a woman's voice is part of her body and thus part of her sexual being. In connection with the parallel understanding of her sexuality as active and even potentially aggressive, it is then necessary for society to control or limit women's voices.[69] The legal opinions offered on these forums are somewhat more nuanced and generally do not prohibit women from speaking in public per se (based on the sunnah that women did speak to the Prophet Muhammad directly and in public in the seventh century), but that "it is not permissible for a woman to speak in a soft or alluring voice" because "men may be tempted by that."[70]

In the context of prayer, adhan, and Qur'an recitation the issue of who decides when a woman's voice is alluring and thus tempting is connected to questions of spiritual practice but also legal concepts of validity. Those who spoke against the woman-led prayer often invoked not only Islamic legal regulations against such innovation in ritual practice but also objections to a woman in front of a male or mixed congregation on grounds that this female presence and the sight (and voice) of the woman would distract men from their concentration on worshiping God.

The organizers' decision to invite a woman as mu'adhdhin (muezzin) for the prayer was, like the gender of the khatibah and imama, a matter of claiming spiritual and societal equality and of "sounding" their protest at the exclusion of women's voices from the realm of ritual and leadership.

That context matters for the discussion of women's voices is evident in the vastly different approaches to women as Qur'an reciters in the geographically distant locations of Egypt and Indonesia. Kristina Nelson's groundbreaking study of the sound dimensions of the Qur'an and its recitation in the Egyptian context points to the construction of a discourse on public Qur'an recitation that is, at least now, exclusively male. Nelson writes that women tend to be less musical in their recitation and less well trained, while male reciters can become quite famous and will be broadcast on TV and radio. And while some women in the early twentieth century did rise to acclaim as Qur'an reciters, the practice was always surrounded by public controversy.[71] Similarly, a legal opinion issued by the Indian Darul Iftaa, associated with the Deoband school, allows women to speak on religious radio shows but categorically prohibits them from performing Qur'an recitation and Islamic songs because "it is not permitted for a woman to raise her voice melodiously in the presence of a non-Mahram man."[72]

In contemporary Indonesia, Rasmussen points out, "things are radically different. While a woman would not lead a religious ritual where men were present, she would certainly recite in the company of men in myriad contexts. . . . Furthermore, the vocal and musical artistry of women's recitation is in no way inferior to their male counterparts."[73] Rasmussen's ethnographic study of Indonesian schools of Qur'an recitation for women and their recitation practices makes clear that female Qur'an reciters are many and that their presence, training, and practice is not an exception in the Indonesian context.[74]

Michael Muhammad Knight recalled after the Friday prayer that Suhayla el-Attar's first pronunciation of the adhan had a profound impact on him: "The first adhan to really kill me in a while, it was beautiful in a way that you can't get from a man."[75] And Sarah Eltantawi, one of the prayer's organizers, proclaimed, "The beautiful voices of women have been excluded from this beautiful ritual and that, too, will end today."

FROM THE SEPARATION of Muslim women's presence in American mosques by means of curtains, barriers, and one-way mirrors to the reclaiming of gendered and mixed-gender spaces in the same mosques, from women's activism inside and outside mosques and community centers, this chapter has aimed to demonstrate how the 2005 prayer event has contributed to existing debates in Muslim communities about physical and metaphorical spaces for women and the roles of Muslim women as leaders. Discourses on leadership, different kinds of leadership roles, and women's activism can clearly be linked to earlier discussions of women's exegetical projects for gender justice and equality on the one hand and the importance of authority on the other. That authority and leadership are not synonymous but rather have to be understood as separate but related concepts becomes clear through deeper analysis of how the authority to interpret can be self-assumed as well as bestowed on the individual by a community. Only the building of interpretive communities, however transient or temporary, translates exegetical authority into changes on the ground. Similarly, leadership qualities and positions can be assumed by an individual, but it is only through community building efforts that leadership can lead to a transformation of existing communities and societies. American Muslim women have not only participated in such transformations but also documented their experience and reflections in a variety of texts. These texts, as they relate to the theme of space, leadership, and voices, also connect these discourses back to the prayer and its symbolic claim to all three: space, leadership, and voice. Muslim women's claims to their voices and their right to speak on their own behalf and on behalf of other Muslim women and men were audibly performed in the prayer event. Their "voices" were amplified through different media, linking voices, leadership, and space to media representations and production.

7

Media, Representation(s), Politics

The dominant narrative of the Muslim woman in Western discourse from
about the eighteenth century to the present basically states, often in
quite sophisticated ways, that the Muslim woman is innately oppressed;
it produces Muslim women who affirm this statement by being either
submissive nonentities or rebellious renegades—rebellious against their
own Islamic world, that is, and conforming to Western gender roles.

Mohja Kahf, *Western Representations of the Muslim Woman*

This assertive statement by the American Muslim scholar, novelist, and poet
Mohja Kahf serves as a thought-provoking introduction to this chapter, not
least because it allows insight into the debates surrounding the representation of Muslim women and the connection of such representations to American Muslim women's writings and their active engagement with media
production. This chapter analyzes the media dimension of the woman-led
prayer and its connection to representations of American Muslim women.
One purpose of the prayer, to challenge the "dominant narrative of the
Muslim woman," overlaps with the active engagement of American Muslim
women writers with various forms of media. The "success" of this challenge
depends on the nature, dynamics, and politics of media production on the
one hand and on the possibility of many different "readings" of such media
products on the other.

Representations of "the Muslim Woman"

Muslims have long decried the mostly negative nature of media representations of their religion and their communities, and a significant body of
research is available to understand better the dynamics and politics of rep-

resentations of Islam and Muslims.[1] Edward Said in his *Orientalism*[2] and *Covering Islam*[3] has provided us with the foundational analytical tools for understanding the power of representation by others through a discussion of both the colonial discourses from which the stereotypes of Muslims originate and more contemporary representations in various forms of media. Stereotypes and misrepresentations do not only do injustice to the perception of others; they also have the power to influence the realities of those who are stereotyped.

The image of the oppressed and silenced Muslim woman is only second to the even more pervasive image of the violent Muslim extremist male and its association with terrorism. These negative images are complementary and interdependent in their assumption that the violent and oppressive nature of Muslim men necessitates and produces the silent, victimized, and oppressed Muslim woman. Several American Muslim women scholars have explored representations of Muslim women in their work. Leila Ahmed, in her groundbreaking *Women and Gender in Islam* (1992), has analyzed the marriage between colonialism and feminism, especially in the nineteenth century, through which the image of the oppressed Muslim woman was not only cemented but also put to direct political use.

> Even as the Victorian male establishment devised theories to contest the claims of feminism, and derided and rejected the ideas of feminism and the notion of men's oppressing women with respect to itself, it captured the language of feminism and redirected it, in the service of colonialism, toward Other men and the cultures of Other men. It was here and in combining the languages of colonialism and feminism that the fusion between the issues of women and culture was created. More exactly, what was created was the fusion between the issues of women, their oppression and the cultures of Other men. The idea that Other men, men in colonized societies or societies beyond the borders of the civilized West, oppressed women was to be used, in the rhetoric of colonialism, to render morally justifiable its project of undermining or eradicating the cultures of colonized people.[4]

Mohja Kahf has argued in her book, *Western Representations of the Muslim Woman*, that this image of the oppressed Muslim woman was a product of the eighteenth and nineteenth centuries and that applying the lens of Orientalism further back into the past effectively obscures earlier historical contexts for the production of a variety of other representations of Muslim women and their purposes for contextualized politics and histories.[5] Rather, Kahf's study of Muslim women in "Western" literatures from the twelfth to the nineteenth centuries demonstrates that the transformation of the Muslim woman from a strong-willed queen with sometimes "intimidating sexuality" in medieval European literature to the helpless veiled woman in the harem was a slow process, taking place over several centuries and yielding to different and entirely Western contexts, that is, with no correlation to the actual roles of Muslim women in corresponding centuries.[6]

In the introduction to her book, Kahf contends that "'the Muslim woman is being victimized' is the common axis undergirding a wide variety of Western representations. The narrative about the Muslim woman is so diffuse as to be part of conventional wisdom in the Western world."[7] She elaborates that this narrative can be called on in media and cultural production without further explanation, with the vocabulary for recognizing the veil, seclusion, polygamy, and other symbols for the Muslim woman's victimization already firmly in place. It can be called on for entertainment and polemical as well as political purposes. It is thus important not to lose sight of particular contexts, histories, and political variables. Rather than perpetuate the assumption that Muslim women and Muslims more generally have been and are being stereotyped and misrepresented in various parts of the "West" in much the same way, I focus on the particularity of representations of Muslim women in North American media contexts. Such media contexts are also contingent on different forms of media: television, books, news media (print and otherwise), the Internet, and documentary films. Each medium follows its own logic of production and involves a variety of actors producing and consuming them; and many of their dynamics have changed as a result of the introduction and spread of increasingly sophisticated technologies. Access to various forms of media for consumption as well as production, and interest in them, varies greatly according to factors such as class, education, and political orientation.

Media Representations of American Muslims

Is there a difference in the representations of Muslims generally and American Muslims? Do the images of American Muslim women, if there are any, differ significantly from those of Muslim women outside of North America?

In my first paper on the writings of American Muslim women in 2005 I confidently asserted that American Muslim women were for the most part absent from public and media representations. Who could name an important American Muslim woman? How often does one see American Muslim women on television shows having actual roles other than the victim of a Muslim man's crime or quietly and veiled opening the door for the detective to take away the Muslim man? This confidence in the invisibility of American Muslim women has since been replaced by an awareness of the number of readily available representations and by an increasingly sophisticated body of research analyzing such representations. The writings of American Muslim women show a trajectory over several decades, with scholarly materials appearing somewhat earlier than popular texts in book form or other print media. There is, however, a significant difference in the way American Muslims are represented in American media as opposed to representations of Muslims elsewhere. Two possible reasons come to mind. First, American Muslims have, over the past decades but increasingly after 9/11, actively and intentionally participated in media production, both in existing mainstream media outlets and in their own Muslim media outlets. Second, especially in the "War on Terror," distinctions between domestic Muslims and those other Muslims abroad were an important tool for identifying who would be perceived as a threat to American national security and under what circumstances. Mahmood Mamdani's formulation of the distinction between "good Muslims" and "bad Muslims" as a tool of control reflects this dynamic.[8]

Studies of media representations and images of American Muslims and their political purposes paint a rather confusing picture. Nacos and Torres-Reyna, in a study of stereotyping and media coverage of American Muslims before and after 9/11, based on a statistical survey of leading newspapers and news shows on television, found that not only did the news coverage of American Muslims increase in the immediate aftermath of 9/11 (which would be rather unsurprising), but that there was a significant increase in positive representations of American Muslims as well.[9] In particular, there were a growing number of thematic news frames and human interest stories about American Muslims, thus humanizing members of the various American Muslim communities. The authors found that American Muslims were discussed in the context of civil liberties rather than domestic terrorist threats and that more attention was paid to their lives, circumstances, and experiences. However, the coverage turned increasingly negative again after the first anniversary of 9/11.[10] Nacos and Torres-Reyna also make a connection between media coverage of American Muslims and public opinion surveys. Among their findings were that Americans more often had a decided opinion about Islam and Muslims and that their public sympathy for American Muslims was higher than that for Islam generally.[11]

Evelyn Alsultany has offered a thoughtful and critical analysis of the "sympathetic" portrayal of Arab Americans in two episodes of the TV show *The Practice*, aired in 2001 and 2002, respectively. Alsultany demonstrates that even where court cases seem concerned with civil liberties and the right of Arab Americans to be treated equally, the court decisions in both episodes reinforce and justify the racialization and racialized discrimination of Arab Americans on account of their otherness and threat to national security. She notes that while the representation of Arab and Muslim Americans increased after 9/11 (and so did the presence of sympathetic portrayals), such representations were ultimately used for other purposes.

> The rhetoric of the nation in danger, through news media and TV dramas, has become accepted as truth and common sense. . . . 'crisis' is used to justify racist views and practices; to racialize Arabs, Arab Americans, Muslims, and Muslim Americans as threats to the nation, and hence to use them as the contemporary racialized enemy through which the nation defines its identity and legitimizes its abuse of power.[12]

In another study in the same volume, which also assesses media coverage and representation of Arab Americans and Muslim Americans before and after 9/11, the authors are far more critical of the portrayal of both communities and their individual members as dangerous because of their divided loyalties (as immigrants tied to other countries), as "distinctly devout," and as hampered by their devotion to Islam in participating in the American nation. In article after article, their loyalty is questioned, their religious practices are exoticized, and their connection to international Muslims and Muslim movements is implied.[13] The authors close by arguing that "the elision between Arab Americans and Muslim Americans and what is represented as 'fanatical,' 'violent, 'terrorist,' U.S.-hating Muslims around the world, has set the stage for surveillance, policing, harassment, and incarceration." They call for "more accurate representations" and hold newspapers as well as other media outlets accountable for "their contribution to larger racializing projects."[14]

The three studies surveyed here demonstrate the complexity of media representations of American Muslims,[15] but none of them has paid specific attention to the issue of gender and the representation of American Muslim women. Other studies have focused on representations of Muslim women but not on American Muslim women specifically. What follows is a reflection on the particular politics of American Muslim women's media representation and their implications for American Muslim communities and gender discourses.

An even cursory survey of articles about American Muslim women in the *New York Times* and the *Washington Post* reveals the dynamics of their representation. There is no shortage of human interest stories about American Muslim women, especially after 9/11. They range from the Muslim prom queen to fashion designers of modest Muslim clothing, from Muslim homeschoolers to American Muslim poets, and from hijab-wearing women athletes to the issue of domestic violence in Muslim communities.[16] Many of these articles have been contributed by a handful of journalists, among them, Neil MacFarquhar, Andrea Elliott, Tara Bahrampour, Laurie Goodstein, and Andrea Uddin.

Heather McCafferty has produced a useful case study of the representations of Muslim women in the *New York Times* over a period of several years. Her thesis is not focused on American Muslim women, but she finds, too, that even nuanced articles often reinforce the impression of the "otherness" of American Muslims vi-à-vis non-Muslim Americans.[17]

American Muslim Women in the Media: The Prayer and Beyond

The dynamics of representation, stereotypes, and self-representation are best discussed in a deeper analysis of the media representations of three American Muslim women: Amina Wadud, Asra Nomani, and Mohja Kahf. All three have been engaged in self-representation in various media, conscious of what they see as stereotypes and misrepresentations of Muslim women, and in their own ways all three have been determined to challenge and change media images of Muslim women.

The debate surrounding the 2005 prayer event was carried out largely through various forms of media. It was on Internet sites, in chat rooms, in television news shows, and in newspaper articles and editorials that the prayer was initially discussed and the parameters of the debate established.

The other significant purpose of the prayer was to challenge existing stereotypes and monolithic perceptions of Muslim women as oppressed and silent. The organizers of the prayer intended to use the expected and invited mainstream media attention (both national and international) to counter perceptions of Muslim women as incapable of "speaking for themselves" but also as a homogeneous group, veiled and victimized by Muslim men. Thus the prayer was not only a performance of gender justice, an embodiment of gender-egalitarian tafsir, and an attempt at building new interpretive communities and reclaiming Muslim history and tradition; it was also an act of active and intentional self-representation against pervasive, hegemonic, and powerful reductions of the image of "the Muslim woman." A closer look at the self-representation and participation in media production of Nomani, Wadud, and Kahf, an early supporter of Daughters of Hajar and the prayer event,[18] reveals that all three women emphasize their agency in representing themselves. However, their attempts at changing public images of Muslim women are restricted by pervasive, powerful, and historically constructed images of them.

The prayer was announced to the public several weeks before it took place on March 18, which created media interest as well as room for internal Muslim debates about its intention, nature, permissibility, and politics. While the intent to change media images and public perceptions of Muslims, especially Muslim women, is not always clearly stated by the organizers before or after the prayer, it becomes apparent from the setup and organization that media attention was of vital importance for the organizers. The announcement on MuslimWakeUp on March 13, 2005, stated that the organizers were "looking to make arrangements for an Internet broadcast of the historic event, and more information will be published on the details of the broadcast as soon as we have them." This broadcast never materialized, and only fragments of the extensive footage have found their way into documentary films about Nomani and Wadud.

The woman-led prayer was widely covered by media outlets and heavily attended by representatives from many media organizations, both American and international. A Google News search performed in 2007 found hundreds of articles from newspapers and online news sites around the globe. Stories in the *New York Times*, the *Los Angeles Times*, and *Arab News*, on National Public Radio, and in the *Washington Post* as well the *Pakistan Times* described the event and reflected different perspectives and responses to the prayer in the mediated debate before and after the event.[19] Wadud and Nomani appear as central figures for the prayer, one having provided the scriptural and interpretational justification and the other having been the driving force of its organization. News stories describe the positions and motivations of Wadud, Nomani, and other organizers and participants on the one hand and the various arguments against the prayer on the other. Many articles also contain quotes from scholarly experts on Muslims in America. For the most part, news reporters stayed away from engaged or celebratory representations of the event.

In addition, numerous organizers and participants of the prayer have published accounts and opinion pieces about the prayer and its impact. The focus on Nomani and Wadud allows for a closer look at the ways in which each woman participated in media production and representation while being powerfully defined and described in the media products of others. An analysis of newspaper articles by and about the novelist, scholar, and poet Mohja Kahf completes the picture.

At the Front of the Mosque: Asra Nomani

Nomani has written extensively about herself, most notably in her book *Standing Alone in Mecca*, which details her journey and transformation as an American Muslim woman.[20] Nomani is vocal about her perspectives on the world and engaged in professional media production. The initiative to organize a woman-led prayer—a significant step beyond her earlier demand for women to have equal access to prayer spaces in American mosques—in her own story forms the next logical step in her activist agenda. She recalls the opportunity to organize the event in conjunction with a planned conference of the Progressive Muslim Union and the suggestion to approach Amina Wadud about leading the prayer.[21]

Two days after the prayer event, on March 20, 2005, she recalled her experiences in detail. She cites the courage of the participants and the exhilaration and pride in the event and points out that the prayer was also a way to take their "faith back from the extremists who had tried to define Islam on Sept. 11, 2001."[22] She describes the beauty of men and women greeting each other with respect, the fact that a woman "freely" nursed her baby during the prayer, and that angry protesters outside threatened the women and men inside with eternal hellfire. Here, as in most of Nomani's writings, we see at work an aesthetic of moral righteousness in which Nomani's position is verbally associated with beauty and light, while the "others," those disagreeing with her, come across as wrong and unreasonable.

Nomani represents herself as liberated, thoroughly American and thus modern, and religious in a very comfortable, American way. Her approach to scripture and tradition, her drawing on postenlightenment ideals of individual rights, equality, and justice all reinforce the impression of her as familiar and only mildly exotic. She is exotic only in ways that are appreciated within the American mainstream as a spicy addition to the melting pot of American society and culture. In presenting this image of herself—one that is not void of religiosity—she challenges the stereotype of Muslim women as oppressed and veiled. Nomani's agenda involves, consciously or not, shattering the monolithic perception of all Muslim women as similar, voiceless, and silent.

Contrary to the title of her book, which points to her lone struggle for women's rights, her project of gender reform has included various forms of alliance and community building. She early on enlisted the support of her family, especially her father, in her demands to her hometown's Muslim community. Before her march on the Morgantown mosque to demand access for women to its main hall in June 2004, she founded Daughters of Hajar, evoking the courage and endurance of this Qur'anic figure as an example for contemporary Muslim women to follow.[23] And the prayer itself was an act of community building, the creation of a network of like-minded activists, however temporary.

Nomani is aware of the power of the media to communicate ideas and demands. As a journalist and writer she has seen firsthand the impact media coverage can have on the real lives of real people. Thus, her writings, books, articles, and op-ed pieces taken together speak of a consciously planned act of performance, meant to further her activist agenda. Nomani is also prominently featured in media products conceived by mainstream journalists, as in Paul Barrett's book on American Muslims and the 2009 documentary *The Mosque in Morgantown*.

The woman-led prayer is important for Nomani's trajectory of activism and media representation but by no means its ending point. It involves her pilgrimage adventure with her son and family in 2003, praying in the main hall of the Morgantown mosque in 2004, and the posting of her "99 Precepts for Opening Hearts, Minds and Doors in the Muslim World" on the door of the mosque in Morgantown in early 2005. In her visits to mosques across North America during the Muslim Women's Freedom Tour (often on camera or accompanied by a journalist) she encountered hostility and rejection, sometimes threats, and occasionally support from other Muslim women and men.[24] Later in 2005 Nomani decided to lead a prayer herself. She performed an afternoon prayer (not a Friday prayer) on the campus of Brandeis University, leading both men and another woman in prayer.[25]

As a journalist and thus an active participant in media production, No-mani has developed a mutually dependent and fruitful relationship with media outlets. In an interview right before the prayer, she said:

> Basically, like most journalists, I got into the field to make the world a better place. I can't think of any way to better use the skills that I've gotten as a truth-teller than to bring about some sort of fairness and equity and inclusion in the world. I think when I really reflect on it, I became a solid journalist, I think, because of the principles that my parents taught me as a Muslim; integrity and ethics are vital to being a journalist. So I simply want the same principles to be practiced in my Muslim world, because I've seen the alternative.[26]

She has agency in this production process but is also—inadvertently or not—used for the representational purposes of others. In a *Slate* article titled "Veiled Babes," Nomani relates the results of her research on veiled models for book covers and her discussions with her own publisher about the cover of her book: the hardcover edition showed her wearing a white headscarf; the paperback edition with a slightly modified title[27] features a glamour shot of Nomani with uncovered hair and wearing a pink blazer.[28] In her article she argues that the second picture of her represents her and her ideas much better than does the veiled picture. Otherwise, she found that designers and publishers tend to use the same images from picture databases with no regard for context but in clear identification of available "frames" for Muslim women. The article thus reveals the politics of mar-keting books on Muslim women and demonstrates that Nomani is aware of such dynamics in media production. Overall, while Nomani has been celebrated in media outlets as an alternative voice to stereotypes, her story serves as a revelation of the hidden lives of Muslim women and as a liberal trope. Through the representational choices of her own person and of the adversaries to her campaigns, Nomani has contributed to the reproduction of stereotypes of Muslims (especially those in the Muslim world) as "other" in media representations, including other Muslim women.

"Feminist Rosa Parks Style:" Asra Nomani in the Media

In addition to her own writings on the prayer and her activist agenda, No-mani has been widely featured in various forms of media. Nomani's role in the prayer event, her march on the mosque, and the Muslim Women's

Freedom Tour were the subjects of several articles,[29] as well as a chapter in Barrett's *American Islam: The Struggle for the Soul of a Religion*, published in 2007. Aside from the similarity in title (Nomani's is "A Woman's Struggle for the Soul of Islam"), the book features Nomani's story under the chapter heading "The Feminist."[30] She is "the feminist," not one of many but the quintessential example of a Muslim type. Barrett discloses that he has known Nomani since they worked for the *Wall Street Journal* in the early 1990s. The chapter provides a wealth of personal information about Nomani's family, upbringing, and hometown. Her story is one of empowerment and struggle, adversity posed by those who refuse to support her and her important and legitimate campaign, and ultimately redemption, even if a lonely one. The last line of the chapter reads, "Nomani took a step back, straightened her posture, and prepared to pray in a line of her own."[31]

Throughout the story, Nomani is described as standing up to her adversaries and braving their threats and insults. Barrett finds it necessary to describe her physically, as a petite woman with charcoal hair.[32] He also points on several occasions to the fact that she wears scarves (in various colors) only while praying. Muslim women disagreeing with her wear a headscarf or even a face veil, reinforcing the picture of women who are not only oppressed and veiled but also limited in their intellectual discernment by the "veil." Her male Muslim adversaries are heavy or sturdily built, emphasizing the David and Goliath picture in the mind of the reader.

Barrett is acutely aware of the representational dimension of Nomani's agenda:

> The collision of these expectations turned out-of-the-way Morgantown into a battlefield over women's status in Islam. Nomani, determined to praise God in the same room as men, outraged male worshippers by conducting a defiant pray-in. Rather than retreat to a special women's balcony, she simply stood behind the men. The offended worshippers . . . condemned her as insolent, and they made an issue of another transgression, one that would have scandalized orthodox believers of most faiths: Nomani has borne a son out of wedlock after a brief relationship with a Pakistani Muslim. . . . Nomani fought back, branding her antagonists fundamentalists, men who viewed modern women with contempt. As the confrontation escalated—in part because of her deft publicity skills—she became the catalyst for a broader national debate over the future of Islam in America.[33]

In Barrett's writing, Nomani is not flawless, and he takes pains to present other people's opinions of her, including accusations that she is only interested in publicity. One of her critics accuses her of exposing the Morgantown mosque (and by default American Muslims) to the ridicule of non-Muslims.[34] Barrett's work is based on interviews and meetings with Nomani. He also quotes from email communication between Nomani and others, indicating Nomani's role in providing information to Barrett. Overall, the emerging picture of Nomani is one of a tireless fighter for the rights of women, willing to stand up for her ideas and standing strong in the face of rejection and adversity. She is American and Muslim proudly and shows no hesitation taking on the traditions and mistakes of her religion. Barrett's representation of Nomani reinforces the picture Nomani has developed of herself in her own writings.

In the writings of other journalists, Nomani has been hailed as struggling "Rosa Parks style,"[35] as the "Muslim Sojourner Truth," and as following the traditions of Martin Luther in Germany and Martin Luther King Jr. in the United States.[36] These allusions to civil rights struggles and important African American figures align well with Nomani's own civil rights rhetoric in regard to Muslim women's rights. Nomani's drawing on the imagery and history of the civil rights movement and American history (as in her Bill of Rights) also renders her contributions to discourses and media representations more legible to other (non-Muslim) Americans than to global Muslim communities. It points to her active participation in media representations and to her own framing of the events as produced by, in, and for American dynamics of Muslim discourse. We have seen the drawing of parallels between struggles against racial and gender discrimination earlier in the works of Wadud and Silvers as well.[37] Such parallels provide legitimacy to gender reforms and potential hope for similar success.

There is a strong emphasis on Nomani's status as a lonely fighter, eager and willing to build alliances, but ultimately the only one who can carry out the struggle. This image is perpetuated in the 2009 documentary *The Mosque in Morgantown*, which follows Nomani from the early attempts at reform in her Morgantown mosque through the New York prayer and into Nomani's continuous work to gain equal mosque access for women. In the *Washington Post* online segment "Georgetown/On Faith," posted on May 20, 2009, Jacques D. Berlinerblau, professor at Georgetown University, describes Nomani as follows: "In person, Ms. Nomani is every bit as intelligent, intense and witty as she is on film. Having spent the first half of my scholarly career writing about heretics, let me assure you that she is the real deal!" The segment with and about Nomani is titled "Asra Nomani: Bad Girl of Islam."[38] This is yet another shift, this time from the lone hero-ine of women's rights to an emphasis on Nomani as an antihero, admirable but heretical while still capable of speaking on behalf of Muslim women worldwide. We are reminded of the two categories of Muslim women that Kahf had identified as constructed by colonial Western discourse, and it is her second category that may fit Nomani's representation: "rebellious rene-gades—rebellious against their own Islamic world, that is, and conforming to Western gender roles."[39]

Gender Justice in a Prayer: Amina Wadud

While Wadud is no stranger to the media, her presence as a scholar and spokeswoman for women's rights differs in many ways from that of Nomani. Wadud has spent much more of her time being an academic and an activist. Wadud has occasionally been mentioned in media coverage for her exegeti-cal work on the Qur'an, as in a 1996 *New York Times* article on the Malaysian women's advocacy group Sisters in Islam, which Wadud joined while teach-ing in Kuala Lumpur in the early 1990s. In the article Wadud states, "For 14 centuries the Koran has been interpreted almost exclusively by men. . . . [I]t is only in the past two decades that women have begun to say, let's look at this text and come up with our own conclusions[,] . . . and voila, some of them are not the same as the men came up with."[40] Wadud was among several Islamic studies scholars interviewed for the PBS *Frontline* documen-tary *Muslims* in 2001, and her interview appears on the PBS website as per-manent teaching material. Here she is not reduced to someone who can speak about women's issues and Qur'an interpretation. Rather the inter-view covers a range of questions, from Islamic resurgence to, of course, women's issues. Wadud is most vocal about her exegetical work and the emerging group of progressive Muslims addressing these and many other issues of reform and change in the Muslim world. The interview transcript features a head shot of Wadud wearing a hijab.[41]

Wadud has written in *Inside the Gender Jihad* about her participation in the prayer but has otherwise been reluctant to comment on it.[42] In the book she dedicates a section in the last chapter, "Stories from the Trenches," to her perspective on the prayer.[43] In a preceding section, devoted to a speaking event at a mosque in Toronto, Wadud complains in passing about the sensationalism surrounding that event:

> How any issue is treated in the public frenzy that the media might help to enflame is not a reflection of the actual context, commitment, complexities, or intentions of those who were participants in the forum out of which the media frenzy grew. Public access to information is a much better goal of all aspects of free press and publicity than the role that the media now seems to play in the lives of people seeking information. The media shapes those issues, which are being presented in accordance to the currency of their sensationalism with complete disregard for the actual events being reported and the extent to which the events are located within the trajectories of Islamic history and experience for over fourteen hundred years.[44]

It is clear that Wadud defines media broadly but also that she has an expectation of impartiality and objectivity that seems unrealistic. Her frustration with the aftermath of the controversy explains her later reluctance to be interviewed and thus repeatedly represented and shaped by someone else's perspective and agenda. Regarding the prayer, there is one notable exception, an article based on an interview with her, written by Thomas Bartlett for the *Chronicle of Higher Education*. The fact that the *Chronicle* is not a news media outlet but rather a weekly paper, primarily read by people in academia, may have persuaded her to agree to this interview.[45] Wadud is also at the center of a 2006 documentary titled *The Noble Struggle*, directed by Elli Safari.[46] Both Bartlett's and Safari's representations of Wadud and the prayer are discussed below.

Wadud's agreement to serve as the leader of the prayer and to give the khutbah was in many ways a logical culmination of her work as a scholar and activist. Nomani tells us that Wadud accepted the invitation without hesitation. Wadud reportedly had reservations and concerns for her safety, and she anticipated controversy and debate. In Wadud's account we are taken from her affiliation with the Progressive Muslim Union in 2004 (and her subsequent disagreement with them) through the planned conference at Harvard (which never took place) to a renewed invitation to lead a prayer and give the khutbah in New York. Wadud points to the central role of Nomani, who according to Wadud "was on a tour for her recent book publication, and was able to secure needed funds from her publishers, in order to actually assist the plan to come to fruition."[47] Later Wadud acknowledges Ahmed Nassef, Asra Nomani, and Saleemah Abdul-Ghafur as the organizers who communicated with Wadud in preparation for the event.[48]

In her narrative Wadud's suspicion of journalists is confirmed when she is confronted with their presence not just at the location of the prayer event but in front of her, effectively blocking the direction of the qibla. She writes:

> I took self-responsibility at that moment to remember what the prayer represents: an act of devotion to That which is beyond our eyes' vision, as could be disturbed by the weakness of our hearts. If we settle our hearts back to Allah, then and only then can we complete the worship as intended. That is what I did. The cameras and the media disappeared before my heart and no longer presented a distraction to my eyes.[49]

Wadud's dread of another media frenzy, mirroring the one following her khutbah in 1994, had moved her to focus all her energies on the preparation of the khutbah and keeping with traditional prayer procedure.

In the last paragraph of her prayer story, Wadud also points to the fact that she viewed the media presence and attention as a disturbance and an invasion of sacred space and that it took all her energy to concentrate on leading the prayer: "I was not facing the media, they were inappropriately located in the direction of the prayer, as the organizers later told me, because they could not be controlled."[50] In the passage quoted above Wadud has described how she managed to turn her attention away from the media representatives and back to the ritual at hand. In reflecting on the role of sensationalism in shaping her public image, she writes:

> To many people, worldwide, I am only known through sensationalist controversies. That is understandable. I hope they will eventually come to understand that sensationalist responses to certain public actions are not the basis of, and never can be the goal of, my identity quest as a female in Islam. For this reason I rejected all invitations to do further interviews relating to the congregational prayer in New York City when those invitations were clearly expecting to gain more attention by publishing articles and presenting news programs focused on the event just because it had gained such attention. That is an unfortunate consequence of addressing issues of gender within today's climate of sensationalism.[51]

Her critique of media sensationalism mirrors her earlier critique of intra-Muslim debates focusing on the form rather than the substance of her sermons, both in 1994 and in 2005. The media coverage of Wadud at the prayer event confirms her fear that the symbolic significance of the woman-led prayer would effectively erase her important and more complex interpretive contribution and the larger exegetical implications of her work.

"The Quiet Heretic": Amina Wadud in the Media

Compared to Nomani, Wadud and her role as the leader of her prayer received only brief news media attention, while international and American debates among Muslims continued for quite some time, with her at the center.[52] In part the lesser degree of media attention is related to Wadud's refusal to act as a source for journalists after the prayer. A brief analysis of two articles in the *New York Times*[53] and a longer feature in the *Chronicle of Higher Education* provide some comparison to Nomani's media representations.[54] The two *New York Times* articles by Andrea Elliott mention Wadud and Nomani as central to the prayer. Nomani comes across as the organizer, while Wadud is described as a professor at an American university. In the first article, Wadud is "Ms. Wadud"; in the second one she becomes "Dr. Amina Wadud.' Confusing prayer leadership and Friday khutbah, Elliott writes:

> It was not the first time Dr. Wadud, an Islamic studies professor at Virginia Commonwealth University had led a mixed-gender prayer, she said: she gave a sermon at a Friday prayer in South Africa in 1994. Yesterday, her sermon centered on the idea that men and women should treat each other as equals, and not presume Allah to be male.[55]

The *Chronicle* feature is more elaborate and proudly declares that Wadud had previously rejected most interview requests. Bartlett shares with the reader Wadud's conversion story and feels the need to mention that she is African American, her age, and the fact that she wore "a lime-green head scarf and pink slippers"[56] when he interviewed her at her house, surrounded by piles of paper from chapters of her new book, *Inside the Gender Jihad*. In this academy-oriented publication, he insists on calling her Ms. Wadud instead of Dr. Wadud. He takes her scholarly work seriously but also uses much space to discuss threats and safety concerns after the prayer and incorporates opinions on the prayer from scholars and Wadud's daughter.

The article stays clear of generalized statements about Muslim women and does not allow itself to participate in the reproduction of stereotypes. Statements are specific, attributed to interviewees, and contextualized. The title, however, evokes the same imagery we find in media depictions of Nomani—a lone heroine and heretic.

It is possible to conclude that the fact that Wadud is a scholar and that she is American-born and African American makes it difficult for the media to allude to some of the staple stereotypes about Muslim women. Wadud is not exotic and foreign, certainly not silent and oppressed, and in her language of resistance there are strong notes of an older struggle for civil rights and racial justice. In applying a social justice discourse to gender issues in Islam and in her attempt to resolve the "issues" from within the Islamic tradition, she defies simplistic representations. Except for the fact that she, at least at the time, wore hijab, journalists were harder pressed for ways to make her the Muslim other in conventional ways.

Wadud's suspicion of and reluctance to participate in media representation is obvious from many of her statements. Nevertheless, she has been an active participant in the ongoing negotiation between American Muslim women and the media. In publishing a memoir, however interlaced with scholarship, and in sharing personal experiences and reflections, she has made herself available for multiple readings of her life. Her book has received more scholarly than public attention, likely because of the complexity of her writing. Wadud also agreed to be filmed for a documentary focused on her.[57] The film's description exclaims:

On March 18, 2005, Amina Wadud shocked the Islamic world by leading a mixed-gender Friday prayer congregation in New York. THE NOBLE STRUGGLE OF AMINA WADUD is a fascinating and powerful portrait of this African-American Muslim woman who soon found herself the subject of much debate and Muslim juristic discourse. In defying 1400 years of Islamic tradition, her action caused global awareness of the struggle for women's rights within Islam but also brought violence and death threats against her.

Filmmaker Safari follows this women's rights activist and scholar around the world as she quietly but with utter conviction explains her analysis of Islam in the classroom, at conferences, in her home, and in the hair dresser's shop. Wadud explains how Islam, with its promise of justice, appeals to the African American community. And she links the struggle for racial justice with the need for gender equality in Islam.

> Deeply engaging, this film offers rare insights into the powerful con-
> nections between Islam, women's rights, and racial justice.

This description is sensational because it plays on established expectations: Wadud defies fourteen hundred years of Islamic tradition, singlehandedly and alone, like Nomani in her struggle for the soul of Islam. "Rare insight" might just allude to Wadud's reclusive attitude, but it simultaneously evokes images of hidden and veiled Muslim women and their secluded societies.

The film is powerful and well produced. It reflects a deep appreciation for Wadud's ideas and struggles. Safari portrays Wadud as standing alone as well but visually challenges some of the earlier representations of her in the media. One example is Wadud's choice to be filmed at home and at her hairdresser, without hijab, a choice consistent with a passage in her book in which she explains that she has come to the conclusion that hijab is not mandatory and that she consequently wears it only for official occasions.[58]

Wadud's presentation in various media is a list of exceptions, in reality and in representation. As a scholar, she is uncomfortable with reductionist images and impatient dealing with the consequences of such reductionism. Her choice to largely avoid participation in media production (except for her book and the documentary) and the sensationalism surrounding discussions on Islam and gender make her less interesting from a media perspective. The issue of race and racialized representation certainly also plays an important role. Whereas Nomani happily participates in media events and the production of images, Wadud secludes herself, thus leaving the playing field to others.

"Courageous for a Muslim Woman": Mohja Kahf

The media presence and engagement of Mohja Kahf, a fellow academic as well as fiction writer and poet, is an example of how the deeper understanding of media dynamics and the production of constructed representations can be handled in a very different way. Kahf was involved in the events leading up to the prayer, most notably as one of those who participated in Nomani's defiant march on the mosque in Morgantown in 2004.[59] Kahf also wrote a poem, published on MuslimWakeUp the day before the prayer:

> *Dedicated to the hesitators who care about the issue*
> *but won't declare their support for today's Jum'ah.*
>
> By Mohja Kahf

The Waiting Room

Dare? Go? Act? No,
let's wait. Maybe
this valiant, embattled task
has integrity. In theory,
we're with you, but.
We're waiting for the perfect time
We're waiting for the leaders without flaw
Maybe it is the revolution, but.
Where's the guarantee?
We shall risk nothing.
Should it prove true,
we'll call it ours and say,
We believed with the believers!
Here in the Waiting Room.[60]

Tinged with her characteristic humor, the poem teases those who are not willing to take any risks on the question of whether Muslim women can and should lead congregational prayers.

In an article in the *New York Times*, published in 2007, veteran writer on American Muslims, Neil MacFarquhar, draws on one of Kahf's poems, "Hijab Scene #7," to draw attention to Kahf and her work.[61] The article is titled "She Carries Weapons; They Are Called Words" and describes Kahf's poetry, her reception at a poetry reading at the Arab Cultural and Community Center in New York, and her own thoughts on her writing. MacFarquhar, too, as if to demonstrate the news media's disregard for academic achievements, insists on calling her Ms. Kahf, despite her Ph.D. degree and her position as associate professor at the University of Arkansas, where she teaches comparative literature. Otherwise, MacFarquhar's portrayal attends to the complexity of Kahf's writings as well as to her position vis-à-vis American Muslim communities. In a move reminiscent of Bartlett's description of Wadud's clothing during an interview, MacFarquhar finds it necessary not only to address the issue of hijab but also to draw a direct connection between Kahf, the author, and the protagonist of the story, Khadra Shami. He explains some of Kahf's considerations in Khadra's trajectory and her decision that Khadra "remain veiled, at least along the lines that Ms. Kahf is herself—she covers her hair for public appearances, but lets it slip off in restaurants and is less than scrupulous about it on hot days."[62]

Otherwise, MacFarquhar attends to the issues that Kahf brings up in the interview, including the emergence of American Muslim literature as a genre, the complications of writings from an "ethnically" determined space with all the expectations from both American audiences and Muslim communities, and, again, Kahf's satirical perspective on the stereotype of the Muslim woman. The article also mentions Kahf's infamous "Sex and the Ummah" column on MuslimWakeUp and describes it as "rather graphic" and as having "drawn ire, even a death threat, from the orthodox."[63]

Kahf also appears in a 2003 article on Arab American writers, by Dinitia Smith, published in the *New York Times*. Smith chooses to describe her as follows: "The women's writing is increasingly daring. Mohja Kahf, a Syrian-American, considers herself an Islamic feminist. She is photographed wearing a traditional head scarf, but her work is explicitly erotic, courageous for a Muslim woman and virtually unthinkable in the previous generation."[64] A Muslim woman with a headscarf who writes things erotic *and* courageous *and* considers herself an Islamic feminist is still considered a surprise and a challenge to the stereotype of "the Muslim woman." Ironically, the article ends with an excerpt from a poem by Suheir Hammad rejecting the exoticizing of herself and other women of color: "Don't wanna be your exotic / like some delicate fragile colorful / bird imprisoned caged."[65]

Kahf herself has written articles for major newspapers, notably an opinion piece for the *Washington Post*, published in October 2008.[66] The article, titled "Spare Me the Sermon on Muslim Women," powerfully refutes many of the common stereotypes of Muslim women and satirically exaggerates her own obsession with scarves. Moving from a description of her scarf collection and her determination to never save money on a great scarf to describing the joy of covering body and hair for the daily prayers to her own story of selecting her husband to her legal right to sexual satisfaction, Kahf embodies her conviction of the need for dual critique by pointing out her critique of "Muslim misogyny (which at times is almost as bad as American misogyny)." In a short list, she brings in all the arguments, historical, legal, and exegetical, for why Islam is a great religion for women and ends by saying, "Yet even all that gorgeous history pales when I open my closet door for the evening's pick: teal georgette, pink-and-beige plaid, creamy fringed wool or ice-blue organza? God, why would anyone assume I would want to give up such beauty? I love being a Muslim woman."

The online responses to the article ranged from applauding her for her courage to challenge stereotypes to angry accusations that she did not want to see the inherent misogyny of Islam. The literary tool of exaggeration and satire was lost on many of the commentators. Kahf's attempt to change perceptions by engaging with them satirically allows for a direct connection to the larger issue of the politics and political uses of Muslim women's representation in the media.

Writing about American Muslim Women

In addition to newspaper articles and documentaries, journalists have portrayed and described American Muslim women in a number of popular nonfiction books. As in Barrett's chapter on Nomani, we find third-person portraits of a number of women discussed here.

Donna Gehrke-White, in a book with the unfortunate and misleading title *The Face behind the Veil: The Extraordinary Lives of Muslim Women in America*,[67] provides thoughtful and nuanced portraits of several women. In her category "The Changers" we meet again Sarah Eltantawi, Ingrid Mattson, Azizah al-Hibri, and Riffat Hassan. In each vignette Gehrke-White provides a biographical sketch and some discussion of what it is the woman in question is trying "to change." Linda Brandi Cateura's *Voices of American Muslims* contains among its twenty-three profiles one of Asma Gull Hasan in which Cateura asks Hasan whether American Muslim women will have leading religious positions in their communities and whether Hasan would consider marrying a non-Muslim man.[68]

Geneive Abdo's *Mecca and Main Street: Muslim Life in America after 9/11* contains a chapter titled "Women in the Changing Mosque," which juxtaposes Ingrid Mattson's approach to reform in Muslim communities, including awareness building of the marginalization of women in mosques, with Wadud and the 2005 prayer. The chapter does not mention Nomani or her role in the event but instead describes the various (mostly negative) reactions to the prayer and seems to blame Wadud for the furor it caused.[69] In an op-ed in April 2005, Abdo had accused Wadud of willingly accepting the threats to her life and of potentially producing a backlash for Muslim women "struggling to win new freedoms."[70] Another chapter in Abdo's book, "The Child-Bride in the Dix Mosque," describes customary marriage among Yemeni immigrants in Dearborn and the oppressive structures and stubborn clinging to "tradition" of the mosque's imams.[71]

In Krista Tippett's *Speaking of Faith* (based on the NPR radio show she hosts) we briefly meet Ingrid Mattson and Leila Ahmed in a discussion of

Muslim women's rights and representations and the potential for reform in Islam.[72]

At least one Muslim writer has edited a comparable collection of portraits: Melody Moezzi's *War on Error: Real Stories of American Muslims*[73] features a chapter on Nomani in which Moezzi not only retells the story of Nomani's activism and trials but also reports that Nomani invited her to lead a prayer in her (Nomani's) backyard, which made her realize a potential in herself she did not know she had. Nomani is portrayed yet again as controversial but also as courageous, honest, and fighting for the rights of all Muslim women.

Politics and Political Uses of Representation(s)

Kahf and others have identified the colonial and imperial purposes of the image of the veiled, oppressed, and secluded Muslim woman as well as the constructedness of that image. Kahf has also pointed to the disconnect between the image and the realities of Muslim women's lives and the fact that struggles to acknowledge and change Muslim women's oppression past and present could not draw their analytical strength or arguments from Western representations of Muslim women.

The 2005 prayer and the writings of American Muslim women as part of the recent past need to be examined in terms of their connection to the direct political uses of the image of the Muslim woman, specifically for the "War on Terror" and the wars in Afghanistan and Iraq. Many scholars have critiqued the abuse of media representations of oppressed Muslim women for the public preparation for war and the need to liberate them. This rhetorical marriage of occupation and liberation is not new, as pointed out by Leila Ahmed in her analysis of British colonial ideologies and rhetoric justifying the colonization of Egypt and other Muslim territories. Ahmed has also pointed us to the connection between Western feminism and colonialism.

Charlotte Weber has offered a nuanced portrait of feminist Orientalism in the early twentieth century as embodied in the work of the International Alliance of Women, thereby adding more detailed historical insight into the workings of explicitly feminist groups at the end of the colonial period. Taking Ahmed's 1982 article and Edward's Said's *Orientalism* (1979) as starting points for her inquiry, Weber comes to the conclusion that while Western feminists assessed women's power and authority based on their own perceptions of access to the public sphere, overlooking the degree of social influence Muslim women possessed and failing to see Muslim women's own assessment of their status and needs, she also argues that some Western feminists traveling in the Middle East formed lasting and powerful relationships with Muslim women, born of a genuine if naive understanding of female solidarity.[74] However, ultimately, she contends, Western feminists, based on their comparative "liberatedness," failed to recognize the opportunity to more radically critique Western patriarchy and develop broader definitions of feminism.[75]

Scholars such as Lila Abu-Lughod,[76] miriam cooke,[77] Saba Mahmood, and Charles Hirschkind[78] have critically assessed the construction of Afghan women as pawns in the weeks and months leading to the war in Afghanistan in 2001 but going back to 1997 when the Feminist Majority "adopted the cause of Afghan women."[79] Abu-Lughod's reflections, aptly titled "Do Muslim Women Really Need Saving?" ponders the ethical dilemmas of a feminist academic and anthropologist in taking sides for or against the "liberation" of Muslim women and powerfully critiques the construction of a picture in which there can only be two choices. Abu-Lughod concludes by cautioning that feminists of the twenty-first century should not replicate the projects of colonial powers or Christian missionary women of the nineteenth century and instead creatively consider ways to change geopolitics in order to achieve a world in which Afghan women can have "safety and decent lives."[80]

The juxtaposition of the oppressed lives of women in Afghanistan and Iraq and the prevalence of practices such as "honor killings"[81] and violence against women with the lives and struggles of American Muslim women, even when it changes the perceptions of the latter, still serves political purposes outside their control and interests. The humanization of American Muslims, especially women, and the recognition of their Americanness afford them a measure of real-life improvement and protections. However, framed representations such as the lone hero, the rebel, and the Hijabi with a voice also serve as representational exceptions to the rule. With generally good intentions of "normalizing" American Muslims, journalists, too, participate in the flattening of critical discourses and nuanced readings of the realities of American Muslim lives.

American Muslim women are increasingly also agents of media representations. They are part of transnational and international women's activist and communication networks, and they are uniquely situated to address issues of media representation and politics. They can be torn between outside expectations and inside critique, as well as between commitments to American Muslim minority communities and worldwide communities of Muslim women. In their quest for self-representation they sometimes run the risk of othering other Muslim women by being taken as the exception to the rule or by reemphasizing the oppression and silence of Muslim women elsewhere.

The representation of American Muslim women in various forms of media is complex and nuanced and should always be assessed in particular contexts and with concrete examples. Acutely aware of the widespread perceptions of Muslim women as oppressed and silent, some have chosen to actively participate in media production and to challenge what they see as misrepresentations and stereotypes. The organizers of and participants in the woman-led prayer enacted the prayer as a ritual performance but also as a media performance. Nomani, Wadud, and Kahf (as well as other American Muslim women) are simultaneously constructed as media personalities by others and attempting to construct themselves as such. Their agency in defining media representations of themselves as American Muslim women is limited by the existing representational models as the antidote to other Muslims.

Both Nomani and Wadud (and Kahf in her novel and poetry) have contributed to a particular genre of American Muslim writings, namely, memoirs and autobiographical narratives. These texts follow a somewhat different pattern of representational politics, and their authors have to negotiate the politics of the liberal publishing market.

8

Memoirs, Narratives, and Marketing

We are Muslim women who have cleared our own paths and created ourselves both because and in spite of Islam and other Muslims. Our American Muslim identity is not linear, nor can it be shed or separated. It just is.

Saleemah Abdul-Ghafur, *Living Islam Out Loud*

This collective self-description is as much descriptive as it is programmatic. *Living Islam Out Loud*, published in 2005 and edited by Abdul-Ghafur, one of the organizers of the woman-led prayer, joined a growing number of similar texts—memoirs and personal or autobiographical narratives written by American Muslim women. Reading a number of such texts together reveals that these works form a subgenre of "speaking out" literature that is united by three broad goals: challenging and changing monolithic representations of Muslim women, engaging and negotiating Muslim communities in North America, and creating, defining, and saving American Muslim women's Muslim faith identities. In these three goals they mirror the woman-led prayer event, and, not incidentally, several of the organizers of and participants in the prayer have contributed narrative pieces to this genre. In the last section of this chapter I discuss the connection of these three goals with the dynamics and politics of the liberal American publishing market. The materials analyzed here constitute another aspect of American Muslim women's engagement with media production and representation. The arguments put forward thus offer an extension and deeper engagement with issues of media politics and representations.

American Muslim women have written and published autobiographical and personal narrative accounts for more than a decade but in increasing quantities since September 11, 2001. This speaking out literature is produced by American Muslim women who feel the need to claim their voices, to speak for themselves, and to "speak out loud." Here I want to focus on several of these texts: Asra Nomani's *Standing Alone in Mecca* (2005), Asma Gull Hasan's *American Muslims: The New Generation* (1999) and *Why I am a Muslim: An American Odyssey* (2004), Leila Ahmed's *A Border Passage: From Cairo to America—A Woman's Journey* (1999), Sumbul Ali-Karamali's *The Muslim Next Door: The Qur'an, the Media, and That Veil Thing* (2008), and a number of edited collections that either consist of such narratives or contain several texts in this genre: *Living Islam Out Loud: American Muslim Women Speak* (2005), *Muslim Women Activists in North America: Speaking for Ourselves* (2004), *Shattering the Stereotypes: Muslim Women Speak Out* (2005), and *Voices of Resistance: Muslim Women on War, Faith, and Sexuality* (2006). While the number of books published on Islam and Muslims has certainly increased exponentially since 2001, along with and prompted by a surge in public interest, it is still worth asking, Why do American Muslim women write and publish personal and autobiographical texts?

Challenging (and Changing) Public Perceptions

The texts convey a sense of urgency, a need to write. Why? One important factor is that the authors recognize the power of existing stereotypes over them and other Muslim women and the political violence inflicted on Muslims in America and the world. Many, especially contributors to the edited collections, preface their stories with reflections on the pervasive stereotypes of Muslim women. Fawzia Afzal-Khan writes that a "crucial aim of this anthology, therefore, is to enlighten readers, both Western and Muslim, about the wide array of thought and behavior embodied in the concept 'Muslim Woman'—so that its monolithic quality may be shattered to reveal the complexities and variety that no such single label can justly contain."[1] Similarly, Katherine Bullock has collected stories of American Muslim women activists because "autobiography is one of the best ways to break down stereotypes. . . . In the West, . . . there is a generic image of what it means to be a Muslim woman—oppressed, silenced, subservient—the placard of 'the veiled woman' that serves to efface individuality and uniqueness."[2] Saleemah Abdul-Ghafur contends in the introduction to *Living Islam Out Loud* that "very rarely do we encounter empowering images of American Muslim women"[3] and declares that one of the main purposes of her anthology is to "humanize American Muslim women."[4]

miriam cooke has argued that it is meaningful to merge the words *Muslim* and *woman* into *muslimwoman* in order to point to the power of an image that "is not a description of reality; it is the ascription of a label that reduces all diversity to a single image." cooke goes on to argue that this label has been employed by neo-Orientalists and Islamists alike to restrict Muslim women but that it is also used as a tool of empowerment by Muslim women.[5] The women writers explored here all reject the label "muslimwoman" and its descriptive power. Instead, they "illuminate the women's unique struggles, dreams, goals, triumphs, and challenges."[6]

The goal of "shattering stereotypes" and replacing them with a multivocal and multilayered picture of the diverse realities, ideas, and interpretations of Muslim women is evident and sometimes even achieved in the edited collections. By their very nature, anthologies of fiction, nonfiction, poetry, and life stories lend themselves to such diversification. Hala Halim, in a review of *Shattering the Stereotypes* contends that the collection of texts "largely succeeds in modifying stereotypes" but warns that the "Muslim Women" in the title may risk "operating from within the terms of discussion dictated by Western neocolonial discourse."[7] This is indeed a larger question and one that needs to be answered whenever the label "Muslim woman" is employed. What are the boundaries of the term? Who decides who is and is not a Muslim woman?

The single-author books approach the goal of changing public perceptions of Muslim women in significantly different ways. Consequently, the books by Hasan, Nomani, Ali-Karamali, and to a degree Ahmed, instead of emphasizing the diversity of Muslim women and their perspectives, experiences, and lives, set out to introduce the reader to "Islam" by presenting their own version of what Islam is. Interweaving information about Islam, sometimes drawing on scholars and scholarly literature, with personal experiences of growing up Muslim, living within Muslim communities, and engaging in Islamic ritual practice, these books attempt to balance authenticity with more or less normative claims about Islam. The discussions of women's Islam is at the same time intended to challenge stereotypes of Islam as an inherently misogynist religion and help negotiate for the authors that their identities as Muslims and women are not in conflict with each other.

The most common strategy to this end is to separate Islam from Muslims, that is, to discuss true, normative Islam as significantly different from the history, practices, and interpretations of Muslims. We have encountered this separation of Islam from Muslims or true Islam from Muslim interpretations in previous chapters in a variety of contexts. The authors of the memoirs and personal stories, too, convey the message in their texts that Islam is good, gender just, perfect, and ethical, while Muslims can and should be criticized for sexism, gender injustices, chauvinism, and male-centered discourses.

Nomani writes, "This book is a manifesto of the rights of women based on the true faith of Islam"[8] and "The prophet was indeed the Muslim world's first feminist."[9] Toward the end of her book, in a chapter titled "Harvesting the Fruits of the Pilgrimage," Nomani concludes that the "freedom of movement, thought and voice" has afforded her the opportunity to be closer to her faith. And: "When I confronted the traditions in my Muslim society, I discovered that the gem of Islam is quite pure and good below the layers of repressive sedimentation."[10]

Hasan's chapter titled "Because Islam Is a Woman's Religion"[11] walks the reader through several familiar arguments: there is an important difference between tradition (or culture) and Islam; the Prophet Muhammad treated women well and as equals; men have historically misread passages of the Qur'an for their own advantage; it is a sign of independence and personhood that Muslim women keep their maiden names when they marry; and polygamy is not actually allowed by the Qur'an. She continues by pointing to historical role models like the Prophet Muhammad's first wife, Khadija,[12] and the mystic Rabi'a al 'Adawiyya.

Ali-Karamali takess a more nuanced approach: "There exists no single Islam, no absolute interpretation of it. . . . This book describes the basic beliefs and practices of mainstream Muslims throughout the world, illustrated with vignettes of life as an American Muslim." Acknowledging the diversity of opinions and the existence of interpretive disagreements among Muslims, she continues, "When faced with a plurality of views, I try to choose the majority view or, simply my own view. My goal is to describe what is common to all Muslims and what is open to various interpretations."[13] However, faced with the daunting task of trying to address all common stereotypes and misperceptions, Ali-Karamali's text also engages in the construction of Muslim "mainstream" and "majority" views.

In an interesting departure from her earlier work, and drawing on her childhood experiences in an Egyptian Muslim family, Leila Ahmed, in her memoir *A Border Passage*, describes the existence of a specific kind of Islam, women's Islam, and how it is distinct from men's Islam:

And the women had, too, I now believe, their own understanding of Islam, an understanding that was different from men's Islam. . . . Islam, as I got it from them, was gentle, generous, pacifist, inclusive, somewhat mystical—just as they themselves were. . . . Being Muslim was about believing in a world in which life was meaningful and in which all events and happening permeated with meaning. Religion was above all about inner things. The outward signs of religiousness, such as prayer and fasting, might be signs of a true religiousness but equally well they might not. They were certainly not what was important about being Muslim.[14]

Here Islam is associated with "feminine" characteristics and the dichotomous relationship between men's and women's Islam is an indication of their unequal value. Ahmed describes men's Islam as obsessed with scripture and proper ritual while failing to appreciate the inner dimensions of faith and the fluidity and inclusiveness of oral discourses and women's community.[15] While on the one hand reinvesting the gendered dichotomies of women's and men's Islam with new meaning, namely, by declaring the attributes of women's Islam to indeed be positive, the dichotomy itself is reinforced. In an analysis of Ahmed's memoir, Bernadette Andrea has argued that Ahmed uses the harem metaphor surrounding her construction of women's Islam in order to challenge the Orientalism of Western liberal feminism and "with other Islamic feminists" develops "the counterparadigm of 'the western women's harem.'"[16]

In presenting this true and gender-just Islam in connection with their personal stories, the authors do more than claim the right to tell their own stories, use their own voices, and share their own experiences in order to change the perception of Muslim women. They also describe their faith journeys, real and internal travels through doubts, convictions, challenges, and transformations.

Journeys to and through Faith

Journeys are personal, and the authors share their doubts, their failures, and their inner struggles with the reader. In all the texts there is an emphasis on the struggle to surrender to the will of God and to simultaneously come to this surrender on their own terms.

Nomani's journey is a literal one. She takes the reader on her pilgrimage to Mecca, which is at the same time a journey through her doubts and fears. She writes, "This is a tale of a journey into the sacred roots of Islam to try and discover the role of a Muslim woman in the modern global community. . . . I was very much at odds with my religion. But instead of turning away from Islam, I decided to find out more about my faith."[17] At the conclusion of her journey, Nomani has defined her life purpose as dedicated to good,[18] and she has decided to raise her son, one of the reasons her authenticity and authority were questioned by Muslim communities, as a Muslim. She concludes, "By traveling with me on my pilgrimage as a baby, Shibli embodied for me the essence of Mecca."[19] Leila Ahmed, in a glowing review of the book in the *Washington Post*, contends that "Nomani's quest to discover if she can commit herself to her faith without compromising her ideals of justice and equality is also profoundly shaped by the ideals of today's liberal America." She describes Nomani as "just part of a growing trend of progressive thought and activism among American Muslims coming of age in these times, compelled to renegotiate their religious heritage in the shadow of 9/11."[20]

Samina Ali, a contributor to *Living Islam Out Loud*, describes her spiritual journey, which leads through a "proper Muslim" childhood, an arranged marriage and its subsequent failure, to her realization that she cannot allow her community to define her Muslim identity. Blamed for the failure of her marriage, she embarks on a life journey that leads her to marry a non-Muslim man from outside her ethnic background. It is not until after she faces a near-death experience that she, as she indicates in the title of her essay, meets God.[21]

Sarah Eltantawi, coorganizer of the 2005 prayer, finds herself on a similar journey, but hers is triggered by the events of September 11. Her spiritual journey centers on the metaphorical image of a forest, beautiful, haunting, and pure, and the weeds that block her view toward the truth. While defending Islam and Muslims publicly, she negotiates her inner tension between longing for God and the many disconcerting realities of Islam: "So there is a forest, a world, a path, a magnetic pull, and it is called Islam, and I am in it surrounded by weeds. At that point in time when I actually clear the Islamic forest for myself of the weeds of sexism, chauvinism, and judgment, what will be left?"[22]

In a moving story of her struggle with surrendering to God, Inas Younis describes her journey from despairing over the autism diagnosis of her young son to the realization that her son may lack the faculties of free will and consciousness but that he is a reminder of God's grace and will. After a tearful struggle to surrender and offer God everything in her life in return for her son's healing, Younis experiences a moment of peace, with her son in her arms, and concludes:

> And I thanked God for giving me the courage to enjoy that moment and every other moment from then on. I thanked God for the permission to make my own decisions without the sanction of some official religious authority. I thanked God for the realization that everything I had ever wanted and asked for was encapsulated in that which I prostrated to Him every time I prayed—my mind—and I thanked Him not only for the permission, but the command to use it.[23]

Here the struggle to surrender is not primarily (and sometimes not at all) related to the position of women in Muslim societies, the question of gender equality, or anything to do with being a woman. At the same time, and if we allow ourselves to extend the boundaries of gendered thinking, each of those other stories also has everything to do with being a woman.

Mohja Kahf's contribution to *Living Islam Out Loud*, "The Muslim in the Mirror," is a story of self-transformation as well. Much like her journalistic pieces, her poetry, and the semiautobiographical novel *The Girl in the Tangerine Scarf* (2006), this essay demonstrates Kahf's way with language, her ability to convey serious and indeed urgent meaning combined with hints of sarcasm and rhetorical exaggeration. Carol Fadda-Conrey has argued that the poetry of Mohja Kahf (and the Palestinian American poet Suheir Hammad) can be read as poetic autobiography, not because "these two poets *consciously* incorporate elements of their personal lives into their poetry or that poems are *purposefully* shaped to act as direct reflections of their lives." Instead, she suggests, the poems are "informed by the poets' experiences as women of color living in the United States."[24] In other words, it is the embeddedness of Kahf and her work in community structures and the politics of the larger society that inform her personal perspectives and experiences as an American Muslim woman.[25] And indeed Kahf's story of transformation takes her from being disappointed with all Muslims to affirming that even though she might have had to find new communities, alliances, and support systems, she is "back and kicking" in her quest to take responsibility as a member of her Muslim community.[26]

As Saleemah Abdul-Ghafur shares her own story of growing up in a Muslim family and marrying a Muslim man who turned out to completely undermine her sense of self and her self-perception as "outgoing, confident, and intelligent,"[27] we are brought back to the connection between identity and community. After seeking a divorce, Abdul-Ghafur has to rebuild her Muslim identity. She concludes her story:

> My path to God has been filled with doubts, difficulty, and ease. The more self-aware I become, the more I feel that I am aligned with God's best plan for me. My faith grows stronger, no longer weakened by external forces. Islam for me is surrender to divine will, spiritual practice, and cleansing my soul of hatred, resentment and jealousy. What I now know is that for me, Islam is fundamentally a way of life emanating from God's mercy. I have been endowed with the nature to live my absolute best life, and only I can determine what that means. The Prophet Muhammad taught us that "To know yourself is to know your Lord." And I am closer to my true self than I have ever been.[28]

Like Abdul-Ghafur, many of the women authors have "created their own paths and created themselves because and in spite of Islam."[29] An exploration of their narratives would not be complete without addressing the ways in which communities are experienced, formed, and negotiated in the texts.

Community Building and Belonging

American Muslim women authors come from a variety of backgrounds in terms of class, education, ethnicity or race, and indeed country. Some have immigrated to the United States and Canada as adults; others came as young children or were born in North America to immigrant parents. Yet others come from African American Muslim and Hispanic families or converted to Islam in various stages of their lives. Their journeys to and through faith are intricately linked with Muslim communities that embrace and support them on the one hand and reject, critique, and ridicule them on the other.

Many women describe the unfailing and loving support of their immediate families and the existence of both male and female role models for their own behaviors and endeavors in their lives. Nomani's parents have been such an unfailing source of support for her struggles, embodied in their acceptance of her and her child, their accompanying her on hajj with her baby son, her father's heated debates with the Morgantown mosque board, and her mother's joining Nomani in claiming prayer space in their mosque.[30]

Abdul-Ghafur describes her upbringing, largely defined by her mother, as protected and circumscribed but experiences a sense of clearing after her divorce when her mother reveals the reasons for her strict upbringing and encourages her to find her own path.[31] At the press conference before the Friday prayer, Abdul-Ghafur described herself as her father's daughter, proud to be a Muslim woman. Precious Rasheeda Muhammad describes how "her parents shaped her into the Muslim woman she is today." As African American Muslims they experienced Islam "as freedom, justice, and equality," offering "sorely needed structural solutions to combat the terror of America's racism." And later: "Through their practical application of Islam, I learned to stand firmly for justice from my father and to be innovative as an educator from my mother."[32] Others, like Khalida Saeed, after coming out as a lesbian to her mother, conclude that there are tight boundaries to family and community acceptance and that while her family may have accepted her not getting married, her opening up to her mother for the reason has left the family little choice but to try to control her while pretending that she is "normal."[33] Many authors reflect on the limitations and restrictions placed on them as Muslim girls growing up, attempting to protect their virginity and their reputation.

The communities the women grew up with are simultaneously comforting and restrictive. In several marriage and divorce narratives, for example, those of Samina Ali,[34] Manal Omar,[35] and Asra Nomani,[36] their communities ostracize and condemn them when they decide to seek divorces. Precious Rasheeda Muhammad, growing up in an African American Muslim community, reflects on the lack of acceptance by other Muslims and the constant challenges to her authenticity as a Muslim and her knowledge of Islam. This tension in American Muslim communities, sometimes described as a dividing line between "immigrant" and "black" Muslim communities, despite their intertwined American histories, and because of their competing claims to authenticity, is transcended in the 2005 prayer event and in many of the women's attempts at building their own communities.[37] Where existing communities, whoever constructs their boundaries and rules, cease to function as communities, the narratives tell us much about the creation and construction of new communities, communities in which the authors can feel they belong.

The woman-led prayer created not only a small and potentially temporary movement but also helped shape the outlines of interpretive communities, both for and against the prayer and women's prayer leadership more generally. Similarly, the bringing together of Muslim women in anthologies such as *Living Islam Out Loud*, *Voices of Resistance*, and *Shattering the Stereotypes* has created networks and communities of women who share similar values, interpretations, and, in many cases, commitments to various forms of activism.

Sarah Husain writes in the introduction to *Voices of Resistance*, "We construct here a multiple-voices text and many-sided vision of our lives as 'Muslim' women by forging ourselves into new creative collectivities. In this process, the category 'Muslim' is rendered anew through our own politics and cultural practices across gender, sexuality, race, and nation."[38]

Bullock constructs a historical narrative of Muslim women's exclusion from the public sphere and their confinement to the private sphere of the family, which she argues runs counter to the early Muslim community and Islamic history. The Muslim women activists in her collection "waste far too much energy combating negative pressures from their own communities — about the right to speak publicly, to be involved in community decision making, and to participate in activities outside the home."[39] The women in her book have overcome such pressures, often with support from husbands and fathers, and their stories are intended to — and have already — inspired other Muslim women and provided "role models for an ultra-marginalized group."[40]

Fawzia Afzal-Khan describes the impact of 9/11 on Muslim individuals and communities, the fear and intimidation but also the need to speak out, against wars and violence and for the creation of new knowledge of each other that in turn would create hope for a more peaceful world. Afzal-Khan, too, aspires to building community through her anthology:

> Indeed, by bringing together and juxtaposing the various Muslim female voices we have heard over these past two years, I hope to bring these voices into dialogue with one another. I hope too that something new and dynamic can emerge from this recognition of shared space and trajectory despite differences in outlook, culture, temperament, expression, and yes, the different relationship we each have to the concept of Islam and its place in our lives and identities.[41]

Abdul-Ghafur describes experiencing a new sense of community when she started working for *Azizah Magazine*, an American Muslim women's magazine first published in early 2001. Meeting other Muslim women with similar questions and ideas and their support eventually led to her participation in the Muslim Women's Freedom Tour and the woman-led prayer in New York City. The website associated with *Living Islam Out Loud* has sustained a virtual community of the contributors to the volume for several years, and, as posted on the site, some of the authors appeared together on radio programs, speaking tours, and events until at least summer 2009.[42]

The communities constructed by American Muslim women writers and activists are built on similar interpretations and values. Their "sisterhood of change" aspires to challenging existing and powerful patriarchal interpretations of the Qur'an and Islamic Law and to changing Muslim communities and societies in smaller and larger ways. In the process the authors engage in double critique or multiple critique, to use miriam cooke's term again, directed simultaneously toward Muslim communities and the surrounding non-Muslim society. Kahf has formulated her own experience of the pressures of this engagement:

> Neither will I swerve away from forthrightly criticizing my beloved faith community because such criticism is seen as aiding and abetting the bigots who are vying to close our charities, to criminalize our beliefs and practices and even our Arabic script, and to isolate us inside a barbed wire of hate. I will not circle my wagons around the mosque, will not yield in fearful worry to the entreaties of the wagon-circlers inside nor to the shouts of the hatemongers outside. I function within this double bind. I strategize around it with every move I make, every piece I write.[43]

However, this sisterhood of change also has limitations and boundaries. In the debate over the prayer women activists and writers were quickly condemned for their transgression of established norms and practices and for their open challenge to patriarchal structures and rules that the women (and men) perceived as stifling and "un-Islamic." It is in response to such accusations and in a reflex of self-defense that women writers draw boundaries and exclude others. In the introduction to *Living Islam Out Loud* Abdul-Ghafur outlines the boundaries of community for the book:

> Most of the books written about Islam and Muslims that are widely accessible to the mainstream are by people of other faith traditions. And many of the books written by American Muslims are about immigrants coping with assimilation, or else they offer conversion stories about why the grass is greener on the Muslim side. This book is about

the first true generation of American Muslim women. . . . We have never lived without Islam, nor did we grow up in Muslim majority countries.[44]

In Nomani's journey, especially during her pilgrimage, the lines are drawn between different kinds of Muslim women. She feels affinity and kinship with women in Mecca, sharing in her prayers and entrusting her son to them, so she can perform her prayers. They are beautiful and wear scarves in different colors.[45] A few days later in Medina it is a "phalanx of women shrouded in black nikab" that steps in front of them and prevents the group from entering the men's section of the Prophet's mosque to see the Prophet Muhammad's grave. They shout in Arabic, and it is in their "stiff spines and firm footing" that their negative intention is embodied. Nomani repeats her description of the women as a "phalanx of women in black" two more times on the same page.[46]

In Hasan's narrative, Muslim men who criticize her representations of Islam and her personal appearance are clearly wrong and even suspicious:

I had just finished speaking about Islam in America . . . , and something I had said had clearly upset this older Muslim man. In fact, I had upset about a half dozen men that evening. Judging from appearances, they were Arab Americans, ranging from in their thirties to one in his fifties at least, and they had waited till the end of my talk to bombard me.[47]

In another episode in her book, it is a Muslim woman who attacks her and whose clothing becomes relevant for her lack of authenticity: "'How dare you say that you are a Muslim feminist?' A young American Muslim woman in a turban-like hijab and skintight jeans was yelling at me. I was quite surprised to be the object of the clear scorn she had."[48]

While there are boundaries to the communities constructed by American Muslim women, it also becomes clear from the writings that communities' boundaries are fluid, negotiated at every turn. Sometimes they coincide with American Muslim institutions and organizations; at other times they are informal networks, formed and unformed in connection with an event, a cause, or over the Internet. Alliances are made and broken, agreements and disagreements negotiated and recorded. American Muslim communities appear as much more than collectives of people associated with mosques or community centers. They are religious, social, cultural, political, interpretive, spiritual, and textual, sometimes simultaneously.

ABOVE I HAVE OFFERED my reading of the three interconnected themes of representation, faith, and community. Especially if read as a genre of literature, speaking out texts by American Muslim women can also be approached from the perspective of literary criticism. We can connect thoughts on "third world" women's writings with the politics of representations and the liberal publishing market.

Life and Literature: Constructing the American Muslim Woman

Kahf has described the scripted options for the representations of Muslim women as "being either submissive nonentities or rebellious renegades—rebellious against their own Islamic world, that is, and conforming to Western gender roles."[49] Do the autobiographical narratives written by American Muslim women conform to either of these "choices"? Do American Muslim women writers inhabit a third space, in "the West" but not entirely of it? How aware are the authors of their contexts and larger frames of intra-Muslim, transnational, domestic, and global politics?

Literary analysis of texts produced by "third world" women writers, especially in light of feminist theory, has developed increasingly complex frameworks for "reading" such texts not only as products of individual authors but also as reflections of their embeddedness in communities and societies and forces of determination in the form of class, race, ethnicity, and gender. Amal Amireh and Lisa Suhair Majaj have chronicled their own experiences of tentative and scripted inclusion as Arab American women in the American academy. Scholars of literature, language, and culture, they found themselves included in academic discourses but confined by "discursive, institutional, and ideological structures" that determined "what they could say and whether they would be heard when they spoke."[50] Drawing on Chandra Talpade Mohanty, who wrote that "the existence of Third World women's narratives itself is not evidence of decentering hegemonic histories and subjectivities,"[51] the authors assert that it is necessary to study both the mediation and the production of texts by third world women for Western publication and consumption and the ways in which such texts are turned into commodities.[52] They also connect the interest in reading texts produced by women in and of the third world to waves of feminist interest in non-Western women and their expression. Second wave feminism in the 1970s and 1980s, with its "Sisterhood Is Global" slogan, emphasized the universal nature of human oppression and a universal human rights discourse as well. While it "encouraged cultural exchange," it also "resulted in an insensitivity to differences among women."[53] These limitations have also been recognized and critiqued in Womanist and Mujerista discourses within and beyond North America.[54]

Amireh and Majaj also make a convincing argument for the significance of literary texts and their significance for global communication and "the production of cultural representations" while calling for an acknowledgment of the power imbalance between the first and third worlds: "the latter produces creative texts that travel to the former to be studied and theorized."[55]

While some of the authors read here have come from third world countries or backgrounds, they are at the same time American. I employ a broad definition of what makes a woman an American Muslim woman; however, their American context is significant for their literary and textual production. Mais AlQutami has offered a comparative analysis of "feminist resistance in American women writers of color" by reading conceptualizations of "the veil" in the work of Mohja Kahf and "the house" in the work of the Chicana writer Sandra Cisneros. AlQutami argues that both Kahf and Cisneros are "U.S. Third World women," a term coined by Chela Sandoval,[56] because they "are perceived in the U.S. through their connection to the Third World and are united in oppositional activity against imperialism and colonialism."[57]

This definition, too, imposes boundaries on the women in question. How do American Muslim women writers fit? Describing them as U.S. Third World women writers erases those who are African American and who while "colored" and minority women are very much American, and it simultaneously erases those who are defined as white in the racialized identification system of the United States. The assumption that all minority women and women of color are united in opposition to imperialism and colonialism forces a political identification onto women who may or may not participate in activities or activism that could be described in this way, and it excludes the possibility of "noncolored" women's activism for the same goals.

The connection between women's writings and feminist readings or inclinations would be highly suspect for at least some of the writers, who often reject the "feminist" label. Stranded in a labyrinth of definitions, as-criptions, and assumptions, authors and readers have to face the fact that each designation carries political connotations, builds alliances, designates boundaries, and delineates activist projects.

Read together as a body of literature, tentatively held together by the designation of their authors as American Muslim women and the nature of their texts as autobiographical or personal narratives, what "picture" if any of the represented American Muslim women would emerge? If it is as-sumed that gender equality, women's rights, and self-empowerment are lib-eral and progressive values, then one striking assertion about all authors in this group would be their "progressiveness." They could certainly be read as "rebellious renegades," even though their numbers suggest that they are not quite such a lone a group of heroines as might appear in their news media representations. While at least some of the authors would reject the label "progressive," others might very well embrace it for its currency in discourses, politics, and, not least, marketing. Delineating the specific ap-proaches of individual authors to issues of gender, race, imperialism, and economic disparity would reveal that there is a wide spectrum of positions, intellectual as well as political. While Nomani probably fits the liberated, critical, and daring American Muslim woman schema best, Kahf uses ironic play with the categories themselves to undermine it. Bullock asserts that Muslim women activists in her volume "reject restrictive interpretations of their role as Muslim women," but they also espouse values such as family, sexual morality, and charity rather than revolutionary changes to Mus-lim communities and societies or global imperialism.[58] The contributors to *Voices of Resistance* on the other hand are united against "all wars the United States (and its allies) have been waging against people of color and the poor all over the globe,"[59] thus espousing an anti-imperialist agenda that recog-nizes exclusion and suffering based on color, race, poverty, and violence. At the other end of the spectrum, Hasan describes the Prophet Muhammad as a capitalist, who starting out as an orphan with nothing became the founder of a world religion, in the process emphasizing charity but not commu-nism.[60] These examples make clear that labels and categories always serve a purpose and that applying them to the authors and their texts may obscure more than it reveals.

One way in which autobiographical narratives of third world women are often read and indeed utilized is by conflating the text and the author, which in turn creates the impression that knowing one woman's story means knowing everything about her "culture," religion, or country. Alternatively, one can also read prepackaged assumptions about a woman's culture, religion, or country into the narrative, so as to reassert preconceived notions (and often prejudices) through reading the text. And while American Muslim women live and write in American contexts, their Muslim, that is, religious (and often ethnically "different") cultures and practices make them part of a category that can only be known in this "othering" way. This tendency is exacerbated by the selection of one text to speak for all American Muslim women, in a curriculum or syllabus, in a book club, or in the review section of the *New York Times*. The individual women writers and their stories become interchangeable as long as they serve their purpose of reinscribing Western superiority while allowing readers to express patronizing sympathy for the plight and/or liberating projects of Muslim women.

While othered and excluded, American Muslim women are also recognized as part of the American religious, cultural, and social landscapes, and they perceive themselves as such, as evident in their confident insistence on both their American and Muslim identities. Their progressive stances and values and their investment in their own "liberation" make them recognizable as American and thus remotely familiar as well. The greatest danger in representational readings of American Muslim women's texts is, then, that, consciously or not, they reformulate and legitimize stereotypes of Muslim women outside North America who are still the "other" women, oppressed, foreign, inaccessible, and silent.

The writings of American Muslim women can also be recognized as part of a longer tradition of American religious women's writings or testimony. Far from accepted and established in their respective faith traditions, especially Protestant Christian and later Catholic and Jewish, women wrote personal narratives and autobiographical texts to express their opinions and concerns and to demand change. In the words of Donna Freitas:

> The claim that women's stories have not been told, heard, or encouraged, that women's voices have either been ignored or stifled, is now a common cry and especially so among feminist theorists over the last several decades. This call has never rung more clearly than among women theologians and religion scholars, however, since institutional religion often bears the brunt of societal responsibility for patriarchy and the systematic marginalization of women, and whether women's voices are heard or silenced. The reason why there is an abundance

of women's voices, stories, and opinions available today—one might claim—is because western women, at least, began to refuse the part of the silent female. Feminist scholars pushed, prodded, retrieved, reworked, demanded, or simply decided what women had to say was smart, engaging, necessary and going to be heard, like it or not. Patriarchy would have to either step aside or make room.[61]

Freitas notably emphasizes that it was "western women" who paved the way and assumes that critiquing and challenging patriarchy is a precondition for their significance.

In a collection titled *In Our Own Voices*, edited by Rosemary Skinner Keller and Rosemary Radford Ruether,[62] chapters address and present writings by Protestant, Catholic, Jewish, black, and American Indian women. Muslim, Hindu, Buddhist, and other "other voices" are markedly absent. This absence is somewhat surprising given the decade or more of Muslim women scholars' inclusion in networks of religious feminists. A useful historical comparison to the trope of the liberated Muslim woman can be found in a particular literary genre of the nineteenth century: a nun's tale of escape and liberation. While such tales were typically not written by Catholic women or escaped nuns and their primary purpose was the production of anti-Catholic sentiments among Protestant Americans,[63] the script of religious oppression (including clothing) and necessary escape of a woman in search of liberation and self-fulfillment is reminiscent of similar stories about Muslim women. The power of this script becomes even more clear below in discussing the politics of publishing texts by (and about) American Muslim women writers.

The selection of texts and authors for this chapter was in part guided by their connection to the woman-led prayer and the nature of their texts. Naturally, many names and texts had to be excluded. However, one group, including the works of Irshad Manji, Ayaan Hirsi Ali, and Azar Nafisi, was excluded for more specific reasons.

"Other Muslim" Women Writers and the Politics of Empire

Although writers like Nomani, Hasan, and Ali-Karamali and editors like Afzal-Khan and Husain already span a wide religious, political, and cultural spectrum and although though their texts can potentially reinforce stereotypes and monolithic representations of Muslim women as much as they challenge them, the impact and reception of their writings pales in comparison to those of writers such as Irshad Manji (*The Trouble with Islam,* 2004), Azar Nafisi (*Reading Lolita in Tehran,* 2003) and Ayaan Hirsi Ali (*The Caged Virgin: An Emancipation Declaration for Women and Islam,* 2006; and *Infidel,* 2007). Sold in large numbers, read in book clubs and high schools, and reviewed in many major newspapers, these texts have enjoyed a popularity that can only be explained by a combination of superior marketing and catering to the established expectations of the marketplace.

Several scholars have taken up extensive critiques of some of these works. Their assessment of the entanglement of "critical" Muslim—or post-Muslim, as in the case of Hirsi Ali—women's writings shall be reproduced here in some detail, in order to situate them vis-à-vis the authors and texts analyzed in this chapter.

In writing about Nafisi, Manji, and Hirsi Ali, the anthropologist Saba Mahmood connects the service to Orientalist tropes of Islamic patriarchy in these autobiographical books (or "native testimonials") to their direct propagation of conservative political agendas in America and Europe and their legitimization of the discursive and actual confrontation between "Islam and the West."[64] Mahmood, however, is more troubled by their endorsement by a range of feminists in the United States.

> A number of well-known feminist critics have endorsed these books. . . . While the authentic 'Muslim woman's voice' partially explains the popularity these books command, it is the emancipatory model of politics underwriting these accounts that provokes such pathos and admiration among its feminist readership.[65]

Mahmood goes on to argue that the direct support of conservative political parties and think tanks for these works should give feminists pause and that it is in the omissions and inaccuracies in the texts that the accounts construct an essential opposition between "Western civilization and Muslim barbarism (or fundamentalism)"; and that feminist calls for women's rights have been utilized in neo-imperial projects to bring democracy and freedom to the Muslim world and its oppressed Muslim women.[66]

Mahmood contends by re-presenting her thesis, so forcefully formulated in her *Politics of Piety* (2005), that

> the liberal discourse on freedom, endemic to various traditions of feminist thought, blinds us to the power that nonliberal forms of reli-

giosity command in many women's lives. If indeed feminists are distancing themselves from the imperial politics of our times, it is crucial that these forms of religiosity be understood, engaged, and respected, instead of scorned and rejected as expressions of false consciousness.[67]

While not supported on the same scale, at least some of the texts discussed here can be criticized for working in a similar direction, while others intentionally challenge both feminist and imperial attempts at making the "Muslim woman" in their own image.

Sherene Razack makes a similar connection between feminism and empire, as well as feminism and racism, in her analysis of the wide success of Irshad Manji's work together with the writings of two Western feminists, Phyllis Chesler and Oriana Fallaci. Razack cautions feminists to question more forcefully their assumptions about Western, secular, liberal, and modernized societies in direct confrontation with culturally and religiously different Muslims whose practices are perceived and critiqued as archaic, premodern, and barbaric. She calls for a feminist reengagement with history, specifically, a historical record of alliances between feminist and colonial forces and their discourses.[68]

In a review article in the *Nation* in 2006, Laila Lalami exposes the work of Hirsi Ali and Manji as factually inaccurate and in the service of Western polemics as well as imperial interests in the Muslim world. She proposes that we "stop treating Muslim women as a silent, helpless mass of undifferentiated beings," have more dialogue and less polemic, and address those aspects of Muslim women's lives caused by underdevelopment, poverty, and illiteracy.[69]

Whether the writings of Nomani, Hasan, Abdul-Ghafur, and others, albeit on a smaller scale, also participate in the new and not so new construction and utilization of imperial feminism is in part connected to the marketing of their writings and how they fare in the liberal publishing market.

American Muslim Women and the Liberal Publishing Market

Whereas Nafisi, Manji, and Hirsi Ali have sold millions of copies of their books and have been translated into several languages, the authors discussed here have had to navigate and negotiate the American publishing market in significantly different ways. A look at their publishers reveals that here, too, the differences are vast and that there is at least a tentative correlation between the publishers that pick up their books and the dynamics of their representation. Asra Nomani is the only author whose book was published by a mainstream press, HarperCollins. Wadud has put in writing what others had suspected—that Nomani in fact used the woman-led prayer in 2005 as a marketing tool for her book.[70] The presence and active involvement of her HarperCollins agent at the prayer event may support this assumption as well. Nomani, who best fits the script of the lone rebel, challenging her community, religion, and culture to conform to her Western values and gender concepts, would have to be the most successful of the women writers in question. Asma Hasan's second book, *Why I Am a Muslim*, was published by Element, an imprint of HarperCollins, thus providing her with about equal market access and publicity. Harper reprinted the book in 2008 under the title *Red, White, and Muslim: My Story of Belief.*[71]

Several of the other volumes have come out from smaller or alternative publishers: *Voices of Resistance*, from Seal Press, a publisher of women's books broadly defined;[72] *Shattering the Stereotypes*, from Olive Branch Press, an imprint of Interlink Publishing, itself an alternative voice on the publishing market. Olive Branch Press has specialized in "socially and politically relevant non-fiction, concentrating on topics and areas of the world often ignored by the Western media."[73] White Cloud Press, the publisher of Sumbul Ali-Karamali's book, Continuum for Asma Hasan's first book, and Beacon Press for *Living Islam Out Loud* are all publishing houses with an interest in religion and religious perspectives. Finally, Katherine Bullock's volume was published by an academic press, the University of Texas Press.

While the authors have all found a publisher, the process itself can be complicated and involve negotiations of content as well as representation. In "On Being a Muslim Writer in the West," Kahf offers a glimpse of the process of writing for an audience and struggling to bring finished texts to that audience by way of convincing publishers of its marketability. In her familiar satirical exaggeration, and restating her thesis about the two available models for Muslim women, Kahf contends that Muslim women can indeed get published but only if they cater to one of the two prefabricated models of Muslim women: victim or escapee. She writes, "No matter how much a Muslim woman may have something different to say, by the time it goes through the 'machine' of the publishing industry, it is likely to come out the other end packaged as either a Victim Story or Escape Story."[74] For the first, the woman should be a "mute marionette" given voice to by a Westerner, have a "meek mother," a "forbidding father," a "rotten religion," a "cruel country," a "vile veil," and/or "stifled sexuality." The alternative escapee story needs at least some of the following elements: "brave battler of a bad birthright," "religion still rotten," "Uncle Sam will set her free," "veiling still vile," "sold on sex," and optionally "Zionist zinger."[75]

These expectations are independent of the identity of the author, Muslim or not, and they can be negotiated to a degree and sometimes even avoided. But, Kahf contends, publishers couch their demands for the presence of these tropes in the language of sales, success, and craft. Kahf then shares several examples of how texts written by Muslim and Arab American women are squeezed and fit into these molds. Authors have the choice to modify their work, reject a contract, or try to find another publisher.

Kahf also points out that the situation of Muslim women writers is complicated by "merciless Muslim readers" who criticize any hint of such representational politics without acknowledging the powerful forces at work and the dire lack of other choices if a woman wants to get published at all.[76] Kahf suggests, based on her own experience, that people should learn from other U.S minorities and their experiences, play with the stereotypes forced onto the stories, resist labels, engage in dual critique, build audiences, and have legal cover and the right to have at least partial control over the publishing process.[77]

Andrea Shalal-Esa asserts that Arab American writers "still have difficulty getting large book contracts with large mainstream publishers and if they do, they find that their works are heavily edited, if not outright censored."[78] She shares stories of authors who are permitted to write only in their "ethnic" or religious category and are required to avoid politically delicate topics such as the Palestinian-Israeli conflict and American foreign policy. Working with smaller and independent publishing houses can result in more editorial control for the author but almost always also means less access to big chain bookstores and the attached higher sales volumes.

THIS DISCUSSION RAISES the often-asked question whether media, including publishing houses, produce and then continually reproduce stereotypes and monolithic, simplified representations; whether they only yield to consumer pressure, thus reproducing and reinforcing existing representations; or whether it is all determined by political actors and interests. There is no simple answer to this question, and the above discussion has shown that interconnected forces and powers are at work in producing and reproducing representations of Muslim women. The writings of American Muslim women are part of this multifaceted landscape in which political projects, media representations, and public opinion inform each other and influence the lives of people here and elsewhere. The authors do not have control over how their texts are received, read, and understood. They offer diverse, complex, and contradictory perspectives on the lives of individual Muslim women in this country. By conforming to the dynamics and stipulations of the liberal publishing market they also have the potential to reinforce existing stereotypes and misperceptions. By presenting American Muslim women as standardbearers of change, transformation, and liberation *and* as critics of Western hegemony, Muslim patriarchy, and static interpretations of Islam, they paint a picture of themselves as liberated, modern, and understandable. The greatest concern, then, becomes the impact of these new representations on existing images of Muslim women elsewhere. Potentially, American Muslim women's freedom to represent, reinterpret, and liberate reinforces the image of the Muslim world as the site of women's oppression and degradation and of religious fanaticism and backwardness. More generally, Muslim women in America are facing the difficult challenge of keeping open the range of definitions of what it means to be Muslim, woman, and American—and many other things—all at the same time.

9

Covers and Other Matters
Concluding Thoughts

My body is not your battleground
My hair is neither sacred nor cheap,
neither the cause of your disarray
nor the path to your liberation
My hair will not bring progress and clean water
if it flies unbraided in the breeze
It will not save us from attackers
if it is wrapped and shielded from the sun

From "My Body is Not Your Battleground," by Mohja Kahf

These lines from Mohja Kahf's poem serve as the introduction to the concluding chapter of this book. Rather than summarize the many dimensions of the discussion offered in these pages, it develops thoughts on those who are not addressed in the book and are in need of further consideration.

The lines above address one important aspect of the study of Muslim women, whether in America or elsewhere, whether in the past or the present, which is the "issue" of hijab, or the Muslim headscarf. No other aspect of Muslim women's studies has received, deservedly or not, more public and scholarly attention. Maybe it is because the hijab is so visible, so obvious, and thus so easy to take as a starting point for thinking about women's roles and status in Muslim societies and communities. Maybe it is about the "mystique" of the veil, the things or human beings hiding or being concealed behind "it," and possibly it is as much about the gaze of those who want to know what is behind the veil. Scholars in many disciplines, feminist or otherwise, have written about the hijab. Increasingly, Muslim women have entered the debate even though it is still not carried out on their terms or within their intellectual parameters. The hijab as a symbol of Muslim women's oppression figures prominently in colonial projects, Muslim modernist reform agendas, and feminist rallies on behalf of Muslim women. Routinely, the hijab appears in newspaper articles, both visually and in description, whenever the topic relates to Muslim women. Each one of the above statements can be supported with a long list of academic articles and books addressing a facet of the topic.[1] Several texts have been dedicated specifically to the topic of hijab in the American context, while every other book on American Muslim women more generally contains at least some reference to the issue.[2]

In this book I have for the most part avoided discussion of hijab. However, many of the women authors discussed in these pages have made their reflections and thoughts on the issue an integral part of their writings. Guided by the way public and academic frames or frameworks determine to a large degree how we formulate our research and writing agendas, and equally often driven by ongoing intra-Muslim conversations about the politics and symbolism as well as the legal, spiritual, personal, and political pros and cons of hijab, Muslim women's writings reflect the many facets of hijab. My decision to avoid focusing on hijab was guided by concerns that it would inevitably distract from other, equally important aspects of Muslim women's ideas and works. Focusing on the outward, symbolic, and visual nature of hijab would have risked overshadowing the many important facets of the discourses that point to more inward and simply other dimensions of Muslim gender debates.

I make two exceptions to this hijab avoidance rule: a brief discussion of the role, presence, and absence of hijab during the prayer event in 2005; and an equally brief reflection on the politics of hijab on the covers of the books analyzed for this study.

Hijab and the 2005 Prayer Event

The visual signification of hijab or any form of clothing covering hair and body is prevalent in American mainstream media representations of Muslim women. In looking at the prayer as a visual performance and as a media event, it becomes clear that here, too, hijab is invested with meaning and used as a tool. The various appearances (or absences) of women's headscarves during the prayer point to the organizers' and participants' perspectives on and utilization of hijab in their intentions to create intra-Muslim debates about woman's leadership, ritual practice, and spiritual equality and to make the prayer event a media event.

An important distinction has to be made between the wearing of hijab for ritual purposes and the covering of hair and body in public and in the presence of men. In the modern period the hijab has been invested with a range of meanings—from piety to social mobility and political protest. And while Muslim women have insisted in many places on their right to choose if they want to cover themselves or not, few if any challenges have been expressed to the need to cover for the performance of ritual prayers and in prayer spaces in mosques. The woman-led prayer departed from this established practice as well. Suheyla El-Attar, the woman who sounded the call for prayer, not only challenged the established role of men as mu'adhdhin but also performed the recitation of the call without a headscarf. Sarah Eltantawi and Asra Nomani both addressed the congregation before the khutbah/prayer without hijab as well. When Saleemah Abdul-Ghafur appeared for the supplications before the khutbah, she had changed her clothes and put on a headscarf. Eltantawi wore a scarf for the prayer as well. Nomani sat through the khutbah and performed the Friday prayers without a headscarf, as did several other women members of the congregation, including Mona Eltahawy. Amina Wadud entered the church premises, attended the press conference, and performed the prayer in the same long, loose-fitting purple robe and headscarf.

Several readings are possible. The range of choices regarding hijab before and during the prayer could be read as pointing to the fact that Muslim women indeed have choices to cover or not to cover, even in this ritual and at the same time very public context. This reading would challenge the prevalent interpretation of hijab as forced on Muslim women by Muslim men and "Islamic norms." It could also be interpreted as demonstrating that American Muslim women have indeed challenged the forced nature of hijab wearing and thus paint a picture of American Muslim women as struggling with their traditions, communities, and men. And finally, the decision to accept the choices made by the women in attendance could also be understood as a challenge to Muslim communities to take up the debate about the importance and significance of hijab. If pushing the boundaries of textual interpretation, challenging the limits of ritual and religious leadership, and rethinking tradition and community were all part of the intra-Muslim agenda of the prayer and if changing public and media perceptions of Muslim women and men were part of that agenda as well, then the negotiated presence and absence of head coverings at the prayer event achieved both on at least a symbolic level.

Judging a Book by Its Cover

The mediated significance and power of hijab is even more pronounced and apparent on the covers of many of the books discussed here. Of the twenty or so books written and edited by American Muslim women, more than half feature a headscarf in some form.[3] Sometimes intentionally critical, like the art photograph by Yasmina Bouziane on Mohja Kahf's *Western Representations of the Muslim Woman* and artistically invested as in the art piece by Shazia Sikander on the cover of *Shattering the Stereotypes*,[4] and sometimes clearly invested in marketing, like the cover of Amina Wadud's *Inside the Gender Jihad* and the original cover of Asra Nomani's *Standing Alone in Mecca*, those making decisions on the cover designs prove to be part of the framing and being framed of Muslim women. Some books feature photographs of the authors; others have Arabic calligraphy or arabesque geometric designs. Most of the books about American Muslim women and even several about American Muslims more generally, like Paul Barrett's *American Islam*, feature girls or women with hijab. *Muslim Women in America* even has a photograph of the 2005 woman-led prayer event on its cover. In wondering about the publishers' choices (which may or may not have the authors' consent), one realizes how limited and politicized the options are. The covers of books about (or by) Muslim women usually include one or more of the following three choices: representations of women through photographs or art pieces, renderings of Arabic calligraphy (often Qur'anic passages), or abstract geometric or floral designs from Islamic art. I have often wondered if choosing calligraphy or arabesque designs reflect the authors' discomfort with pictures and their representational power. Author photographs emphasize the personal, individualized nature of the narrative and provide an opening for relating to the persona of the writer. Asma Gull Hasan and Asra Nomani, on their respective covers, represent themselves as modern, liberated, fashionably dressed, confident, and only mildly exotic. The cover of *Muslim Women Activists in North America* features pictures of almost all the contributors, and notably all but two, on the back cover, wear the hijab. The artwork on *Shattering the Stereotypes* is a painting of a naked, shackled woman with a veil, with eight arms holding a variety of weapons.[5]

Asra Nomani, in an article in *Slate Magazine* in 2006, describes her negotiations with her publisher about the "veil." After Nomani contested the use of her picture in a white scarf for the hardcover edition, her publisher finally relented and issued the paperback edition with a scarfless fashion photo of her. Nomani argues that the scarf does not represent her and her perspective on the veil and that it is a tired symbol for marketing purposes.[6] The picture on the paperback edition of Nomani's book shows her in a pink blazer, with a scarf around her neck. This picture was taken on the day of the 2005 prayer event. The paperback edition also featured a somewhat different title. Changes in cover designs and titles of some of the books in this study may also indicate the negotiation process and/or the force of marketing considerations.[7]

An alternative reading of the covers would emphasize the power of symbols and the easy recognition of such symbols as marketing tools. Much like caricatures, book covers are expected to send an immediately decodable message to the potential buyer, and nuances are often lost in the process. However, choosing a potent even if simplistic and monolithic symbol of Muslim women such as the hijab can be used as a means of resisting the symbol's meaning. If readers buy or choose a book inspired by its cover they may change or at least broaden their perceptions of Muslim women after reading their stories or ideas. In other words, adopting a potent symbol and subverting it through the text itself can be a strategy of resistance.

Wadud's *Inside the Gender Jihad*, featuring one of the cover models Nomani has described as "veiled babes" in her *Slate* article, can serve as a powerful example for such a reading. The woman on the cover wears a white veil, showing only her eyes. She looks vaguely Arab or South Asian. There certainly is irony if not resistance in this choice, considering that Wadud includes a chapter in the book on why, when, and how she wears or does not wear the hijab and that Wadud is African American. Would the book not have sold with her own picture on the cover? Is an exotic, almost entirely veiled "beauty" more interesting or playing more into readers' and buyers' expectations? I do not know if Wadud was happy with the cover, or whether she perceived it as an expression of racial prejudice, as her colleague Mohja Kahf did in deciding to put up a fight with her publisher when she first saw the cover design for her novel, *The Girl in the Tangerine Scarf*. As Nomani describes the incident in her article:

> In May 2006, Mohja Kahf took a dramatic step to protest the original cover that her publisher, Carroll & Graf, designed for her novel The Girl in the Tangerine Scarf: She posted a protest message on Amazon.com. "Cover is offensive to book's author," her headline read. The problem wasn't a face veil. Instead, the original cover showed a young

woman wearing a scarf but with a bare midriff and nose ring and with her eyes cut off by the design. "Half harem tramp," Kahf wrote in an article for Islamica magazine. "How many Muslim woman stereotypes can you even squeeze into one image?" She threatened to pull her book and "pulled out the 'r' word—racism." (She admits it was a veiled threat.) The publishing house relented a little, covering the midriff, removing the nose ring, and showing the eyes, though Kahf notes, "She was still a thin white woman [on the final cover], and the eyes look stoned."[8]

The somewhat playful tone of the *Slate* article and Kahf's satire should not distract from the important and serious concern with race and racism, which needs further thought and attention.

Race Matters

Taking the title of this section from Cornell West's famous book,[9] it is important to begin to address the ways in which studies of American Muslims and American Muslim women more specifically are at once deeply entrenched in issues of race while at the same time demonstrating the many ways in which academic fields and disciplines draw boundaries and fault lines between their approaches, methodologies, and theories. Intentional and creative crossings of such boundaries in the study of American Muslims is a recent phenomenon, as is the conversation among American Muslims, scholars, individuals, and communities on the myriad ways in which American perceptions and experiences of race have informed community relations, religious histories, and contemporary discourses.

Race matters primarily and obviously in the writings of those American Muslim authors and scholars who are African American and thus come with the experiential background for the conversation and with the motivation to address race issues in Muslim communities. Sherman Jackson, Aminah McCloud, Amina Wadud, and Jamillah Karim[10] are among those scholars who have addressed race issues, racial discrimination, and serious historical and contemporary tensions over blackness, whiteness, and the supposed in-betweenness of Muslims of Arab, South Asian, and other heritage. McCloud has in no uncertain terms criticized the attitudes of immigrant Muslims toward African American Muslims and their purported lack of religious authenticity.[11] Jamillah Karim has contributed an ethnographic study of friendships between young Muslim women of South Asian and African American backgrounds chronicling their identity negotiations, community attitudes, and mutual prejudices. Karim has argued, "By acknowledging and respecting difference within the *ummah*, American Muslims will be better able to build bridges across difference."[12] Later she opines that members of both communities she studied need to perceive their steps toward each other as the pursuit of justice and that "correcting the wrong, in this case racism, must not be compromised, but it requires that the wronged person forgive, make excuses for, and look for the good in the one who has committed the wrong."[13] After the death of the Muslim community leader Warith Deen Muhammad in 2008, the Muslim comedian Azhar Usman and the scholar Sherman Jackson both issued statements of apology, Usman on behalf of "immigrant" Muslims and Sherman Jackson on behalf of those African American Muslim scholars who for too long have been trying to be as "authentic" as immigrant Muslims.[14]

The very categories "immigrant" and "African American" or "immigrant" and "indigenous" have even more recently been questioned by those scholars who argue that drawing such lines effectively obscures the interdependent and interconnected histories of all American Muslims, thus academically reinforcing boundaries that members of American Muslim communities are just beginning to question. Edward Curtis writes:

> Although Muslim Americans condemn racial discrimination and prejudice, they live, like most Americans, in a nation divided by race. . . .
> And yet, indigenous and immigrant Muslims have still influenced one another across racial and other social lines that have divided them. They have shared ideas, disagreed with each other, exchanged food, clothes, and other goods. Unearthing the history of Muslims in the United States means showing how Middle Eastern, South Asian, European, African, black, white, Hispanic, and other Muslim Americans have come in contact and sometimes in conflict with one another.[15]

Several scholars now speak of the racialization of Muslim identities, in public perceptions but even more in legal terms. The invisibility of Arab Americans and their struggles to be accepted as white and not as "colored" have been studied in some detail in recent years as well.[16] In all these dimensions, academic, legal, and communal, American Muslims prove to be part of the very fabric of American society, including its internalized racial categories and pervasive racism. I have had to realize that I read and perceive racial categories and racism somewhat differently because I was not socialized in American society. This includes not recognizing, or reading differently, references to race and racism but also cultural and historical references to the civil rights movement and antiracist rhetoric. Joining other scholars in the study of religion, I am determined to include considerations of race along with gender more intentionally in my work. Working across disciplinary lines, scholars in religious studies and those in areas such as ethnic studies, political science, and cultural studies have begun to address such concerns.[17] More work is necessary to bring together approaches to race and religion, as well as gender and religion, and in the case of American Muslim women also Islamic studies, gender studies, and the study of American religions.

Muslim Women and Academia

While the works and ideas of American Muslim women scholars have slowly made their way into the secular academy, both historically and currently, many methodological and theoretical questions await deeper and more thoughtful answers. In this book I have only briefly touched on the many complex issues involved in the presence of American Muslim women in the secular American academy. Within and beyond religious studies, questions of insider/outsider perspectives as long debated in anthropology and other disciplines have affected the ways in which Muslim women scholars (like and unlike their male counterparts) have succeeded in carving out spaces for their multiple and varying perspectives. Afsaneh Najmabadi has described the ways in which a Muslim identity is ascribed to her from the outside and how this ascribed identity conflicts with her self-perception as a feminist in an essay titled "Teaching and Research in Unavailable Intersections."[18] Minoo Moallem, concerned with the inherent ascription as well, asks:

> Am I a Muslim woman? Even to answer this question is to enter the discursive space of race and gender in the condition of postcoloniality. Or to put it another way, I am faced with the impossibility of transgression since either I am required to submit to the "itinerary of silencing" by refusing to answer the question or to adopt a subject position that makes me "pass."[19]

Both scholars represent themselves as feminists but are reluctant to identify as Muslim. Most of the women in this study would express the opposite problem. They, for the most part, have not problematized their Muslim identities, however differently they may understand them to be constituted, but they debate internally and in their writings the possibility of using the label "feminist."

Part of the discomfort of secular feminists such as Najmabadi and Moallem but also Saba Mahmood in recognizing religious approaches as feminist is the uneasy relationship between secular and religious feminists, especially in the American context. This unease is evident in the politicized ways in which feminist writers opt for religious or ethnic designations such as Arab American feminist versus Muslim American feminist. While Christian and Jewish feminists embarked on religious reinterpretation projects several decades ago, Muslim women did not enter this conversation until the 1980s. Some scholars, such as Aysha Hidayatullah, have argued for the utility of studying the intersections between Christian, Jewish, and Muslim feminist agendas and projects. Hidayatullah has traced some of the ways in which Christian and Jewish feminist thinkers are referred to and reflected on in the scholarly work of American Muslim women.[20] Hidayatullah has also written an article specifically on the ways Elizabeth Schuessler-Fiorenza, one of the foremost Catholic feminist thinkers in the United States, has been influential for her own thought formation as an American Muslim feminist theologian.[21]

The tempting comparisons of Jewish, Christian, and Muslim feminist approaches to scripture, authority, and leadership and the increasing inclusion of Muslim scholars in religious feminist projects need to be thought through and critically assessed in order to avoid the easy conclusion that Muslim women scholars are simply catching up with what has been developed and applied in Jewish and Christian contexts. The history of feminist appropriation of Muslim women as a foil for their own demands and the entanglement of early feminism with colonial projects need to be considered more carefully and might require the conclusion that while there are obvious similarities, there are also vast and important differences. Here again, concerns of race and ethnicity need to play a role. Even more recent are the contributions of queer theology and their critique of heterosexual normativity. Both Womanist and Mujerista feminist theologies have long reflected on the white middle-class biases of earlier feminists, religious and secular, and Muslim women will find themselves at the crossroads and intersections of many of these critiques and ascriptions.

Muslim women in the academic study of women and gender in Islam have had to contend with many variations of the insider/outsider debate and have responded in a variety of ways. In the preface to her 1999 American edition of *Qur'an and Woman* Amina Wadud surmised that the prevalent expectation in the study of religion is to be "neutral, sympathetic, or objective" and that non-Muslim scholarship in Islamic studies is alive and well. Wadud asked then whether this might be "one reason for the large number of 'closet' Muslims in Western academia," a privilege she saw confined to those who were converts to Islam and thus showed no indication in their name of their Muslim identities.[22] In addition, those with "Muslim" names have had to make choices and negotiate the identity politics involved in the study of Islam, as the examples of Najmabadi and Moallem demonstrate. Significant numbers of scholars with "Muslim" names or from Muslim backgrounds have presented their scholarship as detached from their religious identities, if they even perceive themselves as having such identities. On the other hand, Muslim scholars of an earlier generation, including prominently Fazlur Rahman (d. 1988), Ismail al-Faruqi (d. 1986), and Seyyed Hossein Nasr, have produced an oeuvre and legacy of Muslim normative and exegetical as well as programmatic scholarship that have left an indelible mark on the generations of Muslim scholars in North America succeeding them. The central role of Fazlur Rahman for American Muslim women's exegetical work has been discussed in earlier chapters. Muslim women scholars (along with their male counterparts) thus not only negotiate Muslim insider perspectives and approaches but also the equally or even more contentious issue of religiously prescriptive or normative scholarship in the secular American academy. Muslim women have been afforded small but protected spaces to carry out such work. While there can certainly be detected a patronizing attitude of helping Muslim women in their "liberation" and support for very particular exegetical projects—those perceived as liberal and progressive—the American academy has provided alternatives to direct intracommunal debate and possible conflict, namely, a space in which ideas of reform and transformation can be discussed with at least less of the existential threat of excommunication. Much more reflective work and scholarship on the dynamics of Muslim women scholars' work as part of and beyond academic spaces needs to be carried out in order to understand how the rethinking of tradition, new and not so new hermeneutics and exegetical projects, and negotiations of religious and scholarly authority take place.

And equally important, as Muslim scholars and Muslim women scholars we urgently need to carry out our own work, exegetical and otherwise,

while more intentionally reflecting on methodology, politics of representation and identity, and our equally important activist commitments.

Women, Men, and Gender

There is an obvious tendency in Muslim women's studies and more generally in women's studies to focus on women in order to level poignant critiques of the construction of male behaviors, values, and perspectives as
normative in human society. This focus on women in gender studies has
also been an important and powerful way to generate or unearth data, material, and further insights into the lives, experiences, and perspectives of
half of humanity. Rita Gross has described the inclusion of women in the
humanities as the transformation of androcentric studies into androgynous
approaches, which in turn would simply (and not so simply) acknowledge
and take as their departure point the full humanity of women.[23]

In more recent debates among feminist scholars, the institutional limitations of women's studies as part of the academy, the emergence of a feminist "orthodoxy," and the danger of reserving a small corner of the academy
for the study of half of humanity have been argued and countered by various scholars.[24] In the context of this book and the communities involved,
it has become quite clear that the sole focus on women, women's writings,
and women's perspectives may run the risk of obscuring the many ways in
which men, as supporters and detractors, are involved in the formulation
and continuing debates on gender discourses among American Muslims.
The interplay of male and female perspectives and the impossibility of as-
cribing particular attitudes to members of each sex have become apparent.
Some work is now being done in the field of Muslim masculinity, primarily
related to sexual identities and attitudes. A broader lens and more natural inclusion of debates about masculinity and femininity beyond sexual
practice or inclination are necessary to achieve a fully inclusive and more
complex picture. One useful site for future research and my intention to
more fully reflect on both sexes is in the ways in which American Muslims
have approaches issues of domestic violence in their communities, on a discursive level and on more practical levels. For example, Muslim scholarly
approaches to interpretations of Q 4:34 need a fuller and more nuanced
treatment in scholarship, especially in connection and combination with
Muslim grassroots efforts and communal as well as institutional strategies
to address domestic violence. Organizations such as the Peaceful Families

Project, Karamah, but also initiatives such as Muslim Men against Domestic Abuse,[25] formed after the murder of Aasiya Zubair in February 2009,[26] are among the Muslim community efforts to address a phenomenon that is not unique to Muslim communities and societies. Nevertheless, the particular Muslim strategies and initiatives in the American context deserve further attention.

Transnational Dimensions

It is clear from the writings and activist engagements of American Muslim women as well as more generally for American Muslims that the American dimensions of their discourses, politics, and experiences are intricately linked with their transnational counterparts. As Edward Curtis writes, "Telling the story of Muslim America also means tracing the connections of Muslim Americans to Muslims abroad. American Islam is a drama that has unfolded on a global stage marked by international crossings."[27]

American Muslim women scholars and activists have been part of transnational women's networks and organizations and have left their intellectual and activist mark on Muslim women's movements globally. American Muslim intellectuals have often claimed that America provides them with the freedom and environments necessary for developing contemporary Muslim discourses and interpretations free of state coercion and political threat. While this may very well be too rosy a picture of the ways American Muslims have been treated by the American government and while it also does not account for the various direct involvements of American Muslims with government projects and representations, it is true that the intellectual production of American Muslims has made its mark on global Muslim thought. The trajectories of American Muslim discourses, their continuous interchanges with Muslim intellectuals elsewhere and the negotiation of different epistemological traditions, need further and deeper consideration.

Conclusion

I want to open these final paragraphs with a story that Laury Silvers shared with me a few months before I completed this book.

I don't know if you would be interested in this story for your book or not. I was reminded of it the other day. When Nakia [Jackson] and I were doing the woman-led Eid prayer in Boston [in 2006], we gathered at a friend's house the night before with some people for dinner. A friend I had met on an email list, Muhammad B.,[28] asked if he could come to the dinner to give us support. He said he could not come to the Eid prayer as he wasn't certain of the legality of it, but he supported our intentions. He came over and we all talked about women's authority and leadership. Nakia articulated her notion of "Shared Authority" there, which I found very compelling because it did not marginalize men (something none of us wanted to do). It came time for Salat. Muhammad, we knew, was not going to pray behind us, but none of us were concerned. We really appreciated his support even in the face of that. He stepped forward and he asked, with great humility, if we would permit him to lead us. We all readily agreed. He did not assume that he was the leader. He was so humble. He had no entitlement. To us it summed up the "Shared Authority" idea: men are our allies and partners in this process. In any case, I am still so moved by his humility and what it meant for us to be with a man who did not assume his leadership.[29]

Several other public woman-led prayers have taken place after the much-publicized and debated March 2005 event in New York (Boston 2005, Barcelona 2006, London 2007). More important, in less public settings groups and communities of American Muslims have come together over the years to participate in daily, Friday, and Eid prayers in mixed-gender congregations, with men and women taking turns leading and giving sermons. Woman-led prayer as a step toward shared authority has not developed into a "movement," but movement has certainly taken place, and many of these events and developments simply have taken place outside of the purview of public interest or media attention. For it is not media attention or even necessarily public debate that those involved are seeking but rather the continuous negotiation of what it might mean to be an American Muslim in the twenty-first century.

Muslim women and men in North America continue to negotiate religious authority, debate women's leadership in prayer and society, and participate in producing a tafsir of praxis. American Muslim women continue to write and publish their ideas, reflections, and personal stories. Women's exegetical contributions and the many layers of their activist involvement have made gender discourses a central concern for all American Muslims.

Far from an "issue" forced on Muslims by Western colonialists or feminists, gender discourses and debates are owned and negotiated by Muslim communities and individuals as much as by any other member of the global community of human beings. The woman-led prayer event in 2005 has served as a catalyst for many of these debates but also as a lens through which to approach the larger dimensions of these debates even beyond gender. Authority, tradition, community, and leadership, as well as media representations and questions of Muslim self-representation, are at the center of Muslim concerns in North America and for Muslims worldwide.

WRITING ON GENDER inevitably challenges the status quo. This book has been a journey of discovery and realization for me, and it has made me aware of the power of gender discourses in our lives in new and unexpected ways. I did not want to join the field of Muslim women's studies for fear of being confined to it as a scholar and for even greater fear of having to examine my own attitudes, beliefs, and experiences through this prism. In struggling to understand God's intents and expectations, many of the themes and questions explored in this book have been a part of me since I became a Muslim, some even from before. I hope that this book can bridge some of the divides and gaps between Muslims and non-Muslims, scholars and activists, men and women, and that it will facilitate a deeper understanding of the issues we face.

Epilogue

Since I started writing this book, the "issues" of women-led prayer and women's place in American mosques seem to have garnered a new wave of attention. Since 2008 videos, discussion threads, and online debates have appeared, some going back to the 2005 prayer event but not posted until years later. Academic interest in the same topics has also increased, as evident in the work of Sadeghi and Calderini, as well as in the thesis work of Aysha Hidayatullah, Zahra Ayubi, and others.

While media representations of the prayer event and the perspectives and opinions of those in support of women-led prayers often assume staunchly and uncritically liberal positions that take for granted Muslim women's liberation from patriarchy and particular notions of equality, the responses from Muslim community members, scholars, activists, be they male or female, tell a complicated and more nuanced story. When in February 2010 a group of Muslim women walked into the main prayer area of the Islamic Center of Washington, D.C., demanding the right to pray in the back of the main area behind the men rather than in the women's section of the mosque, the mosque leadership called the police and threatened to have the women arrested for disturbing the peace. Immediately hailed by Asra Nomani[30] and Margot Badran[31] as reminiscent of civil rights era protests and reported on Fox News and other channels, this incident demonstrates the significance of the events and debates. It also indicates that the 2004–2005 events are a reflection of larger community dynamics independent of the personalities involved in them. The right to pray in the main hall had been the beginning of Asra Nomani's campaign for Muslim women's rights in the mosque in 2004, and evidently not much had changed. Or maybe change was not taking place in mosques?

Zarqa Nawaz has estimated that the number of mosques with separate prayer areas has grown from under 30 percent to over 60 percent in less than twenty years. Why? I have recently started to consider the possibility that the "lack" of change or change in the opposite direction (from less separation to more separation) may be an expression of an interesting phenomenon: the crisis of religious authority has created a situation in which consensus, the legal concept of ijma', may once again be the consensus of the community and not groups of scholars. In other words, if communities do not want "progress" in gender issues, for whatever reason (outward pressure, increased piety, focus on ritual and cohesion), such progress is simply not going to happen unless discourses and debates convince enough community members of their authenticity and significance. It is the task of scholars, especially those in Muslim women studies, to take their responses and reasons seriously and not to get entangled in liberal discourses that effectively "other" those in disagreement.

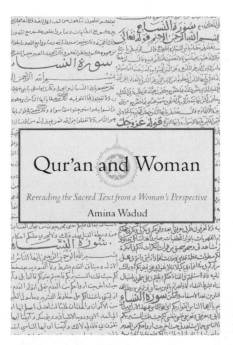

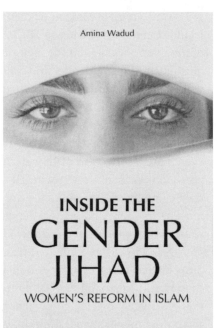

Oxford University Press, 1999   Oneworld, 2006

University of Texas Press, 2002   University of Florida Press, 2004

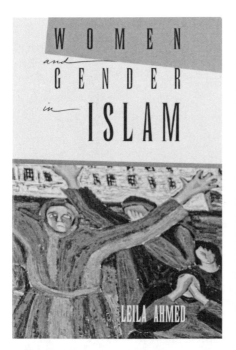

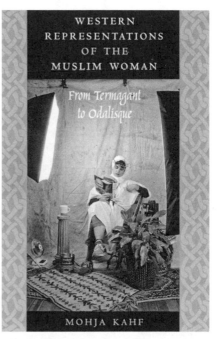

Yale University Press, 1992

University of Texas Press, 1999

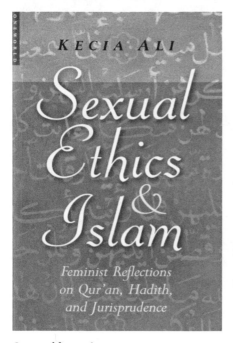

Oneworld, 2006

Harvard University Press, 2010

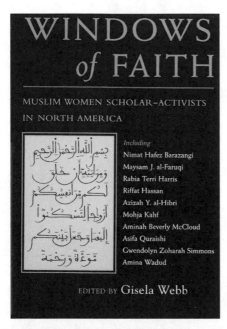

Syracuse University Press, 2000

Olive Branch Press, 2005

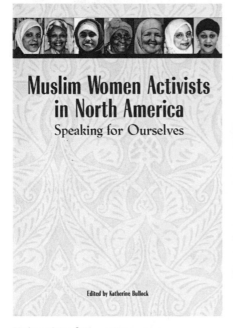

University of Texas Press, 2005

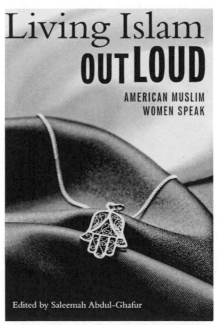

Beacon Press, 2005

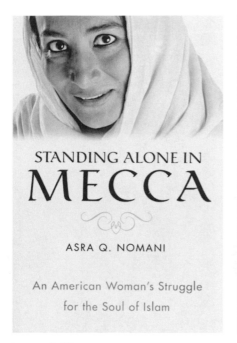

STANDING ALONE IN
MECCA

ASRA Q. NOMANI

An American Woman's Struggle
for the Soul of Islam

HarperCollins, 2005

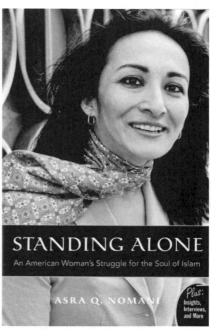

STANDING ALONE
An American Woman's Struggle for the Soul of Islam

ASRA Q. NOMANI

Plus: Insights, Interviews, and More

HarperCollins, 2006

Sumbul Ali-Karamali

The Muslim Next Door

The Qur'an, the Media, and that Veil Thing

"Sumbul Ali-Karamali has provided me with a tremendously valuable window of insight into what it means to honor and live Islam in America's everyday world. *The Muslim Next Door* is both immensely personal and intellectually grounded... One of the most valuable weapons against fear and hatred is exposure to the Other, and this conversational book becomes part of a much-needed, ongoing discovery."
—LALITA TADEMY, AUTHOR, CANE RIVER (AN OPRAH'S BOOK CLUB PICK)

White Cloud Press, 2008

Why
I Am a Muslim
An American Odyssey
ASMA GULL HASAN

Element, 2004

Penguin, 1999

Carroll & Graf, 2006

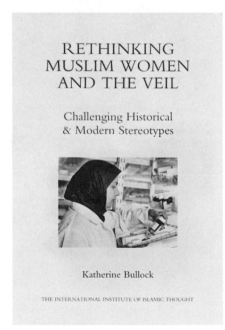

International Institute of Islamic Thought, 2002

Women's Press, 2003

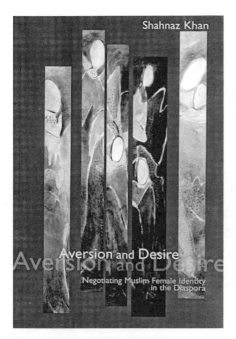

Women's Press, 2002

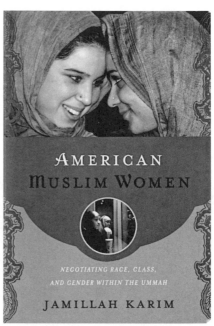

New York University Press, 2009

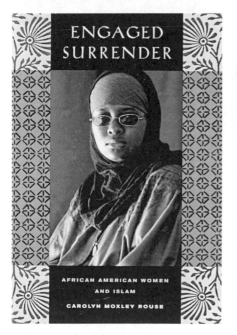

University of California Press, 2004

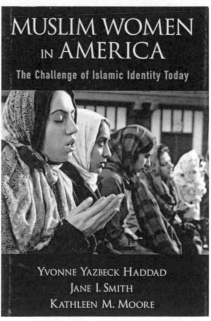

Oxford University Press, 2006

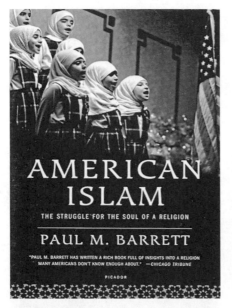

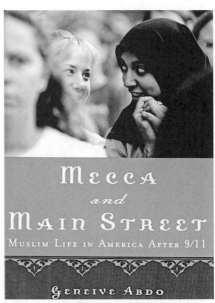

Picador, 2007

Oxford University Press, 2006

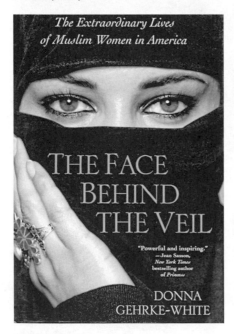

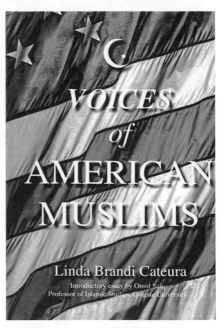

Citadel Press, 2006

Hippocrene Books, 2005

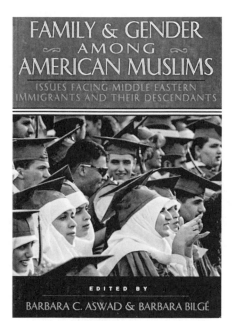

Temple University Press, 1996

AltaMira Press, 2004

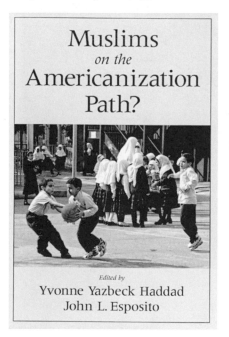

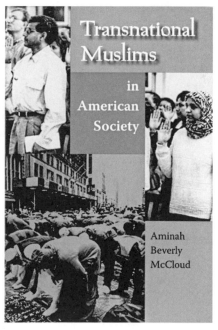

University of South Florida Press, 1998

University of Florida Press, 2006

Notes

Introduction

1   Amina Wadud was professor of Islamic studies at Virginia Commonwealth University in Richmond until her retirement in 2007.

2   Although this book occasionally utilizes poetry such as the stanza by Suheir Hammad in the epigraph, American Muslim women's fiction and poetry have not been included in my analysis for two reasons: the specific dynamics of the worlds of fiction and poetry production and the need to apply a kind of literary analysis, neither of which are within my academic training and knowledge. Thus instead of reading poetry and fiction as reflections of reality, I include them only on occasion and in the case of authors such as Mohja Kahf who have also produced nonfiction and/or scholarly texts.

3   Mamdani 2005.

4   Saba Mahmood writes about feminist theory and activism: "Feminism, therefore, offers both a *diagnosis* of women's status across cultures and a *prescription* for changing the situation of women who are understood to be marginalized, subordinated, or oppressed" (2005b, 10; original emphasis). This same dynamic is at work in the intellectual contributions of many American Muslim women writers and scholars, regardless of whether they describe themselves as feminists.

5   See Asad 2003; and Saba Mahmood, "Interview with Talal Asad: Modern Power and the Reconfiguration of Religious Traditions," February 1996, www.stanford .edu/group/SHR/5-1/text/asad.html (last accessed April 2, 2010).

6   Mahmood 2005b.

7   Mahmood 2005b, 86–91. Mahmood writes, "Hajja Faiza's views on the subject of female circumcision and women's leadership in prayers should not be taken as a sign of a 'moderate position' since her views vary widely in regard to women's place within Islam. If anything, she consistently emphasizes the importance of following the logic of juristic debates and forms of reasoning, which makes her position on the question of gender relations within Islam quite unpredictable" (89–90).

8   Asad 1986, 14.

9   Mahmood 2005b, 115.

10 Hidayatullah 2009b, chap. 1, esp. 68–93. Aysha Hidayatullah is a professor of Islamic studies at the University of San Francisco.

11 I owe the formulation of this insight to a conversation with Ayesha Chaudhry.

Chapter 1

1 I am indebted to Brittany Huckabee and Asra Nomani for sharing this footage of the event with me. Below I quote extensively from my transcription of parts of these video files. Watching the footage has allowed me to gain a significantly different perspective and much deeper understanding of the prayer event, and I am grateful for Brittany's and Asra's generosity.

2 The mediated nature of the prayer event is discussed further in chapter 7.

3 Photographs of the event can easily be found on the Internet. See, for example, several pictures taken and posted by Omar Sacirbey at http://aliciapatterson.org/APF2202/Sacirbey/Sacirbey.html (last accessed January 12, 2011).

4 There are different segregation practices, but they usually involve physically separating men and women from each other. This can mean that women pray in separate rows behind the men or that women pray in a physically separate space, such as behind a curtain, screen, or wall.

5 This overview is based on Nomani's description of the events in the 2006 edition of her book, *Standing Alone*; see 243–246, 308–324. Much of it is also chronicled in the 2009 documentary *The Mosque in Morgantown*, directed by Brittany Huckabee; see www.themosqueinmorgantown.com.

6 References to Hagar (Hajar in Arabic) as a role model for contemporary Muslim women can be found in the writings of several Muslim women scholars and activists, among them Amina Wadud, Hibba Abugideiri, Azizah al-Hibri, and Riffat Hassan, as well as Asra Nomani. See Wadud 2006a, 120–157; Abugideiri 2001a; al-Hibri 2003a; and Hassan 2006. This focus on Hagar is discussed further in chapter 4.

7 Nomani 2006a, 324–330.

8 The Progressive Muslim Union (PMU) was founded in November 2004 by Sarah Eltantawi, Hussein Ibish, Omid Safi, and Ahmed Nassef (personal communication with Eltantawi, April 2010). MuslimWakeUp was founded by Ahmed Nassef and Jawad Ali; the web address was www.muslimwakeup.com. Parts of this once-vibrant site are still available; however, it has not been updated in several years. Its demise is also related to the disintegration of the PMU in late 2006.

9 This information was provided in an article posted on www.muslimwakeup.com, a website associated with the PMU and run by Ahmed Nassef, one of the organizers of the prayer. The article in question is no longer available on the site. Michael Muhammad Knight alludes to the security checks at the entrance in his article "Huggable Islam," posted on March 19, 2005, at www.muslimwakeup.com (last accessed May 20, 2009).

10 MuslimWakeUp! "Make History! Reclaim Our Faith! Endorse Now!" posted March 7, 2005, on www.muslimwakeup.com (last accessed August 29, 2008). Boldface in original.

11 MuslimWakeUp!, "A Statement from the Organizers of the March 18th Woman-Led Jumʿah Prayer," posted March 13, 2005, on www.muslimwakeup.com (last accessed May 20, 2009).

12 Elliott 2005b.

13 These and many of the following quotes from the event were transcribed from the video footage provided by Brittany Huckabee and Asra Nomani.

14 Nomani 2005d.

15 Q 36:58. The passage has elsewhere been translated in a variety of ways. Muhammad Asad translates it as "peace and fulfillment through the word of a Sustainer who dispenses all grace" (Asad 1980, 678); Feisal Abdul Rauf has rendered it "A Greeting of Peace from a Merciful Lord" in his reflections on the dying and death of his father (Abdul Rauf 2007, 175). Hisham Kabbani points to the significance of the verse for Sufi practice and renders it in English: "The Word from a Merciful Lord (for them) is: Peace!" (Kabbani 2004, 314).

16 Both 33 and 100 are traditionally significant numbers for Muslim ritual practice, associated with supererogatory prayers as well as Sufi rituals.

17 I reproduce here selected passages of the available parts of the sermon as transcribed from the video footage. Wadud has published excerpts of the khutbah in her *Inside the Gender Jihad* (2006a, 249–252).

18 Wadud 2006a, 251.

19 Italicized passages in the text of the khutbah indicate passages and phrases spoken by Wadud first in Arabic and then in (her) English translation. Italicized passages enclosed in quotation marks indicate verses from the Qur'an.

20 Nomani 2006a, 290.

21 From her article in the *Daily News*, "My Answered Prayer," published March 20, 2005; available at www.asranomani.com/Writings.aspx (last accessed March 12, 2010). The quotation in the section subhead is also from this source.

22 www.asranomani.com, from the *Daily News*, March 20, 2005 (last accessed September 15, 2008).

23 The following paragraphs are based on several passages in Wadud's books, in which she succinctly describes her view of what transpired. See Wadud 2006a, 246–253.

24 Wadud 2006a, 248.

25 Wadud 2006a, 248.

26 A notable exception is the interview she granted Thomas Bartlett from the *Chronicle of Higher Education*, which resulted in his article, "The Quiet Heretic: A Controversial Prayer Upends a Professor's Life" (Bartlett 2005).

27 This decision and its repercussions for her teaching are documented in the film *The Noble Struggle of Amina Wadud*, directed by Elli Safari, The Netherlands/U.S., 2007, 29 min., color, VHS/DVD (Women Make Movies, www.wmm.com/film Catalog/pages/c699.shtml).

28 See Michael Muhammad Knight, "Huggable Islam," March 19, 2005, www.mus limwakeup.com (last accessed May 20, 2009).

29 Knight 2005. The original novel was spiral-bound and copied at Kinko's. Since then several new editions have been released.

30 See Nomani 2006a, 245.

31 Knight's novels on American Muslims are controversial and provocative and give

rare insight into aspects of American Muslim culture, including Muslim punk and metal music. See Maag 2008. There is a documentary called *Taqwacore: The Birth of Punk Islam* (2009), directed by Omar Majeed; see www.taqwacore.com (last accessed April 25, 2011). A feature film based on Knight's novel is called *The Taqwacores* (2010), directed by Eyad Zahra.

Chapter 2

1   MuslimWakeUp! "Make History! Reclaim Our Faith! Endorse Now!" www.muslimwakeup.com (last accessed August 29, 2008).

2   Wadud 2006.

3   Wadud 2006a, 162. The content of the khutbah is discussed further in chapter 3.

4   Wadud 2006a, 158–186. Na'eem Jeenah, South African Muslim activist and scholar and an organizer of the 1994 event, discusses the nature of the address by quoting Abdulkader Tayob, another South African Muslim scholar and activist, as saying the lecture was a "pre-khutbah talk in a pre-khutbah-less mosque" and situates this description in the context of debates among South African Muslims about *bid'ah* (religious innovation). See Jeenah 1994, 2.

5   I could not determine when this fatwa was issued as the website does not indicate a date.

6   "Fatwa by Dr. Abou El Fadl: On Women Leading Prayer," http://scholarofthehouse.stores.yahoo.net/onwolepr.html (last accessed December 16, 2009).

7   Scrivener 2004.

8   Haddad, Smith, and Moore 2006, p. 65.

9   Uta Lehmann, "Women's Rights to Mosque Space: An Exploratory Study of Women's Access to and Participation in Mosques in Cape Town," unpublished paper presented at Women, Leadership and Mosques: Changes in Contemporary Islamic Authority conference, Oxford University, October 2009. For a broader discussion of gender debates and Islamic feminism in South Africa, see Jeenah 2006. Tarawih prayers are additional congregational or individual prayers carried out after the breaking of the fast in the evening during the month of Ramadan.

10   See Eickelman and Anderson 1999 and 2003a for a collection of articles on new media and emerging alternative public spheres.

11   Eickelman and Anderson 2003a, xi.

12   Eickelman and Anderson 2003a, 6.

13   Lehmann 2009, n. 10.

14   Roxanne Marcotte writes in an article about online Muslim forums in Australia, "For example, the heated debates and discussions on MuslimVillage forums following Amina Wadud's infamous March 2005 leading of a mixed Friday congregational prayer in New York survive on at least three different threads that together generated almost 300 posts and more than 16,000 views from early March to the end of May 2005. These posts provide a snapshot of the hotly debated issue that ensued among participating members of MuslimVillage forums" (Marcotte 2010, n. 12).

15   Safi 2003c, 49.

16 Safi 2003b. The list of contributors also included Farid Esack, Ahmet Karamustafa, Ebrahim Moosa, Tazim Kassam, Scott Kugle, Gwendolyn Simmons, Amir Hussain, Ahmad Moussali, Marcia Hermansen, and Farish Noor.

17 Safi 2003a.

18 Progressive Muslim Union, www.pmuna.org (last accessed March 29, 2006). The website no longer exists.

19 See www.mpvusa.org for more information.

20 For a polemical critique of the PMU, published several days before it was officially founded on November 15, 2004, see "A Comment on the Formation of PMUNA," published November 12, 2004, and signed by the South African activists and scholars Farid Esack and Na'eem Jeenah and the Canadian gender activist Itrath Syed. The document warns that forming the PMU only buys into liberal American rhetoric and the imperial and neocolonial quest to identify "moderate Muslims." See http://commentpmuna.blogspot.com/2004/11/text-of-comment-on-formation-of-pmuna.html (last accessed December 16, 2009).

21 Aslam Abdullah, "Friday Prayers Led by Women," March 9, 2005, www.islamicity.com (last accessed December 16, 2009). Twenty-six readers responded to his post, most of them in support of his argument.

22 Nevin Reda, "What Would the Prophet Do? The Islamic Basis for Female-Led Prayer," March 10, 2005, www.muslimwakeup.com (last accessed August 29, 2008).

23 Sarah Eltantawi, "No, We Don't Have More Important Issues: In Support of Women-Led Prayers," March 12, 2005, www.muslimwakeup.com (last accessed August 29, 2008).

24 Muhammad Afifi al-Akiti, dated March 12, 2005. Al-Akiti's opinion is part of a document that contains a selection of "Fatwas and Legal Opinions on the issue of Women Leading Prayers," posted at http://mac.abc.se/~onesr/d/fwlp_e.pdf on April 5, 2005, and widely circulated on email lists. Many other pieces in the document can be found in other places online but not this one.

25 "A Statement from the Organizers of the March 18th Woman-Led Jum'ah Prayer," March 13, 2005, www.muslimwakeup.com (last accessed May 20, 2009).

26 Amine Tais, "Not Heroic Enough?" March 13, 2005, www.muslimwakeup.com (last accessed August 29, 2008).

27 Abdullah bin Hamid Ali, "Can a Woman Lead Men in Salat?" www.lamppostproductions.com/files/articles/FEMALE_IMAM.pdf (last accessed December 16, 2009).

28 Abu Fatoush, "The Secret of Why Only Men Can Lead Prayers: An Interview with Saudi Scientist Dr. Muhammad Bin Saad An-Nutfah," March 15, 2005, www.muslimwakeup.com (last accessed August 29, 2008).

29 Assembly of Muslim Jurists of America (AMJA; see www.amjaonline.com, March 16, 2005). The fatwa is part of the document cited on http://mac.abc.se/~onesr/d/fwlp_e.pdf, a website titled "Living Islam" that describes itself as middle way, nonextremist and nonmodernist. It posts large numbers of "Islamic documents." Excerpts of the AMJA fatwa were published in the Fatwa section of IslamOnline, www.islamonline.net (last accessed December 16, 2009).

30 Yusuf al-Qaradawi, "Woman Acting as Imam in Prayer," March 16, 2005, www
    .islamonline.net (last accessed October 28, 2008).
31 Muslim Women's League, "Woman-Led Friday Prayer," www.mwlusa.org/topics/
    rights/womanledprayer.htm, posted March 17, 2005 (last accessed April 11, 2010).
    Years earlier, in 1995, MWL published a position paper on political rights of
    women that contained the following passage: "Traditionally, an aspect of leader-
    ship in Islam is the ability of the leader to lead the Muslims in prayer, i.e. act as
    the imam. Many state that women cannot hold positions of leadership because
    women cannot lead men in prayer. However, this argument requires two assump-
    tions which may be invalid. First, one must assume that the leader himself or her-
    self is obligated to lead prayer. Second, one must assume that women cannot lead
    men in prayer." See Muslim Women's League, "An Islamic Perspective on Women
    in the Political System," posted September 1995, www.mwlusa.org/topics/rights/
    politics.html (last accessed April 11, 2010).
32 Mohja Kahf, "The Waiting Room," March 18, 2005, www.muslimwakeup.com (last
    accessed May 20, 2009). See chapter 7 for the text of the poem.
33 Eltahawy 2005b.
34 Ahmed Nassef, "Thank You Sheikh Gumʾa," March 18, 2005, www.muslimwakeup
    .com (last accessed August 29, 2008).
35 This report was then quoted in an online article on *Arab News* reporting on the
    woman-led prayer. See Ferguson 2005.
36 Published by Dar al-Ifta al-Misriyyah, March 22, 2005; see below.
37 The same Aisha al-Adawiya and the organization Women in Islam were the driv-
    ing force behind the formulation of a position paper/pamphlet on women's
    mosque access, published in June 2005. See below for further discussion of the
    pamphlet.
38 Elliott 2005a.
39 Hesham Hassaballa, "What a Damn Shame!" March 18, 2005, www.muslimwakeup
    .com (last accessed August 29, 2008).
40 Louay Safi, "Women and the Masjid between Two Extremes," March 18, 2005,
    www.islamicity.com (last accessed December 16, 2009).
41 Hina Azam, "A Critique of the Argument for Woman-Led Friday prayers,"
    March 18, 2005, www.altmuslim.com (last accessed August 29, 2008).
42 Elliott 2005b.
43 Muzammil Siddiqi, "Woman Imam Leading Men and Women in Salat," March 20,
    2005, www.islamicity.com (last accessed December 16, 2009).
44 Muhammad Tantawi died in March 2010.
45 Ferguson 2005.
46 Suʿad Saleh is featured in the 2009 documentary *Veiled Voices*, directed by Brigid
    Maher, as one of three Muslim women scholars and preachers from Syria, Egypt,
    and Lebanon. The film website describes the protagonists, including Suʿad Saleh,
    as follows: "Women across the Middle East are trying to reclaim their role as
    leaders in Islam. *Veiled Voices* explores in depth the world of three Muslim women

religious leaders, who say women were always meant to be powerful within the religion. Filmed over the course of two years in Lebanon, Syria and Egypt, *Veiled Voices* reveals a world rarely documented, exploring both the public and private lives of these luminary women. Each triumphs over difficult challenges as they carve out a space to lead—both in Islam and in their communities." See www .veiledvoices.com (last accessed February 16, 2010).

47 *ghusl* is the full-body ablution required after intercourse, menstruation, and childbirth.

48 *wudu'* is the smaller ritual of ablution involving washing of the face, hands, and feet.

49 *juloos* is the sitting part of the ritual prayer.

50 Name withheld, "First Fruit of the Prayer," March 21, 2005, www.muslimwakeup .com (last accessed August 29, 2008).

51 'Ali Jum'ah, "Women Leading Friday Prayer: Egyptian House of Fatwa," March 21, 2005, www.islamonline.net (last accessed October 28, 2008). Original emphasis; boldface changed to italics.

52 Jum'ah, "Women Leading Friday Prayer."

53 Lite 2005. See below for the Brandeis event.

54 Zaid Shakir, "An Examination of the Issue of Female Prayer Leadership," March 23, 2005. The text was first published on the Zaytuna website but can no longer be found there. Zaid Shakir reposted the document on his own website on April 22, 2008; see www.newislamicdirections.com/nid/articles/female_prayer_lead ership_revisited/ (last accessed December 16, 2009). The piece was republished in a collection of his essays (Shakir 2007) and in Edward Curtis's *Columbia Sourcebook of Muslims in the United States* (2008).

55 Hussein Ibish, "Erudition as Dead-End: Hina Azam and the Perils of Legal Dogmatism," www.muslimwakeup.com, March 25, 2005 (last accessed August 29, 2008).

56 Rasha Elass, "Islamic Women Break Custom, Lead Prayers," March 25, 2005, www.womensenews.org (last accessed May 20, 2009).

57 The results were published in the first 2005 issue of *Azizah Magazine*, including several quotes from those surveyed. See Al-Dabbous 2005. One especially interesting comment read: "Although this is not a new thing among the Nation of Islam and some Sufi orders, I look forward to the day when female imams will be widespread."

58 Siamack Baniameri, "A Woman Leads Prayers? What's Left of Muslim Men's Dignity?" March 26, 2005, www.muslimwakeup.com (last accessed August 29, 2008).

59 Chu and Mustafa 2005.

60 Eltahawy 2005a.

61 Lindsey 2005.

62 Robert D. Crane, "Shock and Awe in the First Intifada of American Gender Insurgency: Paradigmatic, Strategic and Legal Perspectives," April 2, 2005, www .theamericanmuslim.org (last accessed August 25, 2009).

63 Abdennur Prado, "About the Friday Prayer Led by Amina Wadud," April 4, 2005, www.altmuslim.com (last accessed August 29, 2008). Also posted on http://abdennurprado.wordpress.com (last accessed September 16, 2008).

64 Silvers 2008, 246–252. This text is a partial reprint of the original online post, which can be found at http://nawaat.org/portail/2005/06/03/islamic-jurisprudence-civil-disobedience-and-woman-led-prayer/ (last accessed January 22, 2011).

65 Berger 2005.

66 Wiltz 2005.

67 Sarah Eltantawi and Zuriani Zonneveld, "As You Are You Will Be Led: Khaled Abou El Fadl Leads a Town Hall Meeting on Woman-Led Prayer in Los Angeles," June 19, 2005, www.muslimwakeup.com (last accessed October 28, 2008).

68 "Former Wall Street Journal Reporter Asra Nomani Leads Mixed-Gender Prayer Services," www.brandeis.edu (last accessed April 18, 2008).

69 Nakia Jackson, "Not without My Maybelline—The Advent of Imama Nakia," April 29, 2005, www.muslimwakeup.com (last accessed August 29, 2008).

70 Nakia Jackson, "Nakia Jackson's Eid Khutbah," January 19, 2006, www.progressiveislam.org (last accessed December 16, 2009).

71 Bartlett 2005.

72 For the story of how the booklet came about, see al-Adawiya and Sayeed 2005. The article discusses various positions on women in American mosques and indicates that the conversation about the issue dates back at least to 2001. The online version of the booklet was posted on the CAIR website but was taken down several years ago. I had initially read the appearance of the booklet as a response to the prayer event but found evidence that it had been in preparation for several years. However, the timing of the endorsement and the document's distribution by major national Muslim organizations point to the catalyzing effect of the prayer. At the very least it indicates awareness of the larger issue and its discussion in Muslim organizations and communities.

73 Safi 2005, 61.

Chapter 3

1 Shaikh, raised and now working in South Africa but educated in the United States, might resist this description of herself as American, but her engagement with the works of American Muslim scholars and other religious and feminist scholars effectively makes her part of an intellectual and activist network centered in North America. Her work also mirrors the often transnational activist engagement of many of the women scholars under discussion.

2 Shaikh 2007, 66–89, 70.

3 Shaikh 2007, 70.

4 Badran 2009.

5 Hidayatullah 2009b, 48–59; Shaikh 2003b, 147–157.

6 See Ahmed 1982, 1992.

7   Shaikh 2003b, 155.

8   cooke 2002b, 155. See also cooke 2001.

9   See Hidayatullah 2009b, 58–61. Hidayatullah uses the term *Muslim feminist theologians* throughout her dissertation and also describes herself as one; see Hidayatullah 2009a. See also Shaikh 2003b.

10 Wadud 1999b, xi.

11 Wadud 1999b, xix and note 2. See also Spellberg 1994, 57.

12 Hassan 1990, pp. 95–96.

13 Sayeed 2005; see also Sayeed 2002, 2009. In her dissertation (Sayeed 2005) she explains the decline in numbers in terms of restrictions on travel for women (a common practice among scholars and transmitters) and the connection between women's restricted legal testimony and their reliability as witnesses. The reappearance of larger numbers of women in hadith transmission is in her view related to the shift from oral to textual transmission and other factors. See Sayeed 2005, esp. 158–218, 223–278.

14 Geissinger 2004.

15 Geissinger asserts, however, that she intentionally avoids the "widespread tendency to quarry the past in order to build the present." She goes on to point out that "it is both possible and valid to appreciate the past on its own terms" (Geissinger 2008, 25).

16 This issue is the topic of the next chapter.

17 See further discussion in chapter 4.

18 I owe this important insight to a conversation with Ayesha Chaudhry, who argued that the application of the thematic approach to the Qur'an as advocated by Wadud, Barlas, and others, drawing on the work of Fazlur Rahman, would not necessarily have yielded the same gender-inclusive interpretations because they would still have been defined by their societal circumstances and histories.

19 Wadud 1999b, x.

20 See Mahmood 2005a. In *Politics of Piety* Mahmood questions Western secular feminist assumptions about Muslim women's agency and resistance to the gendered status quo in Muslim societies. See also Mernissi 1987 and 1993 for examples of primary texts.

21 Van Doorn-Harder 2006.

22 See cooke 2001; Badran 1995, 2009. In Egypt Zainab al-Ghazali (1917–2005) and Bint al-Shati' (1913–1998) could certainly be described as intellectual predecessors of the American Muslim women scholars discussed in this book. Margot Badran describes both as supporting a complementary gender model as indigenous to Islam and in distinction to an egalitarian "Western" model; see Badran 2009, 26–38. Interestingly, American Muslim women scholars, with the exception of Nimat Barazangi, have not reflected on their historical predecessors in their work and do not seem to perceive their own work as part of the same intellectual trajectory. Barazangi critiques Bint al-Shati' (her pen name; her real name was 'Aisha 'Abd-al-Rahman) for what she perceives as a complementary gender model falling short of equality. See Barazangi 2004b, 73–79.

23   The overview in this section is indebted to the work of Aysha Hidayatullah, especially Hidayatullah 2009.

24   For a short self-portrait of each scholar, see al-Hibri 2004, 47–54; Hassan 2000, 173–198. Hassan's contribution to Muslim women's rights as human rights is discussed in Svensson 2000. See articles by Riffat Hassan: Hassan 1991a, 1991b, 1998. For works by Azizah al-Hibri, see, e.g., al-Hibri 2000b, 2005a.

25   For analyses of Wadud's hermeneutical strategies, see Abugideiri 2001a, esp. 90–93; Barlas 2006, 97–123.

26   See Barlas 2002, 2006.

27   See Barazangi 2000, 2004b, 2005.

28   See, e.g., Ali 2003, 2006b, 2009.

29   Barlas 2002, 89.

30   Abugideiri 2001b, 14.

31   Grewal 2006.

32   For the role of personal identity in women's exegesis, see Hammer 2009. For a non-Muslim assessment of the question of gender equality in the Qur'an, see Karen Bauer's review article (Bauer 2009). There Bauer contends that modern Muslim scholars in their search for gender justice and equality in the Qur'an have read the text "selectively and ahistorically" and concludes that "the level of discourse in the field of gender in Islam has been hampered by the reticence of modern scholars writing in English to confront the evidence that the Qur'an, on the whole, is not gender-egalitarian" (651).

33   Wadud 1999b, xxii.

34   Wadud 1999b, 14.

35   Wadud 2006a, 2.

36   Wadud 2006a, 24–32. The tawhidic paradigm contends that metaphysically God occupies the highest moral point while human beings are situated on a horizontal axis (30–31).

37   Barlas 2002, 93–128.

38   See Hassan 1998, 2003.

39   Hassan 2005. See a more extensive discussion of Hassan's approach to women's rights in chapter 4.

40   Wadud 1999b, 36–37.

41   Wadud 2006a, esp. 123–124, 188, 192. Wadud's reflections on slavery in the Qur'an are also often linked to more specific reflections on American slavery and its impact on African American men, women, and communities.

42   Barazangi 2004, 70–73.

43   Wadud 1999b.

44   Wadud 2006, 10.

45   Barazangi 2004b, 73. Musawah is also the name of a recently founded international and transnational organization or network of Muslim women who aspire to achieving equality for Muslim women and men by actively implementing change in Islamic law. See the discussion below.

46   Barazangi 2004b, 74–79.

47 Barazangi 2000, 22.

48 These works could and should be called tafsir works so as to acknowledge their own claim to be works of contemporary Qurʾanic exegesis, even though none of them is a complete tafsir text comparable to premodern tafsir works that have typically consisted of a commentary on all Qurʾanic verses and in later generations also commentaries on commentaries. Their departure from premodern methodologies as well as their focus on gender and/or particular passages of the Qurʾan define them as such. They share this feature with many other contemporary exegetical works without a specific focus on gender. For examples, see Taji-Farouki 2004b.

49 Hidayatullah's dissertation identifies exegetical methods employed by what she calls "Muslim feminist theologians" in very similar ways and in much more detail than I can provide here. Her three categories are "Historical Contextualization Method, Intra-Textual Method, and Tawhidic Paradigm."

50 For various assessments of Rahman's significance and his impact on the study of Islam, see Waugh and Denny 1998; Denny 1991; Saeed 2004.

51 Rahman 1982, 7; original emphasis.

52 Rahman 1979, 37–39.

53 Hidayatullah 2009b, 120.

54 The title of a chapter in Hidayatullah's dissertation; see Hidayatullah 2009b, 167. She borrows the term from Wadud and Barlas. See Wadud 1995, 43; Barlas 2002, 16.

55 Hidayatullah 2009b, 167.

56 See Taji-Farouki 2004. Interestingly, the only woman exegete and the only American scholar represented in the volume is Amina Wadud, and the article about her is written by Asma Barlas. See also the chapter on Fazlur Rahman in the same volume; and Saeed 2004.

57 See Rahman 1994 for the following example. Rahman curiously opts for a gender-inclusive translation of Q 50:37, which he renders: "it is a reminder to him/her who has a heart and surrenders his/her ears in witnessing" (2). The Arabic original is the male singular form. The discussion of gender, women in history, and issues of divorce and family and elsewhere polygamy take up four pages in the chapter "Man in Society" (47–51).

58 Bauer 2009, 651.

59 Bauer 2009, 651.

60 Ali 2009.

61 Abou El Fadl 2001b, 94.

62 See Wadud 2006a, 192.

63 Abou El Fadl 2001b: "Importantly, however, since the sole and exclusive Author of the Qurʾan is God, no community of interpretation can possibly become a part of the Authorial enterprise. . . . To state it rather bluntly, this leads to the sanctification of the Qurʾan and the de-sanctification of the *Sunnah*—the Qurʾan is exclusively from God but the *Sunnah* is not" (108). See also 87.

64 Rahman 1979, 67.

65 The evaluation of the authenticity of *ahadith* (pl. of *hadith*) is part of hadith science and is primarily based on an evaluation of the chain of transmission. While the history of these categories is much more complex, ahadith are commonly assessed on a three-point scale ranging from *sahih* (sound) to *hasan* (fair) to *daʿif* (weak). The weight of a hadith in exegetical or legal debates depends to a large degree on its proclaimed authenticity. See Brown 2009, 100–104.

66 See, e.g., Hajjaji-Jarrah's discussion of two commentaries on the question of women's modesty and hijab, where she contends that "Qurʾanic commentators have been, without fail, an integral part in flesh and blood of the historical reality of their time; hence, their commentaries necessarily reflect their interactions with it" (Hajjaji-Jarrah 2003, 182).

67 Yuskaev 2010, 3–4.

68 Mazen Hashem has explored themes and styles of Friday khutbahs in American mosques through a case study of khutbahs in the greater Los Angeles area between 2003 and 2006. See Mazen Hashem, "The Muslim Friday Khutbah: Veiled and Unveiled Themes," October 2009, www.ispu.org/files/PDFs/ISPU%20-%20The_Muslim_Friday_Khutba.pdf (last accessed January 12, 2011); and Hashem 2010.

69 Wadud 2006a. The book contains the entire 1994 khutbah (158–162), followed by Wadud's reflection on the debate over the nature of the 1994 sermon as khutbah or pre-khutbah lecture and its use in South African Muslim gender debates and politics (162–186). The khutbah was transcribed by the late South African activist Soraya Bosch (email communication with Naʾeem Jeenah, November 2009) and printed in the South African Muslim newspaper *al-Qalam*, as part of the discussion of women's mosque participation and leadership. Jeenah has reflected on the khutbah versus pre-khutbah discussion in *al-Qalam* as well; see Jeenah 1994.

70 Wadud 2006a, 181–182. Admittedly, in my first reading of the khutbah I paused to reflect on the validity of offering very personal and female reflections on carrying a child for nine months and then having to let go of that child, both as a reflection of God's will and our willing and willful surrender to God's power. Conditioned by expectations of public roles for men and women, I wondered how men could feel included in such a discourse that clearly privileged women. Yet the opposite, namely, the public privileging of male perspectives and norms in many aspects of our lives, does not usually prompt the same pause.

71 Wadud 2006a, 158.

72 Wadud 2006a, 161.

73 Wadud 2006a, 161.

74 The transcript in the book does not indicate if and how extensively Wadud may have quoted Qurʾanic passages in Arabic, a question that relates to the argument about whether this was a khutbah or pre-khutbah lecture. In her discussion of the event Wadud insists that she gave a khutbah and that its redesignation as a pre-khutbah talk was a political move by the organizers to avoid critique. It seems to have been established practice at least in the Claremont mosque to have a khutbah in Arabic and in vernacular language, distinguishing them by the designations "khutbah" (for the Arabic one) and "pre-khutbah" (in vernacular language)

instead of discussing the ritual innovation of having the khutbah delivered in a vernacular language. See Wadud 2006a, 177–178; Jeenah 1994.

75 The khutbah was transcribed from event footage, as discussed in chapter 1.

76 See Ahmad van Denffer, *Ulum al Quran: An Introduction to the Sciences of the Qur'an*, chap. 5, http://islamworld.net/docs/UUQ/chapter_5.html (last accessed November 17, 2009). Leila Ahmed refers to the story in *Women and Gender in Islam* based on Ibn Sa'd's *Kitab at-Tabaqat* but also points out that in different versions of the story it is Umm Salama who raises the question, or anonymous women, or the wives of Muhammad (Ahmed 1992, 257 n. 11).

77 *iman* is usually translated as faith or belief.

78 Wadud is referring to the debate about the prayer and the multitude of accusations and verbal attacks against her and the organizers of the prayer event.

79 Wadud 2006a. According to Wadud, it was Sa'diyya Shaikh who said, "It made me feel good to *be* a woman," while Wadud's hostess, Najma, said, "I can be who I am. I don't have to be anyone else: I am a Muslim woman" (178–179).

Chapter 4

1 Umm Waraqa was a female companion of the Prophet Muhammad; Hagar is the familiar biblical figure and mother of Abraham's firstborn son, Ishmael; Khadija was Muhammad's first wife (with whom he remained in a monogamous marriage until her death); and 'Aisha was Muhammad's favorite wife during the second period of his mission in Medina. See Ahmed 1992, chap. 3.

2 Calderini 2011, 1. The date of her death is based on Umm Waraqa's mention in a ninth-century compendium of hadith transmitters; see Calderini 2011, 3.

3 Or she participated in the compilation of the Qur'an; the phrase "kanat qad jam'at al-Qur'an" can be translated as either. Calderini translates it as "she knew the Qur'an by heart" (2011, 3). I am grateful to Aisha Geissinger for pointing out to me that both translations are possible and that the meaning is ambivalent.

4 Imam Ahmad Ibn Hanbal, *Musnad*, vol. 8, 405. I am grateful to Jasser Auda for his help tracking the excerpts of hadith compilations and fiqh texts mentioning the hadith of Umm Waraqa.

5 Abu Da'ud, *Sunan*, vol. 1, 161.

6 Calderini 2011, esp. 10–11.

7 Assembly of Muslim Jurists of America (AMJA; see www.amjaonline.com). The fatwa is part of the document posted on http://mac.abc.se/~onesr/d/fwlp_e.pdf. Excerpts of the AMJA fatwa were published in the Fatwa section of IslamOnline, www.islamonline.net (last accessed December 16, 2009).

8 Muhammad al-Akiti, dated March 12, 2005. Al-Akiti's opinion is part of the fatwa collection at http://mac.abc.se/~onesr/d/fwlp_e.pdf.

9 Yusuf al-Qaradawi, "Woman Acting as Imam in Prayer," www.islamonline.net (last accessed October 28, 2008).

10 Hina Azam, "A Critique of the Argument for Woman-Led Friday prayers," March 18, 2005, www.altmuslim.com (last accessed August 29, 2008).

11 Shakir 2008, reposted on his website, www.newislamicdirections.com/nid/articles/female_prayer_leadership_revisited/ (last accessed December 16, 2009).

12 Nevin Reda, "What Would the Prophet Do? The Islamic Basis for Female-Led Prayer" (2005), www.muslimwakeup.com (last accessed August 29, 2008).

13 Ahmed 1992, 118–120.

14 Sadeghi 2006.

15 Elewa and Silvers 2010.

16 Shakir 2005, reposted www.newislamicdirections.com/nid/articles/female_prayer_leadership_revisited/ (last accessed December 16, 2009).

17 The classification is as follows: required (*wajib* '*fard*); recommended (*mandub*); neutral or permissible (*mubah*); disliked (*makruh*); forbidden (*haram*).

18 Tarawih prayers are special congregational (or individual) prayers in the evenings during the month of Ramadan.

19 Shakir 2008, reposted www.newislamicdirections.com/nid/articles/female_prayer_leadership_revisited/ (last accessed December 16, 2009).

20 Yusuf al-Qaradawi, "Woman Acting as Imam in Prayer," www.islamonline.net (last accessed October 28, 2008).

21 Shakir 2008.

22 See note 9 above.

23 Muzammil Siddiqui, "Woman Imam Leading Men and Women in Salat," March 20, 2005, www.islamicity.com (last accessed December 16, 2009); Yusuf al-Qaradawi, "Woman Acting as Imam in Prayer," March 16, 3005, www.islamonline.net (last accessed October 28, 2008).

24 Muslim Women's League (USA), "Women in Society: Political Participation," http://mwlusa.org/topics/rights/polirights.html (last accessed January 6, 2010).

25 "Fatwa by Dr. Abou El Fadl: On Women Leading Prayer," http://scholarofthehouse.stores.yahoo.net/onwolepr.html (last accessed December 16, 2009).

26 Elewa and Silvers 2010, 169–170.

27 The question of authority is more fully explored in chapter 5.

28 Al-Banna 2005. Jamal al-Banna (b. 1920) is the younger brother of the Muslim Brotherhood founder Hassan al-Banna and an Islamic scholar who lives in Egypt. His views on many issues are considered liberal.

29 Her most recent book, *Marriage and Slavery in Islam* (2010) was published after this book was completed.

30 Ali 2006b, xxv.

31 Ali 2006b, xxvi.

32 Ali 2006b, xxvi.

33 Ali 2006b, 7.

34 Ali 2006b, 4.

35 Ali 2009, 99.

36 See Ahmed 1982.

37 cooke 2002b.

38 Al-Hibri 2000b, 55.

39 Al-Hibri 2000b, 54.

40 Al-Hibri 1999.
41 Al-Hibri 2001b.
42 Al-Hibri 2000b.
43 Al-Hibri 2005a, 164.
44 Al-Hibri 2000b, 60.
45 This discussion is based on the first part of Qur'an 4:34. See al-Hibri 2000b, 63–65.
46 Al-Hibri 2005a, 165.
47 Ali 2003, 179.
48 Al-Hibri 2000b, e.g., 70.
49 Hidayatullah 2009b, 63.
50 Karamah: Muslim Women Lawyers for Human Rights, www.karamah.org/about .htm (last accessed January 7, 2010).
51 www.karamah.org/projects.htm.
52 Hassan 1999, 248–250.
53 Svensson 2000, 70. Jonas Svensson offers a more comprehensive evaluation of Hassan's writings in regard to Muslim women and human rights. See Svensson 2000, 67–110.
54 Hassan 1996.
55 Hassan 1996, 370–371.
56 Hassan 1996, 371–380.
57 Hassan 1996, 367–369.
58 Riffat Hassan, "Women and the Qur'an," unpublished manuscript, April 1995. I am grateful to Cangüzel Zülfikar for sharing the manuscript with me.
59 See the organization's website: http://ecumene.org/INRFVVP/index.htm. The site seems to have last been updated with content in 2000.
60 In her essay published in 2000, Wadud discusses various perspectives on the United Nations Convention to Eliminate All Forms of Discrimination against Women (CEDAW) and acknowledges "important strides" while critiquing the secular foundation of the convention (Wadud 2000a, 9–10). In the same volume, Zoharah Simmons describes her participation in the Fourth World Conference in Women in 1995 in Beijing (Simmons 2000).
61 See Wadud 1995, 2003a, 2006a.
62 Most recently, she employed this figure of speech in her blog on the February 2010 attempt of Muslim women in the Islamic Center in Washington, DC, to pray in the main prayer hall. See Asra Nomani, "Let These Women Pray!" *Daily Beast*, www .thedailybeast.com, February 27, 2010.
63 Silvers 2008.
64 Plaskow 1990, 38.
65 See Mernissi 1991, 1993; Ahmed 1992; Sayeed 2005; Geissinger 2008.
66 Ahmed 1986; 1992, 41–63.
67 Hagar is the handmaiden of Sarah, Abraham's wife in the biblical account in Genesis. In the Islamic tradition Hagar is Abraham's second wife (or slave) but the bearer of his first child. Abraham is ordered by God to send her away, and she

finds herself in the desert, searching for water for her child. Her desperate running in the desert is replicated in the Islamic pilgrimage ritual of running seven times between the hills of Safa and Marwa outside Mecca. She is described (in extra-Qur'anic sources) as settling with her son in Mecca, next to the well the archangel Gabriel made appear to quench her child's thirst. Occasionally visited by Abraham, who later builds the Ka'bah with Isma'il, the well of Zamzam became the center of a settlement that then became Mecca.

68 The subtitle of this section is taken from al-Hibri's essay "Hagar on My Mind" (al-Hibri 2003a).

69 Al-Hibri 2003a, 210.

70 Hassan 2006, in Trible and Russell 2006. The volume is a reflection of a renewed interest in Sarah and Hagar as biblical figures and attempts to rethink their roles and significance for contemporary women in the monotheistic traditions. An earlier volume is *Daughters of Abraham: Feminist Thought in Judaism, Christianity and Islam*, edited by Yvonne Haddad and John Esposito (2002).

71 Hassan 2006, 164.

72 Abugideiri 2001a, 88.

73 See Kahf 2001, 32–33 and 31–32 respectively.

74 The poem appears in Wadud's chapter on Hagar in *Inside the Gender Jihad*. Wadud writes that another version would be published and that there was one version on the MuslimWakeUp website, but I could not locate either.

75 Wadud 2006a, 150.

76 Wadud 2006a, chap. 4, 120–157. This is one of Wadud's direct engagements with questions of Islamic Law, however broadly addressed in this text.

77 Wadud 2006a, 87.

78 Wadud 2006a, 113–118.

79 Musawah, www.musawah.org/who_we_are.asp.

80 www.musawah.org/docs/pubs/wanted/Wanted-AW-EN.pdf (last accessed January 7, 2010).

81 Nomani 2006a, 63.

82 Nomani 2006a, 63.

83 Nomani 2006a, 70.

84 Nomani 2005a.

Chapter 5

1 Abou El Fadl 2001b.

2 See Taji Farouki 2004a, 12–16. For historical insight into Islamic education and the role of the 'ulama, see the works of Muhammad Qasim Zaman (2002) and Jonathan Berkey (1992, 2007).

3 Taji-Farouki 2004a, 14.

4 Abou El Fadl 2005, 26.

5 Abou El Fadl 2005, 26–44.

6 Abou El Fadl 2005, 38–39; original emphasis.

7   Abou El Fadl 2001b, 67.

8   Zaman 2002, esp. 1–16; and chap. 2, "Constructions of Authority," 38–59.

9   See Ahmed 1982 for an early critique of this position.

10 Roy 2004, 33–40. Roy also observes anti-intellectualism in religious revivalist movements, echoing Abou El Fadl's assessment.

11 Abou El Fadl 2001b, 86.

12 Abou El Fadl 2001b, 87.

13 Abou El Fadl 2001b, 98–115.

14 Abou El Fadl 2001b, 109.

15 See chapter 4. Also see Abou El Fadl 2001b, 93–94, for his "conscientious pause"; and Wadud 2006a, 192.

16 Hidayatullah 2009b, 31–32.

17 Hidayatullah 2009b, 40. Hidayatullah is quoting Andrew Rippin, *Muslims: Their Religious Beliefs and Practices* (London: Routledge, 2005), 183.

18 See chapter 3 on Qur'anic exegesis.

19 Wadud 1999b, xvii.

20 See e.g., Wadud 2006a, 48, 92, 94, 299.

21 Barlas 2004, 3.

22 Barazangi 2004b, 22.

23 Barazangi 2004b, 41.

24 See Hassan 1990, 94–96; and also Hassan 1999, 249–250.

25 Wadud 2006a, 197.

26 Abdul-Ghafur 2005c, 15.

27 Eickelman and Piscatori 1996, 38.

28 Roy 2004, 153.

29 See Reinhardt 2003, 216.

30 See Barazangi 2004b, esp. 68–112; and Barazangi 2000, 30, where she writes: "Feminist studies and Islam struggle with and against each other in that both are oriented toward a better future for the female by rejecting human hierarchy. From the normative Islamic perspective human hierarchy is rejected as counter to the Qur'anic view of creation and human beings."

31 Wadud 1999b, xviii.

32 Wadud 2006a, 21; see also the chapter "What's in a Name?" 14–54.

33 See chap. 2.

34 Abou El Fadl 2001b, 201. The first goal is the subject of Abou El Fadl's book *Speaking in God's Name*.

35 Ali 2006b, xx.

36 Ali 2006b, xx–xxi. For the last part of her statement Ali relies on Fazlur Rahman.

37 For a direct critique of Azizah al-Hibri, see Ali 2003.

38 Sonbol 1996a, 1–20. This is the introduction to an edited collection titled *Women, the Family, and Divorce Laws in Islamic History*, which through several case studies makes the same argument with regard to the rights and restriction on women in marriage and divorce.

39 Ali 2006b, 109.

40 Ali 2006b, 109.

41 Wadud 2006a, 23.

42 Ali 2006b, 133.

43 Chaudhry 2006, 159.

44 Chaudhry 2006, 163.

45 See Wadud 2006a, "Stories from the Trenches," 217–253.

46 Robert D. Crane, "Shock and Awe in the First Intifada of American Gender Insurgency: Paradigmatic, Strategic and Legal Perspectives," April 2, 2005, www.theamericanmuslim.org (last accessed August 25, 2009).

47 See Muslim Women's League, "An Islamic Perspective on Women in the Political System," posted September 1995, www.mwlusa.org/topics/rights/politics.html (last accessed April 11, 2010); and Chu and Mustafa 2005.

48 See Hammer 2008. Challenges to the scholarly and religious authority of Amina Wadud, who is African American and a convert, often also took the form of questioning her authenticity as a Muslim and her knowledge of Arabic and the Qur'an. Some terms of this challenge were blatantly racist but also highlighted long-standing tensions between African American and immigrant Muslim communities with their intertwined as well as very distinct histories in North America. Recently, several scholars have addressed these divisions; see, e.g., Jackson 2005; McCloud 2006; Karim 2009a, 2009b.

49 See his foreword to Wadud's *Inside the Gender Jihad.*

50 Grewal 2006.

51 See the teacher page of Sunnipath.com, www.sunnipath.com/About/academy Teachers.aspx; and Al-Maghrib Institute's instructor profiles, www.almaghrib .org/instructors.php (last accessed April 16, 2010).

52 See a paper by Margaret Rausch titled "Women Spiritual Guides in Morocco: Agents of Change," presented at the conference "The Politics of Dissent in North Africa," Yale University, February 2009 (www.yale.edu/macmillan/africadissent/ rausch.pdf; last accessed April 18, 2010). At the conference in Oxford in October 2010, "Women, Leadership, and Mosques: Changes in Contemporary Islamic Authority," Margaret Rausch presented a paper on the same topic. At the same conference, Mona Hassan presented her recent work, "Reshaping Religious Authority and Knowledge: State-Sponsored Female Preachers in Contemporary Turkey." The conference proceedings are being prepared for publication in a volume edited by Hilary Kalmbach and Masooda Bano.

53 See Sayeed 2005.

54 Ali 2006b, xxviii.

55 Barlas 2002, xii.

56 Barlas 2006, 269. "Speaking in God's name" is also the title of Abou el Fadl's 2001 book.

57 Barlas 2002, 209–210.

58 Barazangi 2004b, 57.

59 Wadud 1999b, xii.

60 Wadud 1999b, xiii.

61 Barlas, "Still Quarreling over the Qur'an: Five Thesis on Interpretation and Authority," paper presented at the conference "Redefining Boundaries: Muslim Women and Religious Authority in Practice," ISIM, Amsterdam, June 24, 2007, posted at www.asmabarlas.com.

62 See Bakhtiar 2007; she dedicates a whole page of her introduction to the issue of husbands beating their wives with Qur'anic justification. "The question I kept asking myself during the years of working on the translation: How could God, the Merciful, the Compassionate, sanction husbands beating their wives?" (xlviii).

63 Nomani 2006a, 272, 272–277.

64 Khaled Abou El Fadl, "Fatwa by Dr. Abou El Fadl: On Women Leading Prayer," www.scholarofthehouse.org/onwolepr.html. It is not clear from the online document when the fatwa was issued, as it is described as a response to a request by an individual in a particular university context and not related to the New York City prayer.

65 Yuskaev 2010.

66 In response to my roundtable contribution at the 2009 American Academy of Religion meeting, Laury Silvers pointed out to me how important the secular academic space has been for the open formulation of gender-inclusive interpretations and women's participation in feminist and Muslim women's studies. Questions of scholarly authority and the acceptability of particular methodological frameworks both as insiders to their traditions and communities and as active participants in exegetical projects need to be discussed and analyzed in much more depth. See Hammer 2008, an earlier attempt to address this question.

67 Ali 2006b, 152.

68 Ali 2006b, 155.

69 Ali 2006b, 256.

70 Notably, those three are all converts. Mattson is white and Canadian, Yusuf is white, and Shakir is African American. In her M.A. thesis Zahra Ayubi has offered a nuanced analysis and comparison of the works of Wadud and Mattson. Her evaluation of Mattson's work and significance takes into consideration different modes of gender inclusion as well as the politics of inclusion and exclusion both women scholars and leaders have experienced based on their intellectual and activist contributions. See Ayubi 2010.

71 Ali 2006b, 153.

72 Webb 2000b.

73 Sonbol 2005, 221. Sonbol lists a conference titled "Islamic Family Law and Justice for Muslim Women" in Kuala Lumpur in 2001 and a 1999 conference on Muslim marriage contracts at Harvard University (224–225).

74 Sonbol 2005, 222.

75 Barlas 2004.

76 Barlas 2006.

77 Barazangi 2004b, e.g., 46–49, 70–72.

78 Ali 2003.

79 Hidayatullah 2009b, 237–290.

80 This dilemma is present in the work of Aysha Hidayatullah, Ayesha Chaudhry, and Hibba Abugideiri and in my own.

81 Al-Samman 2011.

Chapter 6

1 Nawaz has also included the debate about barriers in mosques into one episode of her very successful sitcom *Little Mosque on the Prairie*, aired on Canadian Public Television. Episode 2 in Season 1 of the show was titled "The Barrier" and comically represented the various community positions on the issue. In early 2011 the show was in its fifth successful season on CBC.

2 Nomani and Eltantawi in particular remarked on the voices of Muslim women during the press conference.

3 According to Azhar Usman, *intizam* in Urdu means "accommodation or arrangement." Email communication, September 22, 2009. The Arabic word *intizam* means "order" or "systematic arrangements," while the root verb *intazama* interestingly has as one of its meanings "to be incorporated." See Wehr 1994, 1147.

4 Azhar Usman, in *Me and the Mosque*, directed by Zarqa Nawaz (2005).

5 Howell 2007, 432–434. The focus in this section on Muslims as immigrants to America is produced by the available literature, but it is still unfortunate in its exclusion of the more complicated and interconnected histories of American Muslims from diverse ethnic, racial, and class backgrounds.

6 See Bagby 2003.

7 Haddad, Smith, and Moore 2006.

8 Haddad, Smith, and Moore 2006, 64.

9 Hafeeza Bell, "Women in Mosques," PBS, www.pbs.org/wnet/religionandethics/week811/p-cover.html, aired November 12, 2004.

10 Ahmed 1999, 120–131.

11 Imam Abdullah Farruuq, "Women in Mosques."

12 For an example of such argumentation, see Gabriel Haddad in response to a question about curtains in mosques posted on www.livingislam.org, one of the many sites available to Muslim seekers for answers to such questions. Haddad is considered conservative in his interpretations. www.livingislam.org/fiqhi/fiqha_e48.html (last accessed October 21, 2009). Haddad argues there that while the sunnah indicates that women and men prayed together, installing a separation between the sexes follows another injunction of the Prophet Muhammad, which is to prevent fitnah in society based on the temptation that women present to men by their mere presence.

13 See Ali 2009, 89.

14 Ali 2009, 90.

15 See chapter 2.

16 Dodds 2002, 33–38.

17 Dodds 2002, 37.

18 See Wan 2009, on the shortage of space in a mosque in northern Virginia. While Wan's article does not mention the exclusion of women from Friday prayers, this is an argument I have encountered in several mosques throughout the United States.

19 Kahera 2002, 128.

20 Kahera 2002, esp. the chapter "Time, Space, and Gender: The Place where the She-Camel Knelt," 118–135.

21 In August 2006 a special committee comprising religious and political figures in Saudi Arabia proposed to create prayer spaces for women in one part of the Grand Mosque surrounding the Kaʿbah, which would have effectively prevented women from accessing the Islamic sanctuary itself, which is where men and women now pray and perform the ritual circumambulation of the Kaʿbah. International public outcry against the plan resulted in the "temporary" abandonment of the idea. The committee cited concerns for women pilgrims' safety and comfort as the main reasons for their proposal. See Syed Rashid Hussain, "No Restriction on Women's Prayer in Kaʿaba" *Dawn Online*, September 12, 2006, www.dawn .com/2006/09/12/top16.htm (last accessed October 21, 2009); also Muslimah Writers Alliance, "Women Face Curbs at Makka," www.muslimahwritersalliance .com/MWA-GMEA4W/Women-Face-Curbs-at-Makka.html (last accessed October 21, 2009). See also the organization's project to foil the proposal, including links, posters, a petition, and a list of endorsers: www.muslimahwritersalliance.com/ MWA-GMEA4W/Home.html (last accessed October 21, 2009).

22 Nomani 2006a, 198.

23 Nomani 2006a, 199.

24 Nomani 2006a, 202.

25 See Wadud 2006a, 17–24, where she describes her understanding of Islam as "engaged surrender," fully aware of the need to interpret and make choices. Wadud rejects a static definition of Islam and describes it thus: "We are all part of a complex whole, in constant motion and manifestation throughout the history of multi-faceted but totally human constructions of 'Islam'" (2006a, 6).

26 Badawi 2005, 55; original emphasis. Jamal Bawadi teaches management and religious studies at Saint Mary's University in Halifax, Canada.

27 See Ahmed 1999, esp. 120–133.

28 The idea of false consciousness is part of Marxist theory and has been applied by feminist theorists to women in particular. For a sophisticated discussion of that debate, not using the term itself but rather focused on issues of agency, autonomy, and resistance, see Mahmood 2005b, esp. chap. 1.

29 Nomani, "Women in Mosques," www.pbs.org/wnet/religionandethics/week811/ p-cover.html.

30 See Bagby, Perl, and Froehle 2001.

31 See Bagby 2003.

32 Haddad, Smith, and Moore, 2006, 64.

33 Haddad, Smith, and Moore 2006, 62.

34 See Nomani 2006a. Also, Paul Barrett's chapter titled "The Feminist," in his *American Islam* (2007), 134–178; and *The Mosque in Morgantown*, directed by Brittany Huckabee (2009), which both chronicle Nomani's struggles.

35 Nomani 2005a, 139–152. The volume also contains her "Islamic Bill of Rights for Women in the Mosque" (Nomani 2005d, 153–154); "Islamic Bill of Rights for Women in the Bedroom" (Nomani 2005c, 155–156).

36 Wadud 2006a, 21.

37 Nomani 2005d, 153.

38 Ingrid Mattson, "Can a Woman Be an Imam? Debating Form and Function in Muslim Women's Leadership," http://macdonald.hartsem.edu/muslimwomensleadership .pdf (last accessed October 20, 2009). The essay is reprinted in part in Curtis 2008; see also Mattson 2008, 252–263.

39 Mattson, "Can a Woman Be an Imam?" 4.

40 Shakir 2008, 167–181.

41 Silvers 2008, 247–248.

42 Abugideiri 2001b, 2.

43 Abugideiri 2001b, 2.

44 One reason for the discussion of Ingrid Mattson here is insistent prompting by several male Muslim scholars in summer and fall 2009. I presented my research in several venues and was repeatedly told that instead of increasing the attention for Nomani and Wadud and advancing their cause, I should focus on "proper" Muslim women leaders and their achievements. Mattson was always the first name mentioned.

45 For a short faculty profile, see http://macdonald.hartsem.edu/mattson.htm; and for her presidential profile, see www.isna.net?ISNAHQ/pages/Ingrid-Mattson-President---US.aspx (both last accessed October 21, 2009).

46 Email exchange with Edward Curtis on July 14, 2009, in which he pointed out that "in 1961, the American Druze Society selected Julie Mullin Makarem as their national leader; in the early 1970s, Zahia Khalil was elected to lead the Federation of Islamic Associations in the United States and Canada, still a major Sunni organization at the time."

47 Another example of a similar trend is Hadia Mubarak, who in 2004 was elected first female president of the Muslim Student Association (National). Mubarak in 2009 was a Ph.D. student in Islamic studies at Georgetown University. See the MSA National website, www.msanational.org/about/boa/ (last accessed October 21, 2009), where Mubarak is listed as a current board member and as a board member of another major American Muslim organization, the CAIR. Mubarak contributes regularly to the *Washington Post*'s OnFaith blog and is the author of an academic article on interpretations of Qur'an 4:34. See Mubarak 2007.

48 Mahmood 2005b, 5–22.

49 Mattson, "Can a Woman Be an Imam?" 6; see Ayubi 2010, 73.

50 Wadud 2006a, 166.

51 Nomani 2005a, 148.

52 See chapter 1, especially references to Umm Waraqa at the press conference.

53 Wadud 2006a, 10; original emphasis.
54 Grabar 1987, 100–102. With reference to its origin and connection with market days and Jewish communities in Medina and their market habits in preparation for the Sabbath, Goitein refers to the one reference in the Qur'an to Friday prayers and argues that the verses in Surah 62 (9–11) emphasize the connection to market activities. See Goitein 1959, 183–195. The dimension of providing a forum for making collective decisions is relevant for the development of the legal concept of *ijma'* (consensus).
55 Plaskow 1991, 9.
56 Wadud 2006a, 248.
57 Haddad, Smith, and Moore 2006, 65–66.
58 Ali 2004.
59 The reasons for these developments and the increase in the number of published personal accounts of American Muslim women is more fully explored in chapter 8.
60 Bullock 2005a.
61 Bullock 2005a, xiii–xix.
62 Afzal-Khan 2005b.
63 Husain 2006b.
64 Nomani said this during the press conference on March 18, 2005.
65 Wadud 2006a, 10.
66 Wadud 2006a, 10.
67 The Arabic term 'awrah is usually translated as "nakedness" but literally refers to the genitals or "weaknesses" of the human body. See Wehr 1979, 769.
68 See, e.g., Sheikh Muhammad Salih al-Munajjid, "Is a Woman's Voice 'Awrah?" www.islmaqa.com/en/ref/26304 (last accessed October 13, 2009); Munawwar Ateeq Rizvi, "Women's Voice—Is it 'Awrah?" http://scholarspen.blogspot.com/2004/09/womens-voice-is-it-awrah.html (last accessed October 13, 2009); and Shaykh Amjad Rasheed "Is a Woman's Voice 'Awra?" http://qa.sunnipath.com/issue_view.asp?HD=3&ID=4835&CATE=368 (last accessed October 13, 2009).
69 See Fatima Mernissi for an early critical discussion of Islamic conceptions of female sexuality as active and potentially aggressive (1987, 27–64).
70 Al-Munajjid on Islam Q&A, see note above.
71 Nelson 1985, 32–51.
72 Muhammad ibn Adam, "Islamic Perspective on Islamic and Ramadhan Radio Stations," www.daruliftaa.com/question.asp?txt_QuestionID=q-23023350 (last accessed September 13, 2009).
73 Rasmussen 2001, 39.
74 Rasmussen 2001. Rasmussen mentions several well-known women reciters, among them Hajjah Maria Ulfa, whose recitation is captured on the CD accompanying Michael Sells's *Approaching the Qur'an* (1999).
75 Michael Muhammad Knight, "Huggable Islam," March 19, 2005, www.muslim wakeup.com (last accessed May 20, 2009).

Chapter 7

1 See, e.g., Said 1997; Karim 2003; Mamdani 2005; Gottschalk and Greenberg 2008.
2 Said 1979.
3 Said 1997.
4 Ahmed 1992, 151.
5 Kahf 1999, 177.
6 Kahf 1999, 5–8.
7 Kahf 1999, 1.
8 Mamdani 2005.
9 Nacos and Torres-Reyna 2007, 1–23.
10 Nacos and Torres Reyna 2007, 25–37.
11 Nacos and Torres-Reyna 2007, 64–66.
12 Elsultany 2008, 227–228.
13 Joseph, D'Harlingue, and Wong 2008, 229–275.
14 Joseph, D'Harlingue, and Wong 2008, 275.
15 Elsultany's is confined to Arab Americans and Joseph et. al. speak of Arab Americans and Muslim Americans (Elsultany 2008; Joseph, D'Harlingue, and Wong 2008). The overlap and differences between the communities and the applicability of terms such as *racialization* to American Muslims need further study. Because historically the majority of Arab Americans were Christians and most American Muslims are not ethnically Arab, but the terms *Arab* and *Muslims* are frequently conflated in public discourse, the study of differences, convergences, and overlaps is complicated and beyond the purview of this book.
16 Only examples can be listed here: see Leigh Brown 2003; Bahrampour 2010; MacFarquhar 2008a; La Ferla 2007.
17 McCafferty 2005, 94–100. One of my favorite *New York Times* articles for discussion is MacFarquhar 2008. It discusses debates over domestic violence in American Muslim communities. The article is nuanced and open to a range of readings.
18 See the poem "Waiting Room" below.
19 For examples, see "Woman-Led Friday Prayer Sparks Controversy in the US," *Pakistan Times*, March 20, 2005; Lite 2005; Ferguson 2005; Elliott 2005a, 2005b.
20 See chapter 8 for an analysis of her memoir in the context of other, similar texts by American Muslim women.
21 Nomani 2006a, 290.
22 www.asranomani.com/Writings.aspx.
23 Nomani 2006a, 308.
24 Watanabe 2005.
25 See pictures and descriptions at www.brandeis.edu/investigate/events/Asra Nomanifullpage.html.
26 Karnasiewicz 2005.
27 The paperback edition is titled *Standing Alone* (2006) rather than *Standing Alone in Mecca* (2005).

28 Nomani 2006a. The pictures for the cover were taken on the day of the prayer event in 2005.

29 Nomani is featured in numerous newspaper articles; see, e.g., Salmon 2003; Goodstein 2004; Wiltz 2005.

30 Barrett 2007, 134–178. The other chapters bear titles with similar identifications, including "The Mystics," "The Imam," and "The Scholar," the latter a portrait of Khaled Abou El Fadl.

31 Barrett 2007, 178.

32 Barrett 2007, 137.

33 Barrett 2007, 135.

34 Barrett 2007, 158.

35 According to her website and her biography; no source cited. The reference to Rosa Parks appears in Goodstein 2004.

36 Berger 2005.

37 Whether such parallels also lead to the racialization of Muslims and/or the feminization of African Americans deserves further thought. For the former see Naber 2008a; and for an example of discussion of the latter, see Higginbotham 1993, 145–146.

38 Jacques Berlinerblau, Georgetown/On Faith, http://newsweek.washingtonpost .com/onfaith/georgetown/2009/05/welcome_to_faith_complex.html?hpid =talkbox1 (last accessed May 21, 2009).

39 Kahf 1999, 177.

40 Mydans 1996.

41 Interview Amina Wadud, Muslims (*Frontline*/PBS), www.pbs.org/wgbh/pages/ frontline/shows/muslims/interviews/wadud.html.

42 Wadud 2006a.

43 Wadud 2006a, 217–253.

44 Wadud 2006a, 246.

45 Bartlett 2005.

46 *The Noble Struggle*, a film by Elli Safari, The Netherlands/US, 2007, 29 min., Color, VHS/DVD (Women Make Movies, www.wmm.com/filmCatalog/pages/c699 .shtml).

47 Wadud 2006a, 248.

48 Wadud 2006a, 253.

49 Wadud 2006a, 253; original emphasis.

50 Wadud 2006a, 253.

51 Wadud 2006a, 247.

52 For primarily positive responses and reflections on the prayer, the special page of the Progressive Muslim Union at www.pmuna.org/archives/pmu_prayer_initia tive/index.php was very helpful. Unfortunately, this site no longer exists.

53 Elliott 2005a, 2005b.

54 Bartlett 2005.

55 Elliott 2005b.

56 Bartlett 2005.

57 Elli Safari, *The Noble Struggle*, 2007.

58 Wadud 2006a, 219–224.

59 Nomani 2006, 243–45.

60 Mojha Kahf, "The Waiting Room" (2005), *www.muslimwakeup.com* (last accessed August 29, 2008).

61 MacFarquhar 2007. For the poem, see Kahf 2003, 39.

62 MacFarquhar 2007.

63 MacFarquhar 2007. The column is also one of Kahf's contributions to American Muslim media production. It was published on the MuslimWakeUp website in 2004 but disappeared together with other content when the site was hacked. For analyses of its content, see Novoska 2005; Bunt 2009, 110–111.

64 Smith 2003.

65 Smith 2003.

66 Kahf 2008b. See also Kahf 2007.

67 Gehrke-White 2006. None of the women portrayed in the book wears a face veil, thus it is clear that the title is to attract attention rather than reflect the content of the book.

68 Cateura 2005, 33–46.

69 Abdo 2006, 137–164.

70 Abdo 2005.

71 Abdo 2006, 37–60.

72 Tippett 2007, 139–140.

73 Moezzi 2007, 118–130.

74 Weber 2001, 132–133.

75 Weber 2001, 152.

76 Abu Lughod 2002.

77 cooke 2002.

78 Mahmood and Hirschkind 2002.

79 cooke 2002, 227. For "About Us," see the Feminist Majority website, www.feminist.org.

80 Abu-Lughod 2002, 790.

81 See a review article by Jacqueline Rose of several recent books on honor killing and the dynamics of its representation and discussion in the "Western" public sphere, Rose 2009.

Chapter 8

1 Afzal-Khan 2005, 4.

2 Bullock 2005, xvii.

3 Abdul-Ghafur 2005a, 3.

4 Abdul-Ghafur 2005a, 6.

5 cooke 2007, 140.

6 Bullock 2005, xvii–xviii.

7 Halim 2006, 146.

8 Nomani 2006a, ix.

9 Nomani 2006a, x.

10 Nomani 2006a, 279.

11 Hasan 2004, 141.

12 See chapter 4 for a discussion of Leila Ahmed's perspective on the model function of Khadija for contemporary Muslim women.

13 Ali-Karamali 2008, 3.

14 Ahmed 1999, 120–121.

15 Ahmed 1999, 120–134.

16 Andrea 2007, 15. Ahmed describes her studies at a women's college in England and her early encounters with the field of women's studies in the United States as harem experiences.

17 Nomani 2005e, ix.

18 Nomani 2006a, 291.

19 Nomani 2006a, 280.

20 Ahmed 2005b.

21 Ali 2005, 19–35.

22 Eltantawi 2005, 160.

23 Younis 2005, 197.

24 Fadda-Conrey 2007, 156; original emphasis.

25 Fadda-Conrey, like other scholars of literature, frames the work of Mohja Kahf and Suheir Hammad as Arab American rather than Muslim American.

26 Kahf 2005b, 138.

27 Abdul-Ghafur 2005c, 12.

28 Abdul-Ghafur 2005c, 15–16.

29 Abdul-Ghafur 2005a, 5–6.

30 Nomani 2006a.

31 Abdul-Ghafur 2005c, 7–16.

32 Muhammad 2005, 37.

33 Saeed 2005.

34 Ali 2005.

35 Omar 2005.

36 Nomani 2006a.

37 Jamillah Karim has written an illustrative ethnography of the relations between African American and immigrant Muslim women and their negotiations of community, authenticity, and interpretation in different US contexts. See Karim 2009.

38 Hussain 2006, 1.

39 Bullock 2005, xvii.

40 Bullock 2005, xvii.

41 Afzal-Khan 2005b, 4.

42 See www.livingislamoutloud.com (last accessed December 8, 2009).

43 Kahf 2005, 131.

44 Abdul-Ghafur 2005a, 3–4.

45 Nomani 2006a, 81.
46 Nomani 2006a, 107.
47 Hasan 2004, 115.
48 Hasan 2004, 51.
49 Kahf 1999, 177.
50 Amireh and Majaj 2000a, 1.
51 Mohanty 1991, 34.
52 Amireh and Majaj 2000a, 2–3.
53 Amireh and Majaj 2000a, 7.
54 See, e.g., the collection *Deeper Shades of Purple* (Floyd-Thomas 2006) and the work of Ada Maria Isasi-Diaz (1996).
55 Amireh and Majaj 2000a, 14.
56 Sandoval 1991.
57 AlQutami 2009. Despite her emphasis on "the veil" in Kahf's work, AlQutami characterizes Kahf as an Arab American writer and only occasionally makes reference to her Muslimness.
58 Bullock 2005, xvii.
59 Hussain 2006, 1.
60 Hasan 2004, 158–159.
61 Donna Freitas, "Expanding the Catholic Canon of Literature to Include Women and Girls," H-Net review at www.h-net.org/reviews/showrev.php?id=12491 (last accessed January 15, 2009).
62 Skinner Keller and Radford Ruether 1995.
63 See Griffin 2004, esp. 27–61.
64 Mahmood 2007, 83.
65 Mahmood 2007, 84.
66 Mahmood 2007, 84.
67 Mahmood 2007, 85.
68 Razack 2008, 83–106.
69 Lalami 2006.
70 Wadud 2006a, 248.
71 Hasan 2009.
72 See their website, www.sealpress.com/about.php.
73 See the website of Interlink Publishing, of which Olive Branch Press is an imprint: www.interlinkbooks.com/pages.php?page=about&osCsid=64ba8424892b d13ccof388d2d7dd7aa6.
74 Kahf 2006.
75 Kahf 2006, 1–4. Kahf has also written an essay on the reception, reading, and packaging of the Egyptian feminist Huda Sha'rawi's memoirs, translated by Margot Badran and published in 1986 as *Harem Years: The Memoirs of an Egyptian Feminist* (New York: Feminist Press). See Kahf 2000, 148–172, in which her categories of escapee and victim are complemented by a third category, "pawn."
76 Kahf 2006, 6.

77 Kahf 2006, 7–9.
78 Shalal-Esa 2009.

Chapter 9

1   See, e.g., El Guindi 1999; Bullock 2002; Abu-Lughod 1986.
2   See, e.g., Alvi, Hoodfar, and McDonough 2003; Kopp 2002; Ghazal Read and Bart-kowski 2000.
3   See the collection of images of the book covers at the end of this chapter.
4   Afzal-Khan 2005.
5   Online I have found another, probably later version of this cover in which the stark image has been submerged into other images.
6   Nomani 2006b.
7   Several of the books featured in the appendix have been published with more than one cover, either for subsequent editions or for other geographic markets.
8   Nomani 2006b; Kahf 2006.
9   West 2001.
10 See Jackson 2005, 2009; McCloud 1994, 2006, 2007; Karim 2005, 2009; Wadud 1995, 1999a, 2003.
11 McCloud 2006.
12 Karim 2009, 236.
13 Karim 2009, 242.
14 Azhar Usman, "An Apology" (2008), posted at www.altmuslim.com/a/a/a/2813/ (last accessed December 15, 2008). Sherman Jackson, "Imam WD Muhammad and the Third Resurrection" (2008), posted at www.hahmed.com/blog/2008/09/24/ imam-w-d-mohammed-and-the-third-resurrection-by-sherman-abd-al-hakim-jackson/ (last accessed December 15, 2008). Both were circulated widely on Muslim blogs, websites, and email lists.
15 Curtis 2009, xii.
16 See Naber 2008; Jamal and Naber 2008; Razack 2008; Bayoumi 2007.
17 In January 2010 I participated in an interdisciplinary workshop at Columbia University that addressed many of my concerns about religion and race in the study of American Muslims. Our conversations showed how differently emphases are placed on race and racial categories in different fields and that while scholars in religious studies may have resisted more sustained inclusion of race into their considerations, race can, on the other hand, like other categories, quickly over-power other dimensions including religion. Some scholars at the workshop argued that the study of American Muslims can ultimately be reduced to issues of race, while others cautioned that a better weighing of these and other dimensions of American Muslim lives is necessary. In another workshop at Princeton University in March 2010 other scholars questioned the utility of the concept of racialization of American Muslims as a useful analytic tool.
18 Najmabadi 2008, 69–80.

19 Moallem 2005, 55.
20 Hidayatullah 2009b, 68–76.
21 Hidayatullah 2009a.
22 Wadud 1999b, xvi and note 4.
23 Gross 1999.
24 See Scott 2008, which contains essays from 1997 combined with several more re-
    cent works by feminist writers on the topic.
25 See Peaceful Families Project, www.peacefulfamilies.org; Karamah—Muslim
    Women Lawyers for Human Rights, www.karamah.org; and Muslim Men against
    Domestic Abuse at www.mmada.org (last accessed February 12, 2010).
26 The murder was widely covered by the media. See Daisy Khan's OnFaith blog for
    the *Washington Post*, "Turning the Tragedy of Aasiya Zubair Hassan into Action,"
    February 27, 2009, http://newsweek.washingtonpost.com/onfaith/panelists/
    daisy_khan/2009/02/turning_the_tragedy_of_aasiya.html (last accessed April 18,
    2010).
27 Curtis 2009, xii.
28 The name of the individual has been changed to ensure privacy.
29 Email exchange with Laury Silvers, January 17, 2010. In a blog entry in 2007 Sil-
    vers offered the following explanation for "shared authority": "Nakia Jackson has
    called this model "shared authority." It is a good term because it best expresses
    the intention that not only can men and women work together, but also muslims
    who do not otherwise agree can work together. We can all share in the salat. If
    satan cannot come between us in salat, we will not be broken as an umma." See
    "God, uh excuse me, Ali Eteraz has spoken," www.progressiveislam.org, posted
    February 14, 2007 (last accessed February 12, 2010).
30 Asra Nomani, "Let These Women Pray!" *Daily Beast*, www.thedailybeast.com,
    February 27, 2010.
31 Margot Badran, "Ejected from God's House," *Al-Ahram Weekly Online*, http://
    weekly.ahram.org.eg/2010/988/op14.htm (last accessed March 11, 2010). Ba-
    dran's opinion piece in *Al-Ahram* took the controversy to a global audience with
    further reaching implications for transnational Muslim community dynamics and
    debates.

Selected Bibliography

Abdo, Geneive. 2005. "When Islam Clashes with Women's Rights." *Boston Globe*, April 9.

———. 2006. *Mecca and Main Street: Muslim Life in America after 9/11*. New York: Oxford University Press.

Abdul Rauf, Feisal. 2007. "Reflections on Death and Loss." In *Voices of Islam: Family, Home, and Society*, ed. Vincent Cornell, 173–178. Westport, CT: Praeger.

Abdul-Ghafur, Saleemah. 2005a. "Introduction." In *Living Islam Out Loud: American Muslim Women Speak*, ed. Saleemah Abdul-Ghafur, 1–6. Boston: Beacon Press.

———, ed. 2005b. *Living Islam Out Loud: American Muslim Women Speak*. Boston: Beacon Press.

———. 2005c. "Saleemah's Story." In *Living Islam Out Loud: American Muslim Women Speak*, ed. Saleemah Abdul-Ghafur, 7–15. Boston: Beacon Press.

Abou El Fadl, Khaled. 2001a. *And God Knows the Soldiers: The Authoritative and Authoritarian in Islamic Discourse*. Lanham, MD: University Press of America.

———. 2001b. *Speaking in God's Name: Islamic Law, Authority and Women*. Oxford: Oneworld.

———. 2005. *The Great Theft: Wrestling Islam from the Extremists*. San Francisco: Harper.

———. 2006. *The Search for Beauty in Islam: A Conference of the Books*. Lanham, MD: Rowman & Littlefield.

Abou-Bakr, Omaima. 2001. "Islamic Feminism: What's in a Name?" *Middle East Women's Studies Review* 15:4: 1–4.

Abugideiri, Hibba. 2001a. "Hagar: A Historical Model for 'Gender Jihad.'" In *Daughters of Abraham: Feminist Thought in Judaism, Christianity, and Islam*, ed. Yvonne Y. Haddad and John L. Esposito, 81–107. Gainesville: University Press of Florida.

———. 2001b. "The Renewed Woman of American Islam: Shifting Lenses toward 'Gender Jihad?'" *Muslim World* 91:1–2 (Spring): 1–18.

———. 2004. "On Gender and the Family." In *Islamic Thought in the Twentieth Century*, ed. Suha Taji-Farouki and Basheer M. Nafi, 223–259. New York: I.B. Tauris.

Abu-Lughod, Lila. 1986. *Veiled Sentiments: Honor and Poetry in a Bedouin Society*. Berkeley: University of California Press.

———. 2002. "Do Muslim Women Really Need Saving? Anthropological Reflections on Cultural Relativism and Its Others." *American Anthropologist* 103:3 (September): 783–790.

Adams, Lorraine. 2008. "Beyond the Burka." *New York Times*, January 6.

Al-Adawiya, Aisha, and Sara Sayeed. 2005. "Embracing the Mosque as a Shared Space." *Azizah Magazine* 4:1: 110–111.

El-Affendi, Abdelwahab. 2009. "The People on the Edge: Religious Reform and the Burden of the Western Muslim Intellectual." *Harvard Middle East and Islamic Studies Review* 8: 19–50.

Afridi, Mehnaz. 2009. "Review Paper" [Bullock 2005 and Abdul-Ghafur 2005]. *Contemporary Islam* 3:3: 187–190.

Afsaruddin, Asma. 2002. "Reconstituting Women's Lives: Gender and the Poetics of Narrative in Medieval Biographical Collections." *Muslim World* 92:3–4 (Fall): 461–480.

Afzal-Khan, Fawzia. 2005a. "Playing with Images, or Will the RE(A)EL Muslim Woman Please Stand Up, Please Stand Up?" In *Shattering the Stereotypes: Muslim Women Speak Out*, ed. Fawzia Afzal-Khan, 1–18. Northampton: Olive Branch Press.

———, ed. 2005b. *Shattering the Stereotypes: Muslim Women Speak Out*. Northampton: Olive Branch Press.

Ahmed, Leila. 1982. "Western Ethnocentrism and Perceptions of the Harem." *Feminist Studies* 8:3 (Autumn): 521–534.

———. 1986. "Women and the Advent of Islam." *Signs* 11:4 (Summer): 665–691.

———. 1992. *Women and Gender in Islam: Historical Roots of a Modern Debate*. New Haven: Yale University Press.

———. 1999. *A Border Passage: From Cairo to America—A Woman's Journey*. New York: Penguin Books.

———. 2005a. "A Pilgrim's Progress" (review of Nomani's *Standing Alone in Mecca*). *Washington Post*, May 1.

———. 2005b. "The Veil Debate—Again." In *On Shifting Ground: Muslim Women in the Global Era*, ed. F. Nouraie-Simone, 153–171. New York: Feminist Press at CUNY.

Alcoff, Linda. 1992. "The Problem of Speaking for Others." *Cultural Critique* 20 (Winter): 5–32.

Ali, Ayaan Hirsi. 2006. *The Caged Virgin: An Emancipation Proclamation for Women and Islam*. New York: Free Press.

Ali, Kecia. 2002. "Rethinking Women's Issues in Muslim Communities." In *Taking Back Islam: American Muslims Reclaim Their Faith*, ed. Michael Wolfe, 91–98. New York: Rodale and Beliefnet.

———. 2003. "Progressive Muslims and Islamic Jurisprudence: The Necessity for Critical Engagement with Marriage and Divorce Law." In *Progressive Muslims: On Justice, Gender, and Pluralism*, ed. Omid Safi, 163–189. Oxford: Oneworld.

———. 2004. "Acting on a Frontier of Religious Ceremony: With Questions and Quiet Resolve, a Woman Officiates at a Muslim Wedding." *Harvard Divinity Bulletin* [online] 32:4 (Fall–Winter).

———. 2006a. "'The Best of You Will Not Strike': Al-Shafiʿi on Qurʾan, Sunnah, and Wife-Beating." *Comparative Islamic Studies* 2:2: 143–155.

———. 2006b. *Sexual Ethics and Islam: Feminist Reflections on Qur'an, Hadith, and Jurisprudence*. Oxford: Oneworld.

———. 2008. "Marriage, Family, and Sexual Ethics." In *The Islamic World*, ed. Andrew Rippin, 615–627. London: Routledge.

———. 2009. "Timeless Texts and Modern Morals: Challenges in Islamic Sexual Ethics." In *New Directions in Islamic Thought*, ed. Kari Vogt, Lena Larsen, and Christian Moe, 89–100. London: I. B. Tauris.

———. 2010. *Marriage and Slavery in Early Islam*. Cambridge, MA: Harvard University Press.

Ali, Samina. 2005. "How I Met God." In *Living Islam Out Loud: American Muslim Women Speak*, ed. Saleemah Abdul-Ghafur, 19–25. Boston: Beacon Press.

Ali, Syed. 2005. "Why Here, Why Now? Young Muslim Women Wearing *Hijab*." *Muslim World* 95:4 (Fall): 515–530.

Ali-Karamali, Sumbul. 2008. *The Muslim Next Door: The Qur'an, the Media, and That Veil Thing*. Ashland: White Cloud Press.

Alkhateeb, Maha, and Salma Elkadi Abugideiri, eds. 2007. *Change from Within: Diverse Perspectives on Domestic Violence in Muslim Communities*. Herndon: Peaceful Families.

AlQutami, Mais Yusuf. 2009. "Feminist Resistance in Contemporary American Writers of Color: Unsettling Images of the Veil and the House in Western Culture." Ph.D. dissertation, Indiana University of Pennsylvania.

Alsultany, Evelyn. 2008. "The Prime-Time Plight of the Arab Muslim American after 9/11." In *Race and Arab Americans before and after 9/11: From Invisible Citizens to Visible Subjects*, ed. Amaney Jamal and Nadine Naber, 204–228. Syracuse: Syracuse University Press.

Alvi, Sajida Sultana, Homa Hoodfar, and Sheila McDonough, eds. 2003. *The Muslim Veil in North America: Issues and Debates*. Toronto: Women's Press.

Amireh, Amal, and Lisa Suhair Majaj. 2000a. "Introduction." In *Going Global: The Transnational Reception of Third World Women Writers*, ed. Amal Amireh and Lisa Suhair Majaj, 1–26. New York: Garland.

———, eds. 2000b. *Going Global: The Transnational Reception of Third World Women Writers*. New York: Garland.

Andrea, Bernadette. 2007. "Passage through the Harem: Historicizing a Western Obsession in Leila Ahmed's *A Border Passage: From Cairo to America—A Woman's Journey*." In *Arab Women's Lives Retold: Exploring Identity through Writing*, ed. Nawar Al-Hassan Golley, 3–15. Syracuse: Syracuse University Press.

Anwar, Ghazala. 1996. "Muslim Feminist Discourses." In *Feminist Theology in Different Contexts*, ed. Elisabeth Schüssler Fiorenza and M. Shawn Copeland, 55–61. New York: Orbis.

Anwar, Zainah. 2005. "Sisters in Islam and the Struggle for Women's Rights." In *On Shifting Ground: Muslim Women in the Global Era*, ed. Fereshteh Nouraie-Simone, 233–247. New York: Feminist Press at CUNY.

Asad, Muhammad. 1980. *The Message of the Qur'an*. Trans. Muhammad Asad. Gibraltar: Dar Al-Andalus.

Asad, Talal. 1986. *The Idea of an Anthropology of Islam*. Georgetown Occasional Papers. Washington, DC: Georgetown University.

———. 2003. *Formations of the Secular: Christianity, Islam, Modernity*. Stanford: Stanford University Press.

Aswad, Barbara, and Barbara Bilge, eds. 1996. *Family and Gender among American Muslims: Issues Facing Middle Eastern Immigrants and Their Descendants*. Philadelphia: Temple University Press.

Ayubi, Zahra. 2010. "Alimah to Imamah: Muslim Women's Approaches to Religious Authority in the American Context." M.A. thesis, University of North Carolina, Chapel Hill.

Badawi, Jamal. 2005. *Gender Equity in Islam: Basic Principles* Chicago: American Trust Publications.

Badran, Margot. 1995. *Feminism, Islam, and Nation: Gender and the Making of Modern Egypt*. Princeton: Princeton University Press.

———. 2001. "Understanding Islam, Islamism, and Islamic Feminism." *Journal of Women's History* 13:1 (Spring): 47–52.

———. 2009. *Feminism in Islam: Secular and Religious Convergences*. Oxford: Oneworld.

Bagby, Ihsan. 2003. "Imams and Mosque Organizations in the United States: A Study of Mosque Leadership and Organizational Structure in American Mosques." In *Muslims in the United States*, ed. Philippa Strum and Danielle Tarantolo, 113–134. Washington, DC: Woodrow Wilson Center.

———. 2004. "The Mosque and the American Public Square." In *Muslims' Place in the American Public Square*, ed. Zahid Bukhari, Sulayman Nyang, Mumtaz Ahmad, and John Esposito, 323–346. Walnut Creek, CA: Altamira Press.

Bagby, Ihsan, Paul M. Perl, and Bryan T. Froehle. 2001. *The Mosque in America: A National Portrait*. Washington, DC: Council on American Islamic Relations.

Bahrampour, Tara. 2010. "Muslims Turning to Home Schooling in Increasing Numbers." *Washington Post*, February 21.

Bakhtiar, Laleh. 2007. *The Sublime Quran*. Trans. Laleh Bakhtiar. Chicago: Kazi Publications.

Al-Banna, Jamal. 2005. *Jawaz Imamat a-Mar'a Li-l-Rijal* (The Permissibility of Female Prayer Leadership of Men). Cairo: Dar al-Fikr al-Islami.

Barazangi, Nimat. 2000. "Muslim Women's Islamic Higher Learning as a Human Right." In *Windows of Faith: Muslim Women Scholar-Activists in North America*, ed. Gisela Webb, 22–50. Syracuse: Syracuse University Press.

———. 2004a. "Understanding Muslim Women's Self-Identity and Resistance to Feminism and Participatory Action Research." In *Traveling Companions: Feminism, Teaching, and Action Research*, ed. Mary Brydon-Miller, Patricia Maguire, and Alice McIntyre, 21–40. Westport, CT: Praeger.

———. 2004b. *Woman's Identity and the Qur'an: A New Reading*. Gainesville: University Press of Florida.

———. 2005. "Silent Revolution of a Muslim Arab American Scholar-Activist." In *Muslim Women Activists in North America: Speaking for Ourselves*, ed. Katherine Bullock, 1–18. Austin: University of Texas Press.

Barlas, Asma. 2002. *"Believing Women" in Islam: Unreading Patriarchal Interpretations of the Qur'an*. Austin: University of Texas Press.

———. 2004. "Amina Wadud's Hermeneutics of the Qur'an: Women Rereading Sacred Texts." In *Modern Muslim Intellectuals and the Qur'an*, ed. Suha Taji-Farouki, 97–123. New York: Oxford University Press.

———. 2005. "Globalizing Equality: Muslim Women, Theology, and Feminism." In *On Shifting Ground: Muslim Women in the Global Era*, ed. Fereshteh Nouraie-Simone, 91–110. New York: Feminist Press.

———. 2006. "Women's Readings of the Qurʾan." In *The Cambridge Companion to the Qurʾan*, ed. Jane Dammen McAuliffe, 255–272. Cambridge: Cambridge University Press.

Barrett, Paul. 2007. *American Islam: The Struggle for the Soul of a Religion.* New York: Picador.

Bartlett, Thomas. 2005. "The Quiet Heretic: A Controversial Prayer Upends a Professor's Life." *Chronicle of Higher Education* 51:49: A10–12.

Bauer, Karen. 2006. "'Traditional' Exegeses of Q 4:34." *Comparative Islamic Studies* 2:2: 129–142.

———. 2009. "The Male Is Not Like the Female (Q3:36): The Question of Gender Egalitarianism in the Qur'an." *Religion Compass* 3–4: 637–654.

Bayot, Jennifer. 2004. "Sharifa Alkhateeb, Feminist within Islam, Dies at 58." *New York Times*, November 4.

Bayoumi, Moustafa. 2006. "Racing Religion." *New Centennial Review* 6:2: 267–293.

Berger, Rose Marie. 2005. "The Hungry Spirit." *Sojourners Magazine* (June).

Berkey, Jonathan. 1992. *The Transmission of Knowledge in Medieval Cairo: A Social History of Islamic Education.* Princeton: Princeton University Press.

———. 2007. "Madrasas Medieval and Modern: Politics, Education, and the Problem of Muslim Identity." In *Schooling Islam: The Culture and Politics of Modern Muslim Education*, ed. Robert Hefner and Muhammad Q. Zaman, 40–60. Princeton: Princeton University Press.

Bhimani, Salima. 2003. *Majalis al-Ilm: Sessions of Knowledge—Reclaiming and Representing the Lives of Muslim Women.* Toronto: Tsar Publications.

Braude, Ann, ed. 2004. *Transforming the Faiths of Our Fathers: Women Who Changed American Religion* New York: Palgrave.

Brekus, Catherine, ed. 2007. *Reimagining the Past: The Religious History of American Women.* Chapel Hill: University of North Carolina Press.

Brown, Jonathan. 2009. *Hadith: Muhammad's Legacy in the Medieval and Modern World.* Oxford: Oneworld.

Bueno, Eva Paulino. 2000. "Race, Gender, and the Politics of Reception of Latin American *Testimonios*." In *Going Global: The Transnational Reception of Third World Women Writers*, ed. Amal Amireh and Lisa Suhair Majaj, 115–147. New York: Garland.

Bullock, Katherine. 2002. *Rethinking Muslim Women and the Veil: Challenging Historical and Modern Stereotypes.* Herndon: International Institute of Islamic Thought.

———. 2005a. "Introduction." In *Muslim Women Activists in North America: Speaking for Ourselves*, ed. Katherine Bullock, xiii-xix. Austin: University of Texas Press.

———, ed. 2005b. *Muslim Women Activists in North America: Speaking for Ourselves.* Austin: University of Texas Press.

Bunt, Gary. 2009. *iMuslims: Rewiring the House of Islam.* Chapel Hill: University of North Carolina Press.

Burwell, Catherine. 2007. "Reading Lolita in Times of War: Women's Book Clubs and the Politics of Reception." *Intercultural Education* 18:4 (Fall): 281–296.

Byng, Michelle. 1998. "Mediating Discrimination: Resisting Oppression among African-American Muslim Women." *Social Problems* 45:4 (November): 473–487.

Calderini, Simonetta. Forthcoming. "Classical Sources on the Permissibility of Female Imams: An Analysis of Some Hadiths about Umm Waraqa." In *Sources and Approaches Across Near Eastern Disciplines*, ed. Verena Klemm et al. Leuven: Peeters.

———. 2009. "Contextualizing Arguments about Female Ritual Leadership (Women Imams) in Classical Islamic Sources." *Comparative Islamic Studies* 5:1:5–32.

Cateura, Linda Brandi. 2005. *Voices of American Muslims: 23 Profiles*. New York: Hippocrene Books.

Cesari, Jocelyn, ed. 2007 *Encyclopedia of Islam in the United States*. New York: Greenwood Press.

Chaudhry, Ayesha. 2006. "The Problems of Conscience and Hermeneutics: A Few Contemporary Approaches." *Comparative Islamic Studies* 2:2: 157–170.

———. 2009. "Wife-Beating in the Pre-Modern Islamic Tradition: An Inter-Disciplinary Study of Hadith, Qurʾanic Exegesis and Islamic Jurisprudence." Ph.D. dissertation, New York University.

Chaudhry, Lubna Nazir. 2005. "Aisha and Her Multiple Identities: Excerpts from Ethnographic Encounters." *Muslim World* 95:4 (Fall): 531–556.

Chavez, Mark. 1997. *Ordaining Women: Culture and Conflict in Religious Organizations*. Cambridge, MA: Harvard University Press.

Chu, Jeff, and Nadia Mustafa. 2005. "Her Turn to Pray: A Historic Service Signals a New Push by Muslim Women to Reclaim Their Rights in the Mosque." *Time Magazine* 165:13 (March 28): 49.

cooke, miriam. 2001. *Women Claim Islam: Creating Islamic Feminism through Literature*. New York: Routledge.

———. 2002a. "Islamic Feminism before and after September 11." *Journal of Gender Law & Policy* 9 (Summer): 227–235.

———. 2002b. "Multiple Critique: Islamic Feminist Rhetorical Strategies." In *Postcolonialism, Feminism, and Religious Discourse*, ed. Laura E. Donaldson and Kwok Pui-Lan, 142–160. New York: Routledge.

———. 2007. "The Muslimwoman." *Contemporary Islam* 1:1 (Spring): 139–154.

Curtis, Edward. 2002. *Islam in Black America: Identity, Liberation and Difference in African-American Islamic Thought*. Albany: State University of New York Press.

———. 2009. *Muslims in America: A Short History*. New York: Oxford University Press.

———, ed. 2008. *Columbia Sourcebook of Muslims in the United States*. New York: Columbia University Press.

Al-Dabbous, Wessam. 2005. "Out in Front." *Azizah Magazine* 4:1: 32.

Davis, Hilary, Jasmin Zine, and Lisa K. Taylor. 2007. "Interview with Mohja Kahf." *Intercultural Education* 18:4 (October): 383–388.

Denny, Frederick. 1991. "The Legacy of Fazlur Rahman." In *The Muslims of America*, ed. Yvonne Haddad, 96–108. New York: Oxford University Press.

Dodds, Jerrilynn, and Edward Grazda. 2002. *New York Masjid: The Mosques of New York City*. New York: Powerhouse Cultural Entertainment.

Eickelman, Dale, and Jon W. Anderson, eds. 2003a. *New Media and the Muslim World: The Emerging Public Sphere*. Bloomington: Indiana University Press.

———. 2003b. "Redefining Muslim Publics." In *New Media and the Muslim World: The Emerging Public Sphere*, ed. Dale Eickelman and Jon Anderson, 1–18. Bloomington: Indiana University Press.

Eickelman, Dale, and James Piscatori. 1996. *Muslim Politics*. Princeton: Princeton University Press.

El Guindi, Fadwa. 2003. *Veil: Modesty, Privacy, and Resistance*. London: Berg.

———. 2005. "Gendered Resistance, Feminist Veiling, Islamic Feminism." *Ahfad Journal* 22:1 (June): 53–78.

Elewa, Ahmed, and Laury Silvers. 2010. "'I am one of the People': A Survey and Analysis of Legal Arguments on Woman-Led Prayer in Islam." *Journal of Law and Religion* 26:1 (2010–2011): 141–171.

Elia, Nada. 2006. "Islamophobia and the 'Privileging of Arab American Women,'" *NWSA Journal* 18:3 (Fall): 155–161.

Elliott, Andrea. 2005a. "Muslim Group Is Urging Women to Lead Prayers." *New York Times*, March 18.

———. 2005b. "Woman Leads Muslim Prayer Service in New York." *New York Times*, March 19.

Eltahawy, Mona. 2005a. "Meanwhile: Making History at Friday Prayer." *New York Times*, March 29.

———. 2005b. "A Prayer toward Equality." *Washington Post*, March 18.

Eltantawi, Sarah. 2005. "A Meditation on the Clearing." In *Living Islam Out Loud: American Muslim Women Speak*, ed. Saleemah Abdul-Ghafur, 159–173. Boston, Beacon Press.

Esack, Farid. 1997. *Qur'an, Liberation, and Pluralism: An Islamic Perspective on Interreligious Solidarity against Oppression*. Oxford: Oneworld.

———. 2001. "Islam and Gender Justice: Beyond Simplistic Apologia." In *What Men Owe to Women: Men's Voices from World Religions*, ed. John C. Raines and Daniel C. Maguire, 187–210. Albany: State University of New York Press.

Fadda-Conrey, Carol. 2007. "Weaving Poetic Autobiographies: Individual and Communal Identities in the Poetry of Mohja Kahf and Suheir Hammad." In *Arab Women's Lives Retold: Exploring Identity through Writing*, ed. Nawar Al-Hassan Golley, 155–180. Syracuse: Syracuse University Press.

Al-Faruqi, Maysam J. 2000 "Women's Self-Identity in the Quran and Islamic Law." In *Windows of Faith: Muslim Women Scholar-Activists in North America*, ed. Gisela Webb, 72–101. Syracuse: Syracuse University Press.

Ferguson, Barbara. 2005. "Woman Imam, Raises Mixed Emotions." *Arab News*, March 20.

Floyd-Thomas, Stacey, ed. 2006. *Deeper Shades of Purple: Womanism in Religion and Society*. New York: New York University Press.

Gehrke-White, Donna. 2006. *The Face behind the Veil: The Extraordinary Lives of Muslim Women in America*. New York: Citadel Press.

Geissinger, Aisha. 2004. "The Exegetical Traditions of 'A'isha: Notes on Their Impact and Significance." *Journal of Qur'anic Studies* 9:1 (April): 1–20.

————. 2005. "Portrayal of the *Hajj* as a Context for Women's Exegesis: Textual Evidence in al-Bukhari's (d. 870) '*al-Sahih*.'" In *Ideas, Images, and Portrayal: Insights into Classical Arabic Literature and Islam*, ed. Sebastian Günther, 153–180. Leiden: Brill.

————. 2008. "Gendering the Classical Tradition of Quran Exegesis: Literary Representations and Textual Authority in Medieval Islam." Ph.D. dissertation, University of Toronto.

————. 2011. "'Aisha bint Abi Bakr and Her Contributions to the Formation of the Islamic Tradition." *Religion Compass* 5:1 (January): 37–49.

Ghazal Read, Jen'nan, and John Bartkowski. 2000. "To Veil or Not to Veil? A Case Study of Identity Negotiation Among Muslim Women in Austin, Texas." *Gender and Society* 14:3 (June): 395–417.

Goitein, S. D. 1959. "The Origin and Nature of the Muslim Friday Worship." *Muslim World* 49:3 (July): 183–195.

Goodstein, Laury. 2004a. "Muslim Women Seeking a Place in the Mosque," *New York Times*, July 22.

————. 2004b. "Woman's Mosque Protest Brings Furor in the U.S." *New York Times*, July 22.

Gottschalk, Peter, and Gabriel Greenberg. 2008. *Islamophobia: Making Muslims the Enemy*. Lanham, MD: Rowman & Littlefield.

Grabar, Oleg. 1987. *The Formation of Islamic Art*. New Haven: Yale University Press.

Grewal, Zareena. 2006. "Imagined Cartographies: Crisis, Displacement, and Islam in America." Ph.D. dissertation, University of Michigan.

Griffin, Susan M. 2004. *Anti-Catholicism and Nineteenth-Century Fiction*. New York: Cambridge University Press.

Griffith, R. Marie. 1997. *God's Daughters: Evangelical Women and the Power of Submission*. Berkeley: University of California Press.

Gross, Rita. 1999. *Feminism and Religion: An Introduction*. Boston: Beacon Press.

————. 2002. "Feminist Theology as a Theology of Religions." In *The Cambridge Companion to Feminist Theology*, ed. Susan Frank Parsons, 60–78. Cambridge: Cambridge University Press.

Guardi, Jolanda. 2004. "Women Reading the Quran: Religious Discourse and Islam." *Hawwa* 2:3: 301–315.

Haddad, Yvonne, and John Esposito, eds. 2001. *Daughters of Abraham: Feminist Thought in Judaism, Christianity, and Islam*. Gainesville: University Press of Florida.

Haddad, Yvonne, Farid Senzai, and Jane I. Smith. 2009. *Educating the Muslims of America*. New York: Oxford University Press.

Haddad, Yvonne, Jane I. Smith, and Kathleen Moore. 2006. *Muslim Women in America: The Challenge of Islamic Identity Today*. New York: Oxford University Press.

Hajjaji-Jarrah, Soraya. 2003. "Women's Modesty in Qur'anic Commentaries." In *The Muslim Veil in North America: Issues and Debates*, ed. Sajida Sultana Alvi, Homa Hoodfar, and Sheila McDonough, 181–213. Toronto: Women's Press.

Halim, Hala. 2006. "Review of *Shattering the Stereotypes: Muslim Women Speak Out*." *Comparative Studies of South Asia, Africa, and the Middle East* 26:1: 146–147.

Hammad, Suheir. 2005. "My Sister's Prayer." In *Living Islam Out Loud: American Muslim Women Speak*, ed. Saleemah Abdul-Ghafur, 199–201. Boston: Beacon Press.

Hammer, Juliane. 2008. "Identity, Authority, and Activism: American Muslim Women's Approaches to the Qur'an." *Muslim World* 98:4 (October): 442–463.

———. 2009. "Reading Gender in the Qur'an: Text, Context, and Identity in the Work of Amina Wadud." In *Between Orient and Occident: Studies in the Mobility of Knowledge, Concepts, and Practices*, ed. Anke Bentzin, Henner Fuertig, Thomas Krueppner, and Riem Spielhaus, 128–145. Freiburg: Herder.

———. 2010. "Performing Gender Justice: The 2005 Woman-Led Prayer in New York." *Contemporary Islam*, special issue *Muslims and Media* 4:1 (April): 91–116.

Hasan, Asma Gull. 1999. *American Muslims: The New Generation*. New York: Continuum.

———. 2002. "Halal, Haram, and *Sex and the City*." In *Taking Back Islam: American Muslims Reclaim Their Faith*, ed. Michael Wolfe, 117–121. New York: Rodale and Beliefnet.

———. 2004. *Why I Am a Muslim: An American Odyssey*. London: Element.

———. 2009. *Red, White, and Muslim: My Story of Belief*. San Francisco: Harper.

Hashem, Mazen. 2010. "Religious Text in the Modern World: Muslim Friday Khutbahs." *American Journal of Islamic Social Sciences* 27:4 (Fall): 1–22.

Hassan, Riffat. 1990. "An Islamic Perspective." In *Women, Religion, and Sexuality: Studies on the Impact of Religious Teachings on Women*, ed. Jeanne Becher, 93–128. Philadelphia: Trinity Press International.

———. 1991a. "The Issue of Woman-Man Equality in the Islamic Tradition." In *Women's and Men's Liberation: Testimonies of Spirit*, ed. Leonard Grob, Riffat Hassan, and Haim Gordon, 65–82. New York: Greenwood Press.

———. 1991b. "'Jihad Fi Sabil Allah': A Muslim Woman's Faith Journey from Struggle to Struggle to Struggle." In *Women's and Men's Liberation: Testimonies of Faith*, ed. Leonard Gibb, Riffat Hassan, and Haim Gordon, 11–30. New York: Greenwood Press.

———. 1991c. "Muslim Women and Post-Patriarchal Islam." In *After Patriarchy: Feminist Transformations of the World's Religions*, ed. Paula M. Cooey, William R. Eakin, and Jay B. McDaniel, 39–64. New York: Orbis Books.

———. 1996. "Rights of Women within Islamic Communities." In *Religious Human Rights in Global Perspective*, ed. John Witte and J. D. van der Vyer, 361–386. The Hague: Kluwer Law International.

———. 1998. "Feminism in Islam." In *Feminism and World Religions*, ed. Arvind Sharma and Katherine K. Young, 248–278. Albany: State University of New York Press.

———. 2000. "Is Family Planning Permitted by Islam? The Issue of a Woman's Right to Contraception." In *Windows of Faith: Muslim Women Scholar-Activists in North America*, ed. Gisela Webb, 226–240. Syracuse: Syracuse University Press.

———. 2001. "Challenging the Stereotypes of Fundamentalism: An Islamic Feminist Perspective." *Muslim World* 1:1–2 (Spring): 55–69.

———. 2003. "Islam." In *Her Voice, Her Faith: Women Speak on World Religions*, ed. Arvind Sharma and Katherine K. Young, 215–242. Boulder, CO: Westview Press.

———. 2004. "Riffat Hassan—Muslim Feminist Theologian." In *Transforming the*

Faiths of Our Fathers: Women Who Changed American Religion, ed. Anne Braude, 173–198. New York: Palgrave.

———. 2005. "Women's Rights in Islam: Normative Teachings versus Practice." In *Islam and Human Rights: Advancing a U.S.-Muslim Dialogue*, ed. Shireen Hunter with Huma Malik, 43–66. Washington, DC: Center for Strategic and International Studies.

———. 2006. "Islamic Hagar and Her Family." In *Hagar, Sarah, and Their Children: Jewish, Christian, and Muslim Perspectives*, ed. Phyllis Trible and Letty Russell, 149–170. New York: Westminster Knox.

Hendricks, Joie. 2006. "Neither Here nor There: Identity Negotiation and Community Creation among Qur'an Only Muslims on the Internet." M.A. thesis, University of Missouri, Columbia.

Hermansen, Marcia. 1991. "Two-Way Acculturation: Muslim Women in America between Individual Choice (Liminality) and Community Affiliation (Communitas)." In *The Muslims of America*, ed. Yvonne Haddad, 188–204. New York: Oxford University Press.

Al-Hibri, Azizah. 1982. "A Study of Islamic Herstory; Or How Did We Ever Get into This Mess?" *Women's Studies International Forum* 5:2: 207–219.

———. 1999. "Islamic Law and Muslim Women in America." In *One Nation under God? Religion and American Culture*, ed. Marjorie Garber and Rebecca C. Walkowitz, 128–142. New York: Routledge.

———. 2000a. "Deconstructing Patriarchal Jurisprudence in Islamic Law: A Faithful Approach." In *Global Critical Race Feminism: An International Reader*, ed. Adrien Katherine Wing, 221–233. New York: New York University Press.

———. 2000b. "An Introduction to Muslim Women's Rights." In *Windows of Faith: Muslim Women Scholar-Activists in North America*, ed. Gisela Webb, 51–71. Syracuse: Syracuse University Press.

———. 2001a. "Muslim Women's Rights in the Global Village: Challenges and Opportunities." *Journal of Law and Religion* 15:3: 37–66.

———. 2001b. "Redefining Muslim Women's Roles in the Next Century." In *Democracy and the Rule of Law*, ed. Norman Dorsen and Prosser Gifford, 90–100. Washington, DC: CQ Press.

———. 2003a. "Hagar on My Mind." In *Philosophy, Feminism, and Faith*, ed. Ruth E. Groenhout and Marya Bower, 198–210. Bloomington: Indiana University Press.

———. 2003b. "An Islamic Perspective on Domestic Violence." *Fordham International Law Journal* 27:1: 195–219.

———. 2004. "Azizah Al-Hibri—Founder." In *Transforming the Faiths of Our Fathers: Women Who Changed American Religion*, ed. Anne Braude, 47–54. New York: Palgrave.

———. 2005a. "Muslim Women's Rights in the Global Village: Challenges and Opportunities." In *Shattering the Stereotypes: Muslim Women Speak Out*, ed. Fawzia Afzal-Khan, 158–178. Northampton: Olive Branch Press.

———. 2005b. "The Nature of Islamic Marriage: Sacramental, Covenantal, or Contractual?" In *Covenant Marriage in Comparative Perspective*, ed. John Witte and Eliza Ellison, 182–216. Grand Rapids, MI: Eerdmans.

———. 2006. "Divine Justice and the Human Order: An Islamic Perspective." In

Humanity before God: Contemporary Faces of Jewish, Christian, and Islamic Ethics, ed. William Schweiker, Michael A. Johnson, and Kevin Jung, 238–255. Minneapolis: Fortress Press.

Hidayatullah, Aysha. 2009a. "Inspiration and Struggle: Muslim Feminist Theology and the Work of Elizabeth Schuessler-Fiorenza." *Journal of Feminist Studies in Religion* 25:1: 162–170.

———. 2009b. "Women Trustees of Allah: Methods, Limits, and Possibilities of 'Feminist Theology' in Islam." Ph.D. dissertation, University of California, Santa Barbara.

Higginbotham, Evelyn. 1993. *Righteous Discontent: The Women's Movement in the Black Baptist Church, 1880–1920.* Cambridge, MA: Harvard University Press.

Howell, Sally. 2007. "Mosque History." In *Encyclopedia of Islam in the United States,* ed. Jocelyne Cesari, 432–434. New York: Greenwood Press.

Husain, Sarah. 2006a. "Introduction: Iqra! A Poetics of Resistance." In *Voices of Resistance: Muslim Women on War, Faith, and Sexuality,* ed. Sarah Husain, 1–16. Emeryville: Seal Press.

———, ed. 2006b. *Voices of Resistance: Muslim Women on War, Faith, and Sexuality.* Emeryville: Seal Press.

Inji Khan, Nadia. 2009. "'Guide Us to the Straight Way': A Look at the Makers of 'Religiously Literate' Young Muslim Americans." In *Educating the Muslims of America,* ed. Yvonne Y. Haddad, Farid Senzai, and Jane I. Smith, 123–154. New York: Oxford University Press.

Isasi-Diaz, Ada Maria. 1996. *Mujerista Theology: A Theology for the Twenty-First Century.* New York: Orbis Books.

Jackson, Sherman. 2005. *Islam and the Blackamerican: Looking toward the Third Resurrection.* New York: Oxford University Press.

Jamal, Amaney. 2005. "Mosques, Collective Identity, and Gender Differences among Arab American Muslims." *Journal of Middle East Women's Studies* 1:1 (Winter): 53–78.

———. 2009. "The Racialization of Muslim Americans." In *Muslims in Western Politics,* ed. Abdulkader Sinno, 200–215. Bloomington: Indiana University Press.

Jamal, Amaney, and Nadine Naber, eds. 2008. *Race and Arab Americans before and after 9/11: From Invisible Citizens to Visible Subjects.* Syracuse: Syracuse University Press.

Jeenah, Na'eem. 1994. "Mosques and Khutbahs Can Be Exciting, Too." *Al-Qalam,* July.

———. 2006. "The National Liberation Struggle and Islamic Feminisms in South Africa." *Women's Studies International Forum* 29: 27–41.

Al-Johar, Denise. 2005. "Muslim Marriages in America: Reflecting New Identities." *Muslim World* 95:4 (Fall): 557–574.

Joseph, Suad, Benjamin D'Harlingue, and Alvin Ka Hin Wong. 2008. "Arab Americans and Muslim Americans in the *New York Times,* before and after 9/11." In *Race and Arab Americans before and after 9/11: From Invisible Citizens to Visible Subjects,* ed. Nadine Naber and Amaney Jamal, 229–275. Syracuse: Syracuse University Press.

Kabbani, Hisham. 2004. *The Naqshbandi Sufi Tradition Guidebook of Daily Practices and Devotions.* Washington, DC: Islamic Supreme Council of America.

Kahera, Akel Ismail. 2002. *Deconstructing the American Mosque: Space, Gender, and Aesthetics*. Austin: University of Texas Press.

Kahf, Mohja. 1997. "Hajar in America." *Middle East Report* 205 (October–December): 39.

———. 1999. *Western Representations of the Muslim Woman: From Termagant to Odalisque*. Austin: University of Texas Press.

———. 2000a. "Braiding the Stories: Women's Eloquence in the Early Islamic Era." In *Windows of Faith: Muslim Women Scholar-Activists in North America*, ed. Gisela Webb, 147–171. Syracuse: Syracuse University Press.

———. 2000b. "Packaging 'Huda': Sha'rawi's Memoirs in the United States Reception Environment." In *Going Global: The Transnational Reception of Third World Women Writers*, ed. Amal Amireh and Lisa Suhair Majaj, 148–172. New York: Garland.

———. 2001. "'The Water of Hajar' and Other Poems." *Muslim World* 91:1–2 (Spring): 31–44.

———. 2003. *E-Mails from Scheherazad*. Gainesville: University Press of Florida.

———. 2005a. "The Muslim in the Mirror." In *Living Islam Out Loud: American Muslim Women Speak*, ed. Saleemah Abdul-Ghafur, 130–138. Boston: Beacon Press.

———. 2005b. "Muslim Women Rule and Other Little-Known Facts." In *Shattering the Stereotypes: Muslim Women Speak Out*, ed. Fawzia Afzal-Khan, 179–183. Northampton: Olive Branch Press.

———. 2007. "As American as You Are." *Los Angeles Times*, July 25.

———. 2008a. "The Privilege of Being a Woman Muslim." *Los Angeles Times*, October 7.

———. 2008b. "Spare Me the Sermon on Muslim Women." *Washington Post*, October 5.

Karam, Azza. 2002. "Muslim Feminists in Western Academia: Questions of Power, Matters of Necessity." In *Islam in the Era of Globalization: Muslim Attitudes toward Modernity and Identity*, ed. Johan H. Meuleman, 171–188. New York: Routledge.

Karim, Jamillah. 2005a. "Between Immigrant Islam and Black Liberation: Young Muslims Inherit Global Muslim and African American Legacies." *Muslim World* 95:4 (October): 497–513.

———. 2005b. "Voices of Faith, Faces of Beauty: Connecting American Muslim Women through *Azizah*." In *Muslim Networks from Hajj to Hip-Hop*, ed. miriam cooke and Bruce Lawrence, 169–188. Chapel Hill: University of North Carolina Press.

———. 2009a. *American Muslim Women: Negotiating Race, Class, and Gender within the Ummah*. New York: New York University Press.

———. 2009b. "Through Sunni Women's Eyes: Black Feminism and the Nation of Islam." In *Black Routes to Islam*, ed. Manning Marable and Hisham D. Aidi, 155–166. New York: Palgrave).

Karim, Karim. 2003. *Islamic Peril: Media and Global Violence*. Montreal: Black Rose Books.

Karnasiewicz, Sarah. 2005. "A Woman's Battle for the Soul of Islam." *Salon Magazine*, March 16.

Kassissieh, Nicole Nadia. 2005. "'And Say to the Believing Women': The Multiple

Meanings of the Hijab as a Window into Muslim-American Women's Identity." Ph.D. dissertation, Massachusetts School of Professional Psychology.

Khan, Shahnaz. 1998. "Muslim Women: Negotiations in the Third Space." *Signs* 23:2 (Winter): 463–494.

———. 2002. *Aversion and Desire: Negotiating Muslim Female Identity in the Diaspora.* Toronto: Women's Press.

Knight, Michael Muhammad. 2005. *The Taqwacores.* New York: Autonomedia.

———. 2007. *Blue-Eyed Devil.* New York: Autonomedia.

Koon, David. 2007. "Neither Rebel nor Victim: Fayetteville's Mohja Kahf Has a Thing or Three to Say about Women in Islam." *Arkansas Times*, September 13.

Kopp, Holly. 2002. "Dress and Diversity: Muslim Women and Islamic Dress in an Immigrant/Minority Context." *Muslim World* 92:1–2 (Spring): 59–78.

La Ferla, Ruth. 2007. "We, Myself and I." *New York Times*, April 5.

Lalami, Laila. 2006. "The Missionary Position." *Nation*, June 1.

Lee, Felicia R. 2004. "An Islamic Scholar with the Dual Role of Activist." *New York Times*, January 17.

Leigh Brown, Patricia. 2003. "For the Muslim Prom Queen, There Are No Kings Allowed." *New York Times*, June 9.

Lindsey, Alberta. 2005. "Islamic Scholar Hails Actions of VCU Professor—He Says Wadud's Act Is Important for Muslim Women in America." *Richmond Times-Dispatch*, April 2.

Lite, Jordan. 2005. "Imam Rips Woman-Led Prayer." *Daily News*, March 23.

Maag, Christopher. 2008. "Young Muslims Build a Subculture on an Underground Book." *New York Times*, December 22.

MacFarquhar, Neil. 2006. "As Barrier Comes Down, a Muslim Split Remains." *New York Times*, June 25.

———. 2007a. "New Translation Prompts Debate on Islamic Verse." *New York Times*, March 25.

———. 2007b. "She Carries Weapons; They Are Called Words." *New York Times*, May 12.

———. 2008a. "Abused Muslim Women in U.S. Gain Advocates." *New York Times*, January 6.

———. 2008b. "Many Muslims Turn to Home Schooling." *New York Times*, March 26.

Mahmood, Saba. 2003. "Questioning Liberalism, Too." *Boston Review* 28:2 (April–May): 18–20.

———. 2005a. "Feminist Theory, Agency, and the Liberatory Subject." In *On Shifting Ground: Muslim Women in the Global Era*, ed. Fereshteh Nouraie-Simone, 111–152. New York: Feminist Press at CUNY.

———. 2005b. *Politics of Piety.* Princeton: Princeton University Press.

———. 2007. "Feminism, Democracy, and Empire: Islam and the War of Terror." In *Women's Studies on the Edge*, ed. Joan Wallach Scott and E. M. Hammonds, 81–114. Durham: Duke University Press.

Mahmood, Saba, and Charles Hirschkind. 2002. "Feminism, the Taliban, and Politics of Counter-Insurgency," *Anthropological Quarterly* 75:2 (Spring): 339–354.

Majeed, Debra Mubashshir. 2006. "Womanism Encounters Islam: A Muslim Scholar Considers the Efficacy of a Method Rooted in the Academy and the Church." In

Deeper Shades of Purple: Womanism in Religion and Society, ed. Stacey M. Floyd-Thomas, 38–53. New York: New York University Press.

Mamdani, Mahmood. 2005. *Good Muslim, Bad Muslim: America, the Cold War, and the Roots of Terror*. New York: Three Leaves.

Manji, Irshad. 2005. *The Trouble with Islam Today: A Muslim's Call for Reform in Her Faith*. London: St. Martin's Griffin.

Marcotte, Roxanne. 2010. "Gender and Sexuality Online on Australian Muslim Forums." *Contemporary Islam* 4:1 (April): 117–138.

Marquand, Robert, and Lamis Andoni. 1996. "Seriously Tinkering with 1,000 Years of Tradition." *Christian Science Monitor* 88:53 (February 12): 1.

Mattson, Ingrid. 2008. "Can a Woman Be an Imam? Debating Form and Function in Muslim Women's Leadership." In *The Columbia Sourcebook of Muslims in the United States*, ed. Edward Curtis, 252–263. New York: Columbia University Press.

McCafferty, Heather. 2005. "The Representation of Muslim Women in American Print Media: A Case Study of the *New York Times*." M.A. thesis, McGill University.

McCloud, Aminah. 1991. "African-American Muslim Women." In *The Muslims of America*, ed. Yvonne Haddad, 177–187. New York: Oxford University Press.

———. 1994. *African American Islam*. New York: Routledge.

———. 2000. "Legal Issues Facing African American and Immigrant Muslim Communities in the United States." In *Windows of Faith: Muslim Women Scholar-Activists in North America*, ed. Gisela Webb, 136–146. Syracuse: Syracuse University Press.

———. 2006. *Transnational Muslims in American Society*. Gainesville: University of Florida Press.

———. 2007. "Islam in the African American Experience." In *Voices of Islam: Voices of Change*, vol. 5, ed. Omid Safi, 69–83. Westport, CT: Praeger.

Melchert, Christopher. 2006. "Whether to Keep Women out of the Mosque: A Survey of Medieval Islamic Law." In *Authority, Privacy, and Public Order in Islam*, ed. B. Michalak-Pikulska and A. Pikulski, 59–69. Leuven: Uitgeverij Peeters.

Merguerian, Gayane Karen, and Afsaneh Najmabadi. 1997. "Zulaykha and Yusuf: Whose 'Best Story'?" *International Journal of Middle East Studies* 29:4 (November): 485–508.

Mernissi, Fatima. 1987. *Beyond the Veil: Male-Female Dynamics in Modern Muslim Society*. Bloomington: Indiana University Press.

———. 1991. *The Veil and the Male Elite: A Feminist Interpretation of Women's Rights in Islam*. Trans. Mary Jo Lakeland. Cambridge: Perseus Books.

———. 1993. *The Forgotten Queens of Islam*. Minneapolis: University of Minnesota Press.

Mir, Shabana. 2009. "'I Didn't Want to Have That Outcast Belief about Alcohol': Muslim Women Encounter Drinking Cultures on Campus." In *Educating the Muslims of America*, ed. Yvonne Y. Haddad, Farid Senzai, and Jane I. Smith, 209–230. New York: Oxford University Press.

Mir-Hosseini, Ziba. 2006. "Muslim Women's Quest for Equality: Between Islamic Law and Feminism." *Critical Inquiry* 32: 629–645.

———. 2007. "Islam and Gender Justice." In *Voices of Islam: Voices of Change*, vol. 5, ed. Omid Safi, 85–113. Westport, CT: Praeger.

Moallem, Minoo. 2005. "Am I a Muslim Woman? Nationalist Reactions and Postcolonial Transgressions." In *Shattering the Stereotypes: Muslim Women Speak Out*, ed. Fawzia Afzal-Khan, 51–55. Northampton: Olive Branch Press.

Moezzi, Melody. 2007. *War on Error: Real Stories of American Muslims*. Fayetteville: University of Arkansas Press.

Moghadam, Valentine. 2002. "Islamic Feminism and Its Discontents: Toward a Resolution of the Debate." *Signs* 27:4 (Summer): 1135–1171.

Mohanty, Chandra. 1991. "Cartographies of Struggle: Third World Women and the Politics of Feminism." In *Third World Women and the Politics of Feminism*, ed. Chandra Mohanty, Ann Russo, and Lourdes Torres, 1–50. Bloomington: Indiana University Press.

Moosa, Ebrahim. 2003. "The Debts and Burdens of Critical Islam." In *Progressive Muslims: On Justice, Gender, and Pluralism*, ed. Omid Safi, 111–127. Oxford: Oneworld.

Mubarak, Hadia. 2004. "Breaking the Interpretive Monopoly: A Re-Examination of Verse 4:34." *Hawwa* 2:3 (Fall): 261–289.

———. 2007. "How Muslim Students Negotiate Their Religious Identity and Practices in an Undergraduate Setting." *Social Science Research Council*, May 8.

Muhammad, Precious Rasheeda. 2005. "To Be Young, Gifted, Black, American, Muslim, and Woman." In *Living Islam Out Loud: American Muslim Women Speak*, ed. Saleemah Abdul-Ghafur, 36–49. Boston: Beacon Press.

Mydans, Seth. 1996. "Blame Men not Allah, Islamic Feminists Say." *New York Times*, October 10.

Naber, Nadine. 2005. "Muslim First, Arab Second: A Strategic Politics of Race and Gender." *Muslim World* 95:4 (Fall): 479–495.

———. 2008. "Introduction: Arab Americans and U.S. Racial Formations." In *Race and Arab Americans before and after 9/11: From Invisible Citizens to Visible Subjects*, ed. Amaney Jamal and Nadine Naber, 1–45. Syracuse: Syracuse University Press.

Nacos, Brigitte, and Oscar Torres-Reyna. 2007. *Fueling Our Fears: Stereotyping, Media Coverage, and Public Opinion of Muslim Americans*. Lanham, MD: Rowman & Littlefield.

Najmabadi, Afsaneh. 2008. "Teaching and Research in Unavailable Intersections." In *Women's Studies on the Edge*, ed. Joan Wallach Scott and E. M. Hammonds, 69–80. Durham: Duke University Press.

Nassef, Ahmed. 2003. "Tailor Muslim Practices to Fit in America." *Christian Science Monitor*, August 4.

Nelson, Kristina. 1985. *The Art of Reciting the Qurʾan*. Austin: University of Texas Press.

Nomani, Asra. 2004. "Hate at the Local Mosque." *New York Times*, May 6.

———. 2005a. "Being the Leader I Want to See in the World." In *Living Islam Out Loud: American Muslim Women Speak*, ed. Saleemah Abdul-Ghafur, 139–156. Boston: Beacon Press.

———. 2005b. "A Gender Jihad for Islam's Future." *Washington Post*, November 6.

———. 2005c. "Islamic Bill of Rights for Women in the Bedroom." In *Living Islam Out Loud: American Muslim Women Speak*, ed. Saleemah Abdul-Ghafur, 155–156. Boston: Beacon Press.

———. 2005d. "Islamic Bill of Rights for Women in the Mosque." In *Living Islam Out Loud: American Muslim Women Speak*, ed. Saleemah Abdul-Ghafur, 153–154. Boston: Beacon Press.

———. 2005e. *Standing Alone in Mecca: A Woman's Struggle for the Soul of Islam*. San Francisco: HarperCollins.

———. 2006a. *Standing Alone: An American Woman's Struggle for the Soul of Islam*. San Francisco: HarperCollins.

———. 2006b. "Veiled Babes: Why Are Western Publishers So Keen on Shrouded Cover Models?" *Slate Magazine*, November 7.

———. 2007. "A Faith of Their Own: Muslim Women Seek Renewal of Islam." *Sojourners Magazine* 36:3 (March): 8.

Noskova, Martina. 2005. "'Sex and the Umma': Sex and Religion Lived in Mohja Kahf's Columns." *Theory and Practice in English Studies* 4: 115–1119.

Nouraie-Simone, Fereshteh, ed. 2005. *On Shifting Ground: Muslim Women in the Global Era*. New York: Feminist Press at CUNY.

Omar, Manal. 2005. "My Own Worst Enemy." In *Living Islam Out Loud: American Muslim Women Speak*, ed. Saleemah Abdul-Ghafur, 55–66. Boston: Beacon Press.

Peek, Lori. 2005. "Becoming Muslim: The Development of a Religious Identity." *Sociology of Religion* 66:3 (Fall): 215–242.

Plaskow, Judith. 1990. *Standing Again at Sinai: Judaism from a Feminist Perspective*. San Francisco: Harper.

Rahman, Fazlur. 1979. *Islam*. Chicago: University of Chicago Press.

———. 1982. *Islam and Modernity: Transformation of an Intellectual Tradition*. Chicago: University of Chicago Press.

———. 1994. *Major Themes of the Qur'an*. Minneapolis: Bibliotheca Islamica.

Rasmussen, Anne. 2001. "The Qur'an in Indonesian Daily Life: The Public Project of Musical Oratory." *Ethnomusicology* 45:1 (Winter): 30–57.

Rastegar, Mitra. 2009. "Managing 'American Islam.'" *International Feminist Journal of Politics* 10:4: 455–474.

Razack, Sherene. 2008. *Casting Out: The Eviction of Muslims from Western Law and Politics*. Toronto: University of Toronto Press.

Reinhardt, Kevin. 2003. "The Past in the Future of Islamic Ethics." In *Islamic Ethics of Life: Abortion, War, and Euthanasia*, ed. Jonathan Brockopp, 214–220. Columbia: University of South Carolina Press.

Riley, Krista Melanie. 2008. "How to Accumulate National Capital: The Case of the 'Good' Muslim." *Global Media Journal—Canadian Edition* 2:2: 57–71.

Rippin, Andrew. 2001. *Muslims: Their Religious Beliefs and Practices*. New York: Routledge.

Roald, Anne Sofie. 1998. "Feminist Reinterpretation of Islamic Sources: Muslim Feminist Theology in the Light of the Christian Tradition of Feminist Thought." In *Women and Islamization: Contemporary Dimensions of Discourse on Gender Relations*, ed. Karin Ask and Marit Tjomsland, 17–44. Oxford: Berg.

Rose, Jacqueline. 2009. "A Piece of White Silk." *London Review of Books* 31:21 (November 5): 5–8.

Rouse, Carolyn Moxley. 2004. *Engaged Surrender: African American Women and Islam*. Berkeley: University of California Press.

Rouse, Carolyn, and Janet Hoskins. 2004. "Purity, Soul Food, and Sunni Islam: Explorations at the Intersection of Consumption and Resistance." *Cultural Anthropology* 19:2 (May): 226–249.

Roy, Olivier. 2004. *Globalized Islam: The Search for a New Ummah*. New York: Columbia University Press.

Sadeghi, Behnam. 2006. "The Structure of Reasoning in Post-Formative Islamic Jurisprudence: Case Studies in Hanafi Laws on Women and Prayer." Ph.D. dissertation, Princeton University.

Saeed, Abdullah. 2004. "Fazlur Rahman: A Framework for Interpreting the Ethico-Legal Content of the Qurʾan." In *Modern Muslim Intellectuals and the Qurʾan*, ed. Suha Taji-Farouki, 37–66. New York: Oxford University Press.

Saeed, Khalida. 2005. "On the Edge of Belonging." In *Living Islam Out Loud: American Muslim Women Speak*, ed. Saleemah Abdul-Ghafur, 86–94. Boston: Beacon Press.

Safi, Omid. 2003a. "Introduction: The Times They Are A-Changin'—A Muslim Quest for Justice, Gender Equality, and Pluralism." In *Progressive Muslims: On Justice, Gender, and Pluralism*, ed. Omid Safi, 1–32. Oxford: Oneworld.

——, ed. 2003b. *Progressive Muslims: On Justice, Gender, and Pluralism*. Oxford: Oneworld.

——. 2003c. "What Is Progressive Islam?" *ISIM Newsletter* 13 (December): 48–49.

——. 2005. "Shattering the Idol of Spiritual Patriarchy: Towards a Gender-Fair Notion of Prayer in Islam." *Tikkun* 20:4 (July–August): 59–61.

Said, Edward. 1979. *Orientalism*. New York: Vintage.

——. 1997. *Covering Islam: How the Media and the Experts Determine How We See the Rest of the World*. New York: Vintage.

Salmon, Julie. 2003. "A Widow but Spare the Pity." *New York Times*, October 6.

Al-Samman, Hanadi. 2011. "North American Muslim Women's Movements and the Politics of Islamic Feminine Hermeneutics." In *Mapping Arab Women's Movements*, ed. Nawar Al-Hassan Golley and Pernille Arenfeldt. Cairo: American University of Cairo Press.

Sandoval, Chela. 1991. "U.S. Third World Feminism: The Theory and Method of Oppositional Consciousness in the Postmodern World." *Genders* 10: 1–24.

Al-Saqaf, Walid. 2005. "Muslim Activist Wages Gender-Jihad." *Wall Street Journal*, July 6.

Sayeed, Asma. 2002. "Women and 'Hadith' Transmissions: Two Case Studies from Mamluk Damascus." *Studia Islamica* 95: 71–94.

——. 2005. "Shifting Fortunes: Women and Hadith Transmission in Islamic History." Ph.D. dissertation, Princeton University.

——. 2009. "Gender and Legal Authority: An Examination of Early Juristic Opposition to Women's Hadith Transmission." *Islamic Law and Society* 16:2 (Summer): 115–150.

Scott, Joan Wallach, ed. 2008. *Women's Studies on the Edge*. Durham: Duke University Press.

Scrivener, Leslie. 2004. "Woman's Sermon Breaks Tradition at Local Mosque—Student, 20, to Join with Imam—'Not Everyone Has an Open Mind.'" *Toronto Star*, November 13.

Shaikh, Saʿdiyya. 1997. "Exegetical Violence: *Nushuz* in Qurʾanic Gender Ideology." *Journal for Islamic Studies* 17: 49–73.

——. 2003a. "Family Planning, Contraception, and Abortion in Islam: Undertaking

Khilafah." In *Sacred Rights: The Case for Contraception and Abortion in World Religions*, ed. Daniel C. Maguire, 105–128. Oxford: Oxford University Press.

———. 2003b. "Transforming Feminisms: Islam, Women, and Gender Justice." In *Progressive Muslims: On Justice, Gender, and Pluralism*, ed. Omid Safi, 147–162. Oxford: Oneworld.

———. 2004. "Knowledge, Women, and Gender in the Ḥadīth: A Feminist Interpretation." *Islam and Muslim-Christian Relations* 15:1: 99–108.

———. 2007. "A *Tafsir* of Praxis: Gender, Marital Violence, and Resistance in a South African Muslim Community." In *Violence against Women in Contemporary World Religions: Roots and Cures*, ed. Saʿdiyya Shaikh and Daniel Maguire, 66–8. Cleveland: Pilgrim Press.

———. 2009. "In Search of al-Insan: Sufism, Islamic Law, and Gender." *Journal of the American Academy of Religion* 77:4 (December): 781–822.

Shakir, Zaid. 2007. *Scattered Pictures: Reflections of an American Muslim*. Berkeley: New Islamic Directions.

———. 2008. "An Examination of the Issue of Female Prayer Leadership." In *The Columbia Sourcebook of Muslims in the United States*, ed. Edward Curtis, 239–245. New York: Columbia University Press.

Shalal-Esa, Andrea. 2009. "The Politics of Getting Published: The Continuing Struggle of Arab-American Writers." *Al-Jadid* 15:60 (online).

Silvers, Laury. 2006. "'In the Book We Have Left out Nothing': The Ethical Problem of the Existence of Verse 4:34 in the Qurʾan." *Comparative Islamic Studies* 2:2: 171–180.

———. 2007. Review of Ali's *Sexual Ethics and Islam*. *Journal of Middle East Women's Studies* 4:3: 134–136.

———. 2008. "Islamic Jurisprudence, 'Civil Disobedience,' and Woman-Led Prayer." In *Columbia Sourcebook of Muslims in the United States*, ed. Edward Curtis, 246–252. New York: Columbia University Press.

Simmons, Gwendolyn Zoharah. 2000. "Striving for Muslim Women's Human Rights—Before and beyond Beijing: An African American Perspective." In *Windows of Faith: Muslim Women Scholar-Activists in North America*, ed. Gisela Webb, 197–225. Syracuse: Syracuse University Press.

———. 2003. "Are We up to the Challenge? The Need for a Radical Re-ordering of the Islamic Discourse on Women." In *Progressive Muslims: On Justice, Gender, and Pluralism*, ed. Omid Safi, 235–250. Oxford: Oneworld.

Skinner Keller, Rosemary, and Rosemary Radford Ruether, eds. 1995. *In Our Own Voices: Four Centuries of American Women's Religious Writing*. New York: Westminster John Knox Press.

Smith, Dinitia. 2003. "Arab-American Writers, Uneasy in Two Worlds; Immigrant Authors Feel Added Burden since 9/11." *New York Times*, February 19.

Smith, Jane I. 2002. Review of Barlas's "Believing Women" in Islam. *Muslim World* 92:3–4 (Fall): 481–483.

Smith, Susan E. 2007. "Defeating Stereotypes: Memoirs Increasingly Provide Diverse Perspectives, Representations of Muslim Women." *Diverse Issues in Higher Education*, October 4.

Sonbol, Amira El-Azhari. 1996a. "Introduction." In *Women, the Family, and Divorce Laws in Islamic History*, ed. Amira El-Azhari Sonbol, 1–20. Syracuse: Syracuse University Press.

———, ed. 1996b. *Women, the Family, and Divorce Laws in Islamic History*. Syracuse: Syracuse University Press.

———. 2001. "Rethinking Women and Islam." In *Daughters of Abraham: Feminist Thought in Judaism, Christianity, and Islam*, ed. Yvonne Y. Haddad and John L. Esposito, 108–146. Gainesville: University Press of Florida.

———. 2005. "Finding Gender Freedom in Forgotten Laws: Scholarship and Activism in the Service of Personal Status Laws." In *Muslims in the United States: Identity, Influence, Innovation*, ed. Philippa Strum, 213–225. Washington, DC: Woodrow Wilson Center.

Souaiaia, Ahmed. 2004. "From Transitory Status to Perpetual Sententiae: Rethinking Polygamy in Islamic Traditions." *Hawwa* 2:3 (Fall): 290–300.

———. 2007. "She's Upright: Sexuality and Obscenity in Islam." *Hawwa* 5:2–3 (Summer): 262–288.

———. 2008. *Contesting Justice: Women, Islamic Law, and Society*. Albany: State University of New York Press.

Spellberg, Denise. 1994. *Politics, Gender and the Female Past: The Legacy of 'A'isha Bint Abi Bakr*. New York: Columbia University Press.

Stowasser, Barbara Freyer. 1996. "Women and Citizenship in the Qur'an." In *Women, the Family, and Divorce Laws in Islamic History*, ed. Amira El-Azhary Sonbol, 23–38. Syracuse: Syracuse University Press.

———. 1998. "Gender Issues and Contemporary Qur'an Interpretation." In *Islam, Gender, and Social Change*, ed. Yvonne Y. Haddad and John L. Esposito, 30–44. New York: Oxford University Press.

———. 2001. "Old Shaykhs, Young Women, and the Internet: The Rewriting of Women's Political Rights in Islam." *Muslim World* 91:1–2 (Spring): 99–119.

———. 2005. "The Qur'an and History." In *Beyond the Exotic: Women's Histories in Islamic Societies*, ed. Amira el-Azhary Sonbol, 15–36. Syracuse: Syracuse University Press.

Stratton, Allegra. 2005. "A Woman Breaks a Taboo." *New Statesman*, March 28.

Svensson, Jonas. 2000. *Women's Human Rights and Islam: A Study of Three Attempts at Accommodation*. Lund: Lunds Universitet.

Taji-Farouki, Suha. 2004a. "Introduction." In *Modern Muslim Intellectuals and the Qur'an*, ed. Suha Taji-Farouki, 1–36. New York: Oxford University Press.

———, ed. 2004b. *Modern Muslim Intellectuals and the Qur'an*. New York: Oxford University Press.

Tavernise, Sabrina. 2009. "In Quest for Equal Rights, Muslim Women's Meeting Turns to Islam's Tenets." *New York Times*, February 16.

Teipen, Alfons. 2002. "*Jahilite* and Muslim Women: Questions of Continuity and Communal Identity." *Muslim World* 92:3–4 (Fall): 437–459.

Tippett, Krista. 2007. *Speaking of Faith: Why Religion Matters—And How to Talk about It*. New York: Penguin.

Tobin, Theresa Weynand. 2007. "On Their Own Ground: Strategies of Resistance for Sunni Muslim Women." *Hypatia* 22:3 (Summer): 152–174.

Trible, Phyllis, and Letty M. Russell, eds. 2006. *Hagar, Sarah, and Their Children: Jewish, Christian and Muslim Perspectives*. New York: Westminster John Knox Press.

Umar, Nasaruddin. 2004. "Gender Biases in Qur'anic Exegesis: A Study of Scriptural Interpretation from a Gender Perspective." *Hawwa* 2:3 (Fall): 338–363.

Umm Zaid, Saraji. 2002. "Why Every Mosque Should Be Woman-Friendly." In *Taking Back Islam: American Muslims Reclaim Their Faith*, ed. Michael Wolfe, 108–110. New York: Rodale and Beliefnet.

Van Doorn-Harder, Pieternella. 2006. *Women Shaping Islam: Indonesian Women Reading the Qur'an*. Urbana: University of Illinois Press.

Wadud, Amina. 1995. "On Belonging as a Muslim Woman." In *My Soul Is a Witness: African-American Women's Spirituality*, ed. Gloria Wade-Gayles, 253–265. Boston: Beacon Press.

———. 1996. "Towards a Qur'anic Hermeneutics of Social Justice: Race, Class and Gender." *Journal of Law and Religion* 12:1: 37–50.

———. 1999a. "An Islamic Perspective on Civil Rights Issues." In *Religion, Race, and Justice in a Changing America*, ed. Gary Orfield and Holly Lebowitz, 153–163. Washington, DC: Century Foundation.

———. 1999b. *Qur'an and Woman: Rereading the Sacred Text from a Woman's Perspective*. New York: Oxford University Press.

———. 2000a. "Alternative Qur'anic Interpretation and the Status of Muslim Women." In *Windows of Faith: Muslim Women Scholar-Activists in North America*, ed. Gisela Webb, 3–21. Syracuse: Syracuse University Press.

———. 2000b. "Roundtable Discussion: Feminist Theology and Religious Diversity." *Journal of Feminist Studies in Religion* 16:2: 90–100.

———. 2002. "A'ishah's Legacy." *New Internationalist* 345 (May) (online).

———. 2003a. "American Muslim Identity: Race and Ethnicity in Progressive Islam." In *Progressive Muslims: On Justice, Gender, and Pluralism*, ed. Omid Safi, 270–285. Oxford: Oneworld.

———. 2003b. "The Role of Women in the American-Muslim Community and Their Impact on Perceptions of Muslim Women Worldwide." In *Muslims in the United States*, ed. Philippa Strum and Danielle Tarantolo, 171–184. Washington, DC: Woodrow Wilson Center.

———. 2004. "Qur'an, Gender, and Interpretive Possibilities." *Hawwa* 2:3: 316–336.

———. 2005a. "Citizenship and Faith." In *Women and Citizenship*, ed. Marilyn Friedman, 170–187. New York: Oxford University Press.

———. 2005b. Review of Barazangi's *Woman's Identity and the Qur'an*. *Middle East Journal* 59:3 (Summer): 510–511.

———. 2006a. *Inside the Gender Jihad: Women's Reform in Islam* (Oxford: Oneworld).

———. 2006b. Review of Mahmood's *Politics of Piety*. *Journal of the American Academy of Religion* 74: 813–816.

———. 2008. "Foreword: Engaging *Tawhid* in Islam and Feminisms." *International Feminist Journal of Politics* 10:4: 435–438.

Wan, William. 2009. "Abundant Faith, Shrinking Space: Mosques Turn to Synagogues, Ballrooms to Accommodate Growing Membership." *Washington Post*, August 22.

Watanabe, Teresa. 2005. "Breaching the Wall at Prayer." *Los Angeles Times*, June 27.

Waugh, Earle, and Frederick Denny, eds. 1998. *The Shaping of an American Islamic Discourse: A Memorial to Fazlur Rahman*. Atlanta: Scholars Press.

Waugh, Earle, Sharon McIrvin Abu-Laban, and Regula Burckhardt Qureshi, eds. 1991. *Muslim Families in North America*. Edmonton: University of Alberta Press.

Webb, Gisela. 2000a. "Introduction." In *Windows of Faith: Muslim Women Scholar-Activists in North America*, ed. Gisela Webb, xi–xix. Syracuse: Syracuse University Press.

———, ed. 2000b. *Windows of Faith: Muslim Women Scholar-Activists in North America*. Syracuse: Syracuse University Press.

Weber, Charlotte. 2001. "Unveiling Scheherazade: Feminist Orientalism in the International Alliance of Women, 1911–1950." *Feminist Studies* 27:1 (Spring): 125–157.

Wehr, Hans. 1994. *A Dictionary of Modern Written Arabic*, 4th ed. Ed. J. Milton Cowan. Ithaca, NY: Spoken Language Services.

West, Cornell. 2001. *Race Matters*. New York: Vintage Books.

Wiltz, Teresa. 2005. "The Woman Who Went to the Front of the Mosque: Feminist Faces Ostracism—or Worse—for Praying among Men." *Washington Post*, June 5.

Wolfe, Michael, ed. 2002. *Taking Back Islam: American Muslims Reclaim Their Faith*. New York: Rodale and Beliefnet.

Younis, Inas. 2005. "My Son the Mystic." In *Living Islam Out Loud: American Muslim Women Speak*, ed. Saleemah Abdul-Ghafur, 184–198. Boston: Beacon Press.

Yuskaev, Timur. 2010. "The Qur'an Comes to America: Pedagogies of Muslim Collective Memory." Ph.D. dissertation, University of North Carolina at Chapel Hill.

Zaman, Muhammad Qasim. 2002. *The Ulama in Contemporary Islam: Custodians of Change*. Princeton: Princeton University Press.

———. 2005. "The Scope and Limits of Islamic Cosmopolitanism and the Discursive Language of the 'Ulama.'" In *Muslim Networks from Hajj to Hip-Hop*, ed. miriam cooke and Bruce Lawrence, 84–106. Chapel Hill: University of North Carolina Press.

Zine, Jasmin. 2002. "Muslim Women and the Politics of Representation." *American Journal of Islamic Social Sciences* 19:4 (Fall): 1–22.

———. 2004. "Creating a Critical Faith-Centered Space for Antiracist Feminism: Reflections of a Muslim Scholar-Activist." *Journal of Feminist Studies in Religion* 20:2 (Fall): 167–187.

Zine, Jasmin, Lisa K. Taylor, and Hilary E. Davis. 2007. "Reading Muslim Women and Muslim Women Reading Back: Transnational Feminist Reading Practices, Pedagogy, and Ethical Concerns." *Intercultural Education* 18:4 (Fall): 271–280.

Index

Abdo, Genieve, 167

Abdul-Ghafur, Saleemah: and faith journey, 177–178; and imperial feminism, 189; *Living Islam Out Loud*, 171, 172, 176, 177, 180–182, 190; and Morgantown mosque, 16; and Muslim communities, 179, 180–182; and Qur'anic exegesis, 108; and woman-led prayer of 2005, 18, 19, 20–21, 24–25, 29, 31, 41, 139, 161, 171, 179, 181, 195

Abdullah, Aslam, 41–42, 43, 213n21

Abdul Rauf, Feisal, 51, 211n15

Abou El Fadl, Khaled: and gender justice, 40; *The Great Theft*, 102; on hadith tradition, 69, 219n63; on Islamic rulings and regulations, 69, 111; and knowledge/training, 114–115; and Qur'anic exegesis, 68–69, 106; on religious authority, 102–105, 225n10; *Speaking in God's Name*, 68, 100, 104–105; on woman-led prayer, 37–38, 45, 47, 51, 53, 84, 110, 118, 227n64

Abu Da'ud, 79, 80

Abugideiri, Hibba, 62, 95–96, 136–137, 228n80

Abu Zaid, Nasr Hamid, 51–52

activism: and American Muslim women, 61–62, 63, 78, 120, 142–143, 184–185, 203; and community building, 120–123, 181; as embodied tafsir, 56, 57; and gender discourses, 6, 13, 146, 205–206; and Hassan, 61–62, 92–93; and al-Hibri, 61–62, 89, 90, 93; and Muslim women, 59, 88–89, 93–94;

and Nomani, 16–17, 31, 32, 34, 54, 130, 132, 143, 154–156, 164, 168, 185; and Wadud, 33–34, 37, 97, 159, 160, 212n4; and woman-led prayer of 2005, 15–16, 32

Adawiya, Aisha al-, 45, 129, 214n37

Afghanistan War, 48, 168, 169

African American Muslims, 133, 178, 179, 198–199, 235n37

Afsaruddin, Asma, 130–131

Afzal-Khan, Fawzia: *Shattering the Stereotypes*, 143, 172, 173, 180, 187, 190, 196

Ahmed, Leila: *A Border Passage*, 172, 173, 174–175; defining Islam, 174–175; and gender equality, 131; and harem metaphor, 175, 235n16; and Islamic discursive tradition, 81; media representations of, 167–168; and media representations of Muslim women, 148, 168; on Nomani, 176; and role models, 94, 221n76; and woman-led prayer of 2005, 23, 50, 53–54; *Women and Gender in Islam*, 148; and women's spaces in mosques, 128

'Aisha bint Abi Bakr, 59, 78, 80, 94–95, 107, 221n1

Akiti, Muhammad al-, 80, 83–84

Ali, Kecia: and gender justice, 40, 86, 128; on al-Hibri, 90, 121; on interpretation, 113, 120; on Islamic legal rulings, 62, 69, 77, 81, 86–87, 110, 112, 119; on Islamic sexual ethics, 85, 86–88; knowledge/training of, 114, 116; *Marriage and Slavery in Islam*, 222n20;